The Stone Man and the Poet

The Stone Man and the Poet

Barbara Block Adams

iUniverse, Inc.
Bloomington

The Stone Man and the Poet

iUniverse books may be ordered through booksellers or by contacting:

iUniverse
1663 Liberty Drive
Bloomington, IN 47403
www.iuniverse.com
1-800-Authors (1-800-288-4677)

Because of the dynamic nature of the Internet, any Web addresses or links contained in this book may have changed since publication and may no longer be valid.

ISBN: 978-1-4502-7576-7 (sc)
ISBN: 978-1-4502-7577-4 (ebk)

Library of Congress Control Number: 2010917400

Printed in the United States of America

iUniverse rev. date: 1/3/2011

Contents

Acknowledgments

Portions of this book have appeared in slightly different versions in the following publications:

"Cancer Journal: Emotional Triage," *Free Associations* 6, part 4, no. 40 (1997).

"Conversation in the Dark." *When A Lifemate Dies. Stories of Love, Loss and Healing.* Susan Heinlein, Grace Brumett and Jane-Ellen Tibbals, eds. (Minneapolis: Fairview Press, 1997).

"The Gravity Machine." *The Use of Personal Narratives in the Helping Professions: A Teaching Casebook.* Jessica K. Heriot & Eileen Polinger, eds. (Binghamton, NY: Haworth Press, 2002).
"The Gravity Machine" was presented at an AWP Panel, "Writing and Healing II: Writers and Autobiographies," Albany, NY, April 15, 1999.

Some names have been changed to protect the privacy of those who are living.

Cover Photo: Mohonk Mountain, New Paltz, NY Copyright Barbara Adams, 2010

A poem . . . begins as a lump in the throat, a sense of wrong,
A homesickness, a lovesickness....
Robert Frost

I bought us a view of Mohonk Mountain
Where we first made love.
You would have preferred the hill
Where you were born
On your grandfather's stone-filled farm.
"Burying A New England Husband", Barbara Adams

Introduction

"Someday you'll write about me," El often said, after a long discussion or argument about his mercurial moods. No one forced me to carry out El's prediction—his wish, really. Only the burn in my gut drove me to carry it out.

The initial result was the chapter "Cancer Journal: Emotional Triage," written a year after his death. It was composed of excerpts from a journal I kept during El's mortal illness and death—thirteen months, altogether—although this chapter covers only the last two months of his life. I thought that I had carried out his wish. I could let it go.

But "Cancer Journal" turned out to be just the germ, a green shoot, of *The Stone Man and the Poet*. Rosellen Brown wanted to know what led up to "Cancer Journal," making me question myself about our forty-one-year marriage. How had I managed to establish a career while raising four children? How had I survived El's alternating black moods and gentleness? What was wrong with El?

I began writing a book about our families and our life together, chapters emerging willy-nilly, images and events building up, page after page. Making a coherent book out of them seemed impossible, and I gave it up, again and again, for nearly fifteen years.

At least a dozen versions ended up in the trash can. Some chapters survived each purging, stowed in a box in the closet and almost forgotten. I wrote poems to keep my mind busy. But the box in the closet haunted me.

About a year ago, I decided I had to either get rid of it or expose it to the light. I wrote a final draft. Friends and colleagues who read this final version encouraged me. At last, I felt satisfied: I had finished writing about El, and, inescapably, about myself and our long, difficult marriage.

I am deeply grateful to good friends and fellow writers: Jeffrey Berman, who read early drafts as well as the final manuscript with a gentle, fine-tooth comb; Laurence Carr, creative writing teacher, writer, and friend; James Finn Cotter, professor, scholar and poet, and friend to El and me; Lou Salkever, who always believed in El and me; Dr. Barry D. Rosenfeld, for teaching me how to live again; and Christine Crawfis and Bob Miller, directors of the Mohonk Mountain Stage Company, for presenting a staged reading of "Cancer Journal."

I give my deepest love and gratitude to my beloved children—Steve, Amy, Annie, and Sam—who give me a reason to keep trying to do better, and to their beloved spouses/partners—Howie, Barbara, and Lyn. I am so thankful for their existence and love. Finally, I am thankful to my sweet grandchildren, Aaron and Shira, who inspire me with hope for the future.

Barbara Block Adams, September 22, 2010

Chapter I

ASHES

We loved each other; we could have killed each other, like Punch and Judy. It was just a matter of who died first.

"You can't wait for me to die."

I picked up the ironstone ashtray and threw it at El's head. This ashtray had held two of El's lighted cigarettes before I threw it at him. It had been a birthday gift to him several years before, when ashtrays were still considered an appropriate gift. Nobody smoked anymore. Especially our friends. I had never smoked.

The heavy ashtray missed El's head and smashed into the stone fireplace he had built. It did not break, or even chip. But it left a white scar about an inch long on a stone.

Until I had thrown it, it had sat on the coffee table in front of the fireplace. Before that, it had occupied the center of the oak kitchen table, in front of El's chair where he sat and spent most of his waking hours when not working.

El began smoking in the army, when he was eighteen. He smoked when everyone else smoked. Escaping New Hampshire in the army, El dropped his given name, Elwood, along with the "hick" New Hampshire identity. Discharged and college educated, he remained El and kept smoking, even when people started quitting.

El smoked two packs a day, lighting his first cigarette of the day as soon as he woke. When he got out of bed, he lit another cigarette in the bathroom, leaving it to burn on the edge of the vanity. With his first cup of coffee, he smoked two more cigarettes, lighting them with his ubiquitous Bic lighter. He lost at least one Bic a week. When he was shamed into cutting back, filter tips lined up and spilled out the ashtray. I dumped them out, but the stink of stale tobacco lingered everywhere. The bathroom vanity had four burn scars along the edge. I tried to scrub the stains with Comet, but the dark yellow stains had eaten through the Formica.

In the Dhurrie rug in the family room downstairs, there is a round, brown-edged hole. Luckily, wool is fire-resistant. The coffee table and side tables and kitchen table are decorated with black bull's-eye burns. The flagstone floor El installed is immune to burns, of course. My piano, which El bought for me on a birthday when we began teaching, is burn free because he didn't play it.

El's shirts all had tiny, black-edged holes where burning leaves of tobacco had landed and sputtered out. His silk ties—all marred with brown dots. Sports jackets—lapels with burn dots. After he died, I gave them all away. I wonder if the men who got them from the Salvation Army ever noticed these burn patterns.

I used to worry about my own lungs and tried sitting in another room when El was home. This was difficult, if not impossible, because El followed me to wherever I was or what I was doing—into the bathroom when I showered, into the living room when I was reading, and into my study in the corner of the large downstairs room. And into the kitchen when I cooked, sitting at the kitchen table. I bought a "smoke-eating" ashtray with a battery-operated suction device and set it on the table in front of El. It whirred like a baby vacuum cleaner, sucking its tiny lungs out on the smoke from El's cigarettes. The whirring became part of the household noises, but did nothing to clear the air.

Every week, I had to wash the glass over the reproductions on the wall—Manet, Degas, and Van Gogh—wiping off the mustard yellow film. The drapes turned sickly yellow and smelled like stale cigarettes. I had them dry-cleaned, and I washed the cotton curtains every month.

I bought an "ionizer," which was supposed to catch smoke particles and precipitate them into "harmless dust." It was larger than the smoke-eating ashtray and twice as noisy. A twelve-inch, plastic brown box, it roared like a B-29 warming up for takeoff. When El was home, the ashtray, ionizer, ceiling fan, and stove ventilator ran full blast. They helped me believe the air was being cleaned, but the glass over the pictures and the curtains got just as yellow, just as fast.

After much nagging from me and our friends, El finally took a behavior modification class at a local hospital guaranteed to help smokers break the habit. For a month, every week, the group was shown slides of a smoker's bloody yellowed lung tissue, followed by slides of nonsmokers' healthy pink lung tissue; they watched films of lung cancer patients getting worse—coughing, losing weight, and looking skeletal as death overtook the smoker; they listened to testimonials from reformed smokers, as if it were a revival meeting; they listened to doctors and nurses scolding them on their suicidal habit. Summing up, the medical experts said it was a bad, nasty habit that could be changed with behavior modification—if *only* they tried.

El and his group were told to collect all the butts from a week's worth of smoking. El filled a coffee can in four days, a stinking mass of gooey, yellowed plugs. The stink was nauseating. El puffed on a fresh cigarette, inhaling with deep satisfaction, ignoring the remains of used-up tobacco.

One day, a psychologist friend persuaded him to sign up for a hypnotism course, guaranteed to stop him from smoking. After one evening session at a local conference center, El came home laughing hysterically, and smoking. Everyone in the room had succumbed to the hypnotic suggestion to quit smoking, except him. Had El really wanted to quit, he would have observed beforehand that his psychologist friend couldn't stop smoking either, having tried to hypnotize himself. Our doctor at that time (I later dubbed him Dr. Death) was also trying to give up cigarettes. When Nicorette chewing gum first came out, the doctor wrote a prescription for El. The doctor himself chewed the gum assiduously. El stuck a wad of Nicorette in his mouth in the morning, then lit up a cigarette with his coffee. Then the doctor wrote a prescription for the new nicotine patch. I watched El stick it on his bare biceps, hoping it would work. For a whole week, it cut down his craving for nicotine. He stopped coughing and wheezing, and his skin regained some of its healthy pink. By the second week, I caught him smoking *and* wearing the patch. "You're getting double nicotine!" I screamed. So he ripped off the patch.

Finally, for my own sake, I asked El not to smoke inside the house any more. He went outside and sat on the bench on our front porch. The yellow film eased up, and the air in the house smelled better. In cold weather, El sat in the garage, filling a coffee can with cigarette butts. (Behavior modification works!) As the alarming statistics on the relationship between smoking and cancer were published in the media, our friends were no longer allowed to smoke in their houses—no more ashtrays were put out, and no one dared admit smoking any more. One friend put a nice brass sign on the baby grand piano: THANK YOU FOR NOT SMOKING. El fumed (metaphorically and literally) through dinner parties, sneaking into the bathroom for a smoke. On the way home, he'd light up and take a deep drag as I cracked a window. I wouldn't let him smoke in my car. El's car windows were yellow; the upholstery smelled like a dirty ashtray.

Everyone noticed El's cough. Guests arriving at our house would see the can of butts outside the front door if I forgot to empty and hide it before they arrived. Sitting in the passenger seat in his car, I would hear the wheezing as he breathed through his mouth. I nagged, "Do you notice that you are breathing through your mouth?" He'd close his mouth and resume trying to breathe through his nostrils, both of us tense, angry. In less than a minute, he'd open his mouth to suck in enough air for his laboring lungs. "Have you told Dr. M about the wheezing? Ask him to do a chest X-ray," I begged again and again.

The day I threw the ashtray at El, we still did not know he had lung cancer.

A year earlier, during a routine exam, Dr. M had found an aortic aneurysm about to burst. That was a lucky find. El was referred to a surgeon at the Westchester Medical Center who said, "Smoking-related aneurysm." Surgery was needed immediately.

The surgery was dangerous, requiring El to give three units of his own blood beforehand. During the operation, his blood would be shunted to a mechanical circulator (fake heart) until the damaged artery was removed and replaced with a Dacron one. "It will outlast the rest of your body," said the surgeon. I drove El to Westchester three times for the blood giving. He fainted the first time, sitting on a bench outside the lab. I got him into the car. "You hope I'll die," he muttered.

Despite our fears, the surgery went smoothly. El was quickly taken out of post-op and intensive care and returned to his semiprivate room. I leaned over the bed and kissed him. I was relieved and grateful to have my husband back. El glared, "You hoped I'd die, but I made it, no thanks to you." Then he smiled sweetly to the nurse taking his blood pressure. She said to me, "Don't take him seriously. Anger at a spouse is a common post-op occurrence." The doctor came in, smiling. "You're better than new. You'll have to stop smoking, of course."

A week later, I drove El home from the Westchester Medical Center. He lit up a cigarette the minute he got into the car. I screamed, "The doctor said it would kill you!" Ignoring me, El looked angrier than ever.

There are many ways to commit suicide in the modern world, as well as the old one: drowning, hanging, cutting one's throat or wrists, swallowing pills, jumping off a bridge, eating or drinking poison, sitting in a car with the engine running in a closed garage, shooting oneself, jumping into heavy traffic or in front of a train. The list is long and not very creative, considering how many famous and ordinary people have used them. The car-in-the-garage method was high on my own list. Along with jumping off the bridge or in front of a train. But smoking is really very common and easy. It just takes longer.

About a week after we got home from Westchester Medical, I threw the ashtray. I did not want to actually hit him with it. I just couldn't bear any more of his slow suicide.

The ashtray hit the stone fireplace, leaving a half-moon scar on a large stone. In the years since El died, I have never tried to rub it off. In winter, when I build a log fire the way El taught me, I run my fingers over the scar, feeling its hurt like a cavity in a tooth. No one has ever noticed it, not even our grown children and grandchildren. Only I see it and know how it got there.

Regardless of El's anger and many cruelties toward me, I did not want him to die. He was the only person who had ever made me feel safe.

And then, one day, El was diagnosed with terminal lung cancer. We were on Cape Cod with our youngest son Sam, our daughter-in-law, and toddler grandson Aaron, staying in a rented house for two weeks. At the end of the first week, El and I were walking up the long, steep flight of wooden stairs from Nauset Beach to the parking lot. Near the top, I looked back and saw El standing midway, gasping, unable to move. A young man carrying a blanket hooked him under his arm and helped El to the top landing. El continued to suck for air, his face pale and sweaty.

It was a Saturday, and I finally found an open doctor's office in Brewster and drove El there. A woman doctor took El in. He was breathing a bit easier now in the dry, air-conditioned building. A half hour later, the doctor came out with El. He had pneumonia, she said, and gave him two prescriptions. We had another week in our rented house in Eastham. "Should we go home right away?" I asked.

"No hurry," she said. "Finish your vacation. Stop by to pick up your husband's X-rays, and take them to your doctor as soon as you get home." She stared oddly at me. Something was very wrong.

In the middle of the night, El sat up in with a look of terror. "What's wrong?" I asked.

"I can't pee. I have to pee, and I can't."

At three o'clock on Sunday morning, I drove at high speed along Route 6, to Hyannis, an hour away and the only town on the Cape with a hospital. The sun rose over a perfect beach day—cloudless, the salt air dampened with morning dew. By six o'clock, El was able to walk out. They had catheterized him, giving instant relief. One of the meds the Brewster doctor had prescribed causes paralysis of the urethra.

On the way home, I picked up the X-rays and looked at them before getting into the car. Then I hid them in the trunk so El wouldn't ask to see them. Even a layperson could see the orange-sized shadow on his left lung, with a tentacle reaching out around his pharynx.

For the next thirteen months, El underwent three surgeries, radiation, and chemotherapy; he was treated by a dozen or more doctors in two local hospitals and in Sloan-Kettering in New York City. During that year and one month, I tended El around the clock, drove him to the hospitals, shopped for food he could keep down—mostly canned liquids. At the same time, I wondered about my own life: if I would be able to resume teaching in the fall (I had been on sabbatical for the spring term). My own health took a plunge. If El couldn't eat, neither could I. If he couldn't sleep, neither could I. How dare I think of going back to work? I was sinking into depression, but unaware of it. No one told me I was depressed. All the doctors were taking care of El.

Our second grandchild was born on Bastille Day. El sat holding her, his ankles so swollen he couldn't even wear slippers. He had lost forty pounds, down from 150, and his thick brown hair had turned to dry hay. He was unable to use his dentures; his gums were bleeding and raw, and his remaining teeth needed to be pulled but his body could not withstand the extractions. And yet, he smiled toothlessly at Shira and said to her mother, "You done good."

The day El died, I had been awake for over twenty-eight hours at his bedside in Cornwall Hospital. I went home to shower and have coffee. A nurse called me midafternoon. "Come right away. Your husband has had a stroke and is in a coma. We don't know how long he will live."

After the funeral, my friends told me that El had continued to smoke whenever I was out of the house. Rage overtook grief; grief overtook rage. I screamed at El. And blamed myself for not saving him.

This story starts at the end, when my husband died, and I had to look back over four decades of marriage to figure out what had gone wrong.

I was a New Yorker, half Jewish, half Irish, and El was a New England bricklayer, half Irish and half descendant of presidents. We met in college, like two asteroids from distant galaxies colliding in Earth's atmosphere. In the Hudson Valley, where we lived for forty years, he was known as "The Stone Man," the teacher who built fireplaces, and I am known as "The Poet."

This is not a story about smoking cigarettes. It's about a man and woman making a home together out of the ashes of the past.

Chapter II

THE GRAVITY MACHINE

If you are deeply involved with a person in a long marriage, it's difficult to interpret events and behaviors in terms of what seems "normal" and what slides over the line into "abnormal." How to describe El's behavior, the erratic shifts in mood from loving and caring to cruel and punishing?

This is what I told my therapist, Dr. R, a few months after El died: "He would pinch my bottom in the shower, kiss me good-bye, and leave the house for work in a sweet, cheerful mood. When I returned from work, I would find him sitting at the kitchen table glowering in a rage that was palpable in the air around him. He would not speak; neither would he explain why he was angry: Was he angry with me or with someone else? Had something happened at work? He often had run-ins with fellow teachers and with parents. He would sit up till dawn, smoking and drinking coffee, not reading, not writing—just staring into his own thoughts. When he was mad at something, he'd wait until he knew I'd fallen asleep, then tiptoe into the bedroom and flick on the light. As I sat up, disoriented and groggy, he'd begin his indictment of my unforgivable faults: "You no-good bitch, whore. Go get yourself a boyfriend with a big cock. Get out." I hoped the children wouldn't hear, as I sat, unable to reason with this madman who looked like my husband. In daylight, he would apologize and say he'd never do it again. Then he'd bring me a dozen roses ... hold me in his arms as I cried with relief, and believed in him—again.

Dr. R, the therapist assigned to me at Sloan-Kettering as El was dying, was young and handsome. Perhaps too young and too handsome. I wanted to impress him with how independent and smart I was, at the same time I wanted him to take care of me. He never condescended to me, was always kind, but blunt in his feedback. He told me that El's behavior was abuse. Abuse! I had never thought of it that way, believing somehow I deserved it. Dr. R said he couldn't explain *why* El behaved in this double-dealing way, having met El only once, in the hospital, a few weeks before he died. But I felt he could help me understand it and help me deal with my own behavior.

I fell in love with El when we first met. He was older, a vet on the GI Bill, and the first man I'd dated who loved classical music and read Shakespeare (and not only when it was an assignment!). He also knew everything about nature. He could point to a black outline in the sky and say, "Red-tail hawk." He gave me my first taste of venison from a deer he had shot out of season, pan-fried in butter and vinegar. And he read me the "pieces" he'd written about his sly, comic, and cruel relatives in rural New Hampshire. I thought he was a genius. He'd shake his head and blush. "It's not finished yet," he'd say.

"You must! You're a great writer!"

Then, one day I found him sitting on the stairs outside the Student Union. He looked dreadful. "What's wrong? What happened?" I sat down beside him, stroking his back, and he shivered, pulling away from my hand.

"Don't touch me!" These black moods always came without warning. I'd coax him to tell me what was wrong. Frequently, the mood was triggered when a professor criticized his work. He would never go back to that class; he'd take an F rather than drop it. In these moods, he would not make eye contact as he wrung his hands, deriding himself. "I'm no good. I'm worthless. Go get someone on your level." He called me the "queen" of the college, said I was spoiled and too good for him. Then he'd slap himself, hard, on the face, again and again. I was shocked. But I did not recognize the signs of a real mental problem.

After we'd married, I asked myself if his black moods were indeed my fault. I read books on psychology, trying to determine what was wrong. El would say, "Yes, that's it," and start analyzing himself. "Thank you for helping me understand," he'd say, but within fifteen minutes, he would turn and twist his own thoughts until he was again blaming me. "You made me do it," he'd mutter darkly. "You're a snob. Go get somebody else." And he'd slap himself, falling back into his black hole.

Outwardly, El and I were opposites; inwardly, we were much alike—the family victim or outcast. We met by chance, by being in the same place at the same time, among a group of close-knit friends. Though I seemed to be the "lucky" one, the star student, I thought that El was luckier because of his loyal, huge family—Irish on his mother's side, and descended from *the* Adamses on his father's.

I never met Sammit, El's grandfather, the Adams patriarch. His wife, May, had been a schoolteacher before they'd married. Sammit had claimed dominion over his first grandson, El, when El was still in his high chair, pinching the child's cheek to correct bad baby manners—so hard El never forgot.

El's stories about Sammit outweighed all others. Week after week during our courtship, El created vivid portraits of the Adams clan. Reat, El's father (short for Aretus), drank, made children, and built buildings of brick and fifty-pound cinder blocks. He reneged on parental responsibilities, except to slap an envelope of cash on the table at the end of the week, and to slap one or two of his sons at random.

El's mother, Mary, kept her eight children well fed and clean. She washed their clothes in an old machine rigged up outside, and then pushed the clothes through a wringer by hand and hung them on the line. When Reat came home, she had a hot supper ready, put the kids to bed, and piled the dirty dishes in the pantry. The dishes piled up for two or three days until there was no more room on the drain board and there were no clean dishes left. Then, Mary rose an hour earlier than usual, heated cauldrons of water, poured it into the galvanized sink with soap powder, washed the dishes, and then re-filled the sink and rinsed them. After I married El, I watched this dish-washing routine in awe: the pile of dishes, the cauldrons of hot water carried by hand to the sink, pots scraped with a nylon scrubber and salt, and the daughters enlisted as wipers, drying the dishes and putting them away. Until we could afford a dishwasher, it made me obsessive about washing dishes after every meal, no matter how tired I was.

El preferred staying at Sammit's farm in Etna, New Hampshire, most weekends and summers, avoiding his father and noisy siblings and helping with the endless farm chores. He loved nature, and, as long as he didn't do anything wrong, his grandfather treated him kindly—more kindly than his father did, anyway. His grandmother made chicken pie and rolls that were the envy of every other housewife in the area. Compared with home, the atmosphere was peaceful, and El got some loving attention. El loved being in the woods alone. His time on the farm seemed like Eden to El—except for Sammit's unpredictable outbursts. El could mimic Sammit's dulcet voice and vicious follow-up, "Sit up straight at table, boy," he'd say gently, then he'd smack El hard. El would slap his own face to illustrate.

This same grandfather who persecuted his wife, sons, and grandson was locally famous for celebrating the birth of anyone else's child in Etna. When the news reached the farm on the hill that Mrs. So-and-so's daughter had given birth, Sammit would throw his cap in the air and whoop, "Hooray for our side!" Then he would rush off in his Model T to see the baby and give it his blessing, as if he were the unofficial priest. "Hooray for our side!" lingered in the air around him, until his next lashing out at a subservient son, wife, or grandson.

The worst crime Sammit committed against El happened when El was a teenager. Always a loner, El had for company only his slingshot and, later, a twelve-gauge shotgun his uncle Allan had helped him buy. Hunting by himself, El could escape the spoken and unspoken criticism of his manhood from his father and grandfather. Hunting was a manly activity, and even his mother, who hated the killing of wild animals, appreciated the rabbit and venison El brought home, often their only meat. With the other seven children under her feet, El's mother hardly noticed his absence, except when something needed fixing.

One day, a stray dog followed El home from the woods. In the Adams' parlance, any dog not a hunting dog was a "cur." El took the starved beast in, fed it half his lard sandwich, and snuggled it close. His mother shook her head. "Land's sakes! Where did you get that skinny thing?" But she let him keep it in his room. When Reat stumbled home that evening, he laughed sarcastically at the shivering beast.

"You call that a dog?" The dog stayed, however, and El was happy. He had a friend. He could trust this pet as he could trust no human being. He fed it table scraps, slept with it, and named it Scout.

After some months, El came home from school one day and couldn't find Scout. He called, and looked for him everywhere. His mother said, "Ask your father," not looking at him. El waited anxious hours for his father, who finally roared up the steep driveway in his old Buick. Running out, El asked, "Where's Scout?" Reeking of alcohol, Reat said matter-of-factly, "Sammit shot him. What do you want with that dumb cur anyway? He ain't a working dog."

El reeled. Had he been younger, he might have pummeled his father with tiny fists, and then gone to kick his grandfather. Had he been older, he might have killed Sammit. But he could say nothing … do nothing. Tears came to his eyes, much to his father's disgust. El ran into the woods and stayed there until driven in by cold.

I was dumbfounded when El told me this story. I couldn't understand the callous cruelty of his father and grandfather. "Why?" I asked. "What reason did he have to shoot that innocent animal?"

El had tears in his eyes when he explained. "They said he was a nuisance, killed some chickens—maybe. But mostly, it was because Scout wasn't a working dog. My grandfather had just been appointed dogcatcher and wanted to show his authority. Scout was his first legal 'execution' of a stray. Dad and Sammit grabbed Scout, my mother told me later, and drove to the old quarry. They let him out and, as he ran, Sammit shot him. Blind as a bat, but a dead shot."

El told this story over and over, every year, each time just as full of sorrow as if it had happened yesterday. I wondered if Reat and Sammit thought that killing El's pet would cure him of being a "sissy." It seemed like plain sadistic meanness to me.

Other stories El told about these male gods were more benign, encased in the atmosphere of Frost's New England. The reality that underlay all the stories, however, seemed always the same to me: that El was never accepted as a man in the presence of these heroes of his childhood. They were hunters, sportsmen, dog trainers, and bullies who broke El's spirit. To an outsider, these stories might seem innocent and mythic—the legends of the Adamses. But what prompted El to retell them was his unrequited yearning for the love and respect of his father, grandfather, and uncles. Above all else, El wanted their acceptance of his manhood. He never got it. He couldn't win it on their terms—hunting, fishing, and doing brute labor. He thought he might win it with intellectual endeavors, being the first in the family to go to college. But that again was work for "sissies," not men.

When El left for college, he got some encouragement from his Uncle Ben, until El said he wanted to major in English, not science. Ben sneered, "English is for fags," and dropped all interest in El.

His favorite uncle, Allan, laughed, "Have a good time—you'll be back for bird and deer season."

Reat sneered, "You want to be just like them Dahtmouth pinheads. Not one of 'em can do a day's work … man's work."

At the University of New Hampshire, El did well in a creative writing class with Dr. Scudder, for whom he began writing about his family. Dr. Scudder read El's stories to the class saying, "Now this is *real* writing." This praise so terrified El that he cut the class for a week. Dr. Scudder said that he'd still give El an A if he did well on the final exam. El cut the final exam, and Dr. Scudder gave him a C. El had an A average in biology, but cut that final too. Instead of studying, he drank beer all night in bars in nearby Portsmouth. He failed all his other courses.

Back home with his family, El did not tell anyone he'd flunked out of UNH. He tended mason for his father and tried to learn bricklaying so he could get into the tight mason's union. His father wouldn't teach him, but a big Frenchman, Zuke, did. El got into the union and earned good wages in the postwar boom years. In the evenings, he read his stories to his mother and brothers and sisters. They sat, rapt, admiring the big brother who'd gone off to college. Reat would snicker at El's stories, but would compete for attention by telling one of his famous "true" stories.

"Did I tell you about the chicken that crossed the road? Allan was driving and it ran right into our cah—stupid bird, feathers flying and squawking. We stopped and I jumped out and grabbed it. Cooked it that night. Mighty good roasted chicken." El didn't act like a man in the eyes of the Adams men, especially when he stopped hunting. He'd never liked it, and hated killing innocent things.

Dr. Scudder had given El just enough encouragement to write, but it often took him years to actually finish a short "piece," as he called it. He left many unfinished. I typed finished drafts of a few pieces so he could send them to a magazine. "Where should I send it?" he'd ask me. In the 1960s, editors still wrote polite rejections by hand. El got several. Finally, in 1972, one of his pieces was published in *The Saturday Review.* It was a satire, "Life Among the Hogslop Barbarians," making fun of Margaret Mead's popular new studies of primitive tribes. El had a gift for satire and puns that delighted our friends and children. His sense of humor amused everyone.

When El died, I found a box full of his unfinished stories in his large, loopy handwriting on yellow legal pads. The words covered both front and back of the unnumbered pages. My children and I tried sorting them out, wishing he were alive to finish them.

Through a friend who got a professorship at a state college in New York, El was able to start college anew. It is where we met. In his second year, when we were unofficially engaged, a strange obsession took hold of El: a "gravity machine." It would run without fuel or any outside source of energy, run only by the force of gravity circling inside a machine El was trying to design. He stayed up late at night drawing designs, which he showed me. I felt uncomfortable, unable to comprehend this machine that would use only gravity to "work."

"But doesn't it need some outside source to move?" I asked. El shrugged.

On the other hand, he was doing well in advanced courses in embryology and cytology, and had a particular gift for making slides. I was proud of him, certain he had a future in this field. But he was having difficulty with two other courses, physics and statistics. He had no background in math and spent hours trying to learn the math so he could understand the textbooks. He hated the physics professor, a puny man who humiliated him one day when he asked El to read the barometer. El said it was 27.4 (I can't remember the exact number, except that it was unusually low). "That's impossible," smirked the professor. "The pressure never gets that low." The next day, the professor half-apologized, saying that there had been a fluke of low barometric pressure, the lowest on record. But the damage had been done. El would not take an insult from such a puny man who was so lacking in the manhood of his burly male relatives.

El's "gravity machine" would prove he was smarter than the physics professor. "Perpetual motion is the chimera of fools," the professor had said. "Nothing can run without an outside source of energy." As far as El was concerned, the gauntlet had been flung down: he would prove he was the genius ignored by the physics professor, not the idiot and sissy his father had made him out to be.

El stopped studying. For months, he would draw far into the night, filling notebooks with odd diagrams, which he would show to me the next day. They looked something like waterwheels, or swastikas with legs chasing each other inside a circle. Portions were blackened to indicate they were filled with water that was supposed to slosh from one part to another. The whole device would spin around an axis, the sloshing water causing "perpetual" motion in the wheel. "But how would it get started?" I asked, in my ignorance of physics. El sulked, defensive, unable to write formulas and do the essential math.

"I'll have to build a working model," he said. That would take years, a lot of money, and a lab, I thought. He would get no backing from the physics department at the state college. He flunked both physics and statistics. El was certain, however, that he had discovered the secret of the universe. He would become famous as soon as the word got out! He had discovered a source of limitless, clean energy!

El's notebooks full of "gravity machine" drawings are lost. I cannot reproduce any of his designs—just as well.

The gravity machine notebooks piled up, and the semester ended. We were getting married the day after finals, leaving college after two years, and moving to New Hampshire. I was exhausted and wanted to get away from my alcoholic mother who had come back from Florida to invade my life again. I wanted to forget forever my father's abandonment. I wanted to go where no one knew me, to start life anew and have children. I thought El would be a great scientist and a great writer, and I would help him. My own career plans meant nothing to me anymore.

Living in New Hampshire, I saw firsthand the stories of El's family in reality. He had not exaggerated. After our first three children were born, we moved back to New York, to the Hudson Valley, to finish college. It took all my strength to take care of the children, take classes, and keep El from sliding off the rails, day by day. Every positive act was cancelled with an equal or worse negative. He supported us; he resented us. He built fireplaces in summer for the extra money to put us through college, but would come home in a drunken rage. With superhuman effort, we finished our BAs and got teaching jobs.

As our economic circumstances improved, our marriage reached a breaking point. El began three different MA programs, getting As. But he dropped out of each one. He was brilliant in teaching children with emotional and learning problems, and could easily have gotten an MA in psychology, but instead he almost destroyed his teaching career. El was approaching a breakdown and was losing control of his class. Parents complained about the chaos in the classroom the children reported. Then the principal caught him smoking outside, leaving the children unsupervised. The principal, whose personality reminded El of his bullying father, got El suspended indefinitely. El signed himself into the psych ward of a local hospital, then said, "Get me out of here," after two weeks. His psychiatrist hadn't made any headway in figuring out what was wrong with him.

This psychiatric psychoanalyst had been treating El and me for a few years, but things had gone from bad to worse, especially in our marriage. The doctor supported me in my career, holding El at bay, but otherwise he was unsuccessful in comprehending what drove El to such extremes of mood, though he succeeded in persuading El to stop drinking. (Drinking beer was taken for granted in El's family. Nobody kept count). El's abusive attacks on me continued, even while he was heavily dosed with drugs prescribed by his therapist.

In therapy one day, I mentioned El flunking courses while working on a gravity machine. The doctor looked up, "Gravity machine? That's a sure sign of schizophrenia." I was thunderstruck. Schizophrenia? Something was wrong with El, I knew, but this seemed too drastic a diagnosis. Over the years, I had speculated that El had suffered some form of brain damage (he'd been thrown from his grandfather's horse when he was twelve, suffering a fractured skull and a week-long coma), or had inherited some Adams' mental quirk, or suffered psychic damage caused by the brutality of his father and grandfather. The psychoanalyst persisted in his diagnosis of "schizophrenia," however, and prescribed

Trilafon, an antipsychotic medication. I was never quite convinced that he was right. The field of psychotherapy was changing rapidly in the 1970s. The Prozac generation of drugs was just around the corner, and dependence on Freudian theories was weakening. Genetic research was advancing rapidly, locating "markers" for various emotional and physical ailments, from cancer to schizophrenia. Even after El's death, I kept looking for answers to the mystery of El's rages and his self-sabotage, to his alternating funny, gentle nature and his black hatred of himself and me.

Five years after his death, I suddenly remembered a book I'd heard about in high school, *A Mind That Found Itself,* published in 1907. I found a copy of it in the library, then bought one from a company that sold out-of-print books over the Internet. It is a memoir written by Clifford Beers, a well-off young man from New Haven, Connecticut, who suffered a complete breakdown and jumped out of the second-floor window of his family's house. He was put into an asylum where he alternated between depression and delusions. For two and a half years, he was treated in first one, then another mental institution, until he apparently made a full recovery. He decided to write about his illness and treatment in the hope that it would benefit others and improve the treatment of mental illness. *A Mind That Found Itself* became a landmark in the movement to reform the treatment of the mentally ill.

Beers' style of writing was gracious and self-effacing. As I read, I began to notice eerie similarities between the author's and El's behavior. Beers had been diagnosed as a manic-depressive, though I believe diagnosis was then—and is still—an inexact science. In the depressed phase, Beers grew morose and silent, hating himself to the point of suicide. In the manic phase, he was ebullient, certain he was the most brilliant genius in the world. While he was institutionalized, when he was in the midst of a manic phase, he was confined to a cold, padded cell—naked except for his underwear. There was no furniture, nothing but a "drugget," a mat made of felt atop an iron bed. Though freezing with cold and half-starved, Beers felt full of energy and craved to expend it in the blank room. Having nothing else upon which to work, he tore the drugget into strips and then wove them into a crude suit. Every day, the attendants would remove the shredded "suit" and give him a new drugget, which his family had to pay for. Twenty mats, all told. Finally, one day, he tore the mat into strips again, but this time, he tied the ends to the bed and secured the other ends to the transom and window bars. Climbing into this web-like structure, he pulled on the strips until he'd raised the whole bed, *"with me in it*, and was soon dangling in space" (Beers, 1907, 127). Beers wrote that he was certain he had overcome gravity! For weeks, he told the doctors and attendants that his "gravity machine" would make him famous!

> My sensations at this momentous instant must have been much like those which thrilled Newton when he solved one of the riddles of the universe. Indeed, they must have been more intense, for Newton, knowing, had doubts; I, not knowing, had no doubts at all ... For weeks I believed I had uncovered a mechanical principal which would enable man to defy gravity ... Gravity was harnessed—that was all (Beers, 1907,127–28).

Today, we know much more about mental illness than was known when Beers wrote his groundbreaking memoir. New drugs and humanistic psychotherapies have transformed the treatment of mentally ill people who can afford them. Beers luckily got well, given the limitations, ignorance, and primitive treatments of his time, perhaps because he had the advantage of a loving and supportive family, and enough money to obtain the best available treatment.

El and I had no one but each other. My family had failed me completely, and his was downright destructive. Our psychoanalyst prescribed Trilafon, a psychotropic drug used to treat schizophrenia, hoping it would curb his temper, on the theory that he was indeed a schizophrenic. It dulled El's mood slightly, and abetted—if not caused—his impotence. This led to further attacks of anger in El, of course.

I wonder, sometimes, had El lived another ten years, if an anti-depressant and better therapist would have cured him of his alternate black side. He died without any clear diagnosis of what ailed his mind. I don't know which term in the *Diagnostic and Statistical Manual of Mental Disorders, Fourth Edition, 1994*, would fit, if, indeed, any of them would.

Chapter III

HEALTHY BODY, MIXED-UP MIND

"I'm taking an air bath!" El cried, running naked through the back yard of our house, which was surrounded by apple orchards. I ran and locked all the doors, watching from the kitchen window, laughing. Our four kids stared in disbelief, then giggled, since I was laughing. El ran back to the house like a sated satyr, and banged on the door, his skin red as a faun. I unlocked the back door and let him in. The children ran upstairs.

What inspired El's romp was a book we had read. A self-help guru said he took daily "air baths," claiming he absorbed nutriments from the air. Better than a vegetarian diet, and a good way to lose weight!

El's muscled body did not have an ounce of fat. His skin was smooth and ruddy. He smelled like fresh-cut hay. No other man I've known has that innocent, alluring scent of Eden. His body was his strength. His body was also his weakness.

"I could coldcock the son-of-a-bitch." He could. Until he got too old and too sick, El's physical power was apparent in his overdeveloped chest and biceps, which never fit comfortably into a sports jacket of any size. He was the strongest man I have ever met.

El's physical strength came from bricklaying and tending mason, a trade he practiced from the age of twelve until he was nearly sixty. His father Reat had the barrel chest typical of most bricklayers, and the beer belly that characterized the ones who drank—95 percent of most bricklayers drank all day on the job to wash out the mortar dust from their mouths and lungs, and they drank all evening before falling into bed. But El had no belly, just the bulging biceps and triceps, the weight-lifter chest, and rippling back muscles. Compared with his father and most brickies, El was a rookie at drinking, and did so only after work.

El learned how to lay stone and to build fireplaces with his father, following Count Rumford's precise dimensions for the correct ratio of flue to fireplace opening so the fire would draw and not smoke up the house. (The Count was an American-born loyalist employed by the Bavarian government, who wrote about heat and fireplaces.) El became well known for his excellent fireplaces, and built four or five each summer for customers who had heard of him by word of mouth. When people called, they asked for "The Stone Man."

In their brute world of manual labor, a man was measured by his brute strength. Though El became a successful teacher of children with learning disabilities, our friends admired him for his masonry skills. When El finished his bachelor's degree, not only was he the first in the family to finish high school *and* college, his achievement was regarded as "peculiar" and impractical, like learning to stand on your head or juggle oranges.

"You'll never beat me on your best day," said his father Reat. Fred "Aretus" Adams never praised El for his work as a bricklayer, certainly not as a teacher. El's mother Mary named her first-born Elwood, after a boy she'd had a crush on in first grade. El resembled his mother, with a broad forehead, thick Irish hair, deep brown eyes, and the prognathous jaw that made him self-conscious. He thought he looked like an ape. The tough boys in high school nicknamed him "Jaw Breaker." He had a habit of holding one hand over his jaw whenever he talked. From his father, El learned that the only exercise was hard work. Bricklayers walk with their arms rigid, as if holding a trowel in one hand and a brick in the other.

Family lore had it that Reat was descended from "the" Adamses through John Quincy Adams. It was a point of sarcasm and secret pride. El and his father had a gift for story telling, most of which amounted to tall tales based on a minimum of facts. His grandfather Sammit was credited with inventing new words to describe his shock, rage, and joy.

El loved to tell the family's favorite story of Sammit, who, in his seventies, got religion. Hedging his bets, no doubt, on the afterlife, he joined the Etna Baptist Church. His whole family came to watch his baptism: his four grown sons, their wives, grandchildren, and his wife May, sitting in the front row like an army for peace. The minister in his white baptism robe, said the words and blessed George ("Sammit") Adams, facing him, both standing in a tank of water up to their waists. The preacher and a helper then tilted Sammit backwards until his upper body and head were completely under water. Water snorting from his large hairy nostrils, Sammit bolted upright. "Great Caesar's toenails! Are ye trying to drown me, man?" he yelled. His "boys" in the front row laughed uncontrollably. They were, of course, in their late forties by then, but still feared the patriarchal father.

El also could invent creative epithets like his forebear, and use them well along with choice standard swear words. His devout Catholic mother never cursed; always said "Jeezum Crow," when she was surprised. The first time I heard it, I thought it referred to some kind of New England bird. El, however, exuded a string of sons-of-bitches, goddammit-to-hells, whoreballs, and Jesus-whoring-Christs whenever an inanimate object disobeyed his hands or got lost, or a word would not spell itself correctly as he typed it. When things broke, did not fit, or got lost, El blamed "someone"—usually me or our oldest son Steve, the "whoring bastard." If he couldn't spell a word, he would not look it up. He'd call to me from his room, "How do you spell ...?" I'd yell back, spelling it out, and he'd smear on Wite-Out, yelling, "You cocksucker." I was never sure if he meant the word or me.

One day, after I'd complained about hearing "whoreballs" and "cocksuckers" one too many times, he cried happily, "Standard futnuts!" Thereafter, "standard futnuts" became El's favorite expression when he was in a good mood. His "whoreballs" made me envision a transvestite male prostitute. But my favorite of El's cursing neologisms was inspired by the popular television series, *Batman*. Watching the show one night, El summed up the ambiguous relationship between Batman and Robin, using a twist on Robin's "Holy moly, Batman!" El yelled out, "Holy gonads, Batman!"

In college, our friends and I would sit enthralled in the Student Union as El read us his latest piece, written in the middle of the night after he'd dropped me off at my dorm. He would eat up the praise we showered on him, blushing, "It's a rough draft—it needs polishing." One of my favorite stories was called "The Famous Thunderjug," about an actual incident in his childhood, told with ironic humor.

After we married, El asked me to type these pieces up and "correct the grammar" for him—in a word, "polish" them. Between diapers and bottles, I would type a story, not changing the text or adding to it. It was his story, not mine. But I did correct spelling and grammatical errors. When it was finished, El would beam, admiring the neatly typed draft taken from the large, loopy handwritten scrawl on yellow legal pads, written on front and back. "Did you find any mistakes?" he'd ask. Innocently, I'd point out words and sentences I'd corrected for spelling or grammar, and he'd fly into a rage. It was my fault, he somehow felt, that he was ignorant of grammar! I would have to stop him from tearing up the corrected piece.

El's family listened to his stories as he read them as they all sat around the large kitchen table, the center of his family's life. They laughed and slapped the table, recognizing a favorite family story or a particularly crazy relative. El won attention and favor from his younger siblings and his mother in this way. His father would also grin and laugh, then would one-up him with an even more outrageous story based on a true incident, greatly embellished.

Dartmouth, the inaccessible, elitist Ivy League school was only five miles from El's birthplace. Dartmouth, in fact, later bought up all the land of his grandfather's and uncle Allan's farms. Sammit's former property is now home to an expensive residential suburb of Hanover. The Adams men called Dartmouth students "pinheads." Freshmen— and they were all men in those days—wore green beanies and looked like nerds to the "real" Adams men. *Pinhead* was the worst thing an Adams could call another man: "He's just a pinhead who don't know nothing about real work." When El became a teacher, he became—in their eyes—a pinhead.

El believed all his life that his penis was too small to satisfy any woman. In his more sane moments, he attributed this mistaken notion to his plump aunts ridiculing his little wee-wee, when he was a boy of three. "You can't compare the penis of a three-year-old boy to that of an adult man," I argued. I tried to tell him, tactfully, that he was just as adequate as the men I'd had sex with before we met. No logical argument worked to dissolve this injury to his tender manhood. El wanted sex every night. I obliged and usually enjoyed it. But as work took its toll on me, and when his juices slowed, I tried to get him to a less frequent schedule. "We still love each other, sex or no," I reasoned. No soap. Because of medication in his later years, and illness, El became completely impotent many years before his death. He blamed me for it, naturally. El could not accept that he didn't have the body and stamina of his youth. By fifty, his strength was waning, naturally. He didn't have the strength to lay brick any longer. He felt that he'd lost his manhood. But he kept trying to have sex night after night. Failing, he'd snap back the covers, stamp out of the bedroom, and rage for hours.

The pleasure of sex gone, El's chief remaining pleasure was smoking. All day, even at work. He nearly got fired for sneaking outside the school to smoke, leaving his class unattended. He took days off, slept most of the day, and smoked whenever he woke. As his body weakened from smoking and from lack of exercise, so did El's mind seem to lose its vigor and—its saving grace—his sense of humor. He stayed awake most nights until grayness tinged the sky. He began having panic attacks. Once, he insisted I take him to the emergency room, sure he was having a heart attack. The doctors said he'd had a panic attack. If I'd known more then, I would also have recognized El's growing depression: his black moods through which he would sit, not speaking, encased in a black cloud of rage. I wondered again about the cause—genetic or casual abuse? Before I met him, El had broken out into warts all over his face. Though the condition was not life-threatening, he was so ashamed of his appearance (warts, plus the jutting lower jaw), he underwent an experimental cure with doses of mercury. The mercury did indeed cure the warts. Could it have contributed to his mood swings?

Whatever the cause, El's rages and black moods were beyond any normal parameters. After each episode, as the anger subsided, El would promise never to let it happen again. He also begged me to explain what was wrong with him, why it happened. I read books, exploring various theories, but I did not know. Nothing seemed to stop him from bursting into another fury aimed at me.

I had thought El was a strong, intelligent, self-sufficient Yankee who would take care of me, who would always love me. But he could turn into a strange, frightening person who seemed to hate me half the time.

In the 1950s, it was always the woman's fault when a man failed. *Momism*, a misogynist bestseller by Philip Wylie, captured the essence of the '50s' cultural viewpoint toward women who wanted to be more than housewives and mothers, and yet were making sissies out of their boys by too much mothering. Women's magazines agreed, telling their female readers "how to satisfy your man!" Surrounded by this social norm, I felt guilty for wanting more than a kitchen and a floor to mop. I knew there had to be another reason for El's problems. I felt guilty for being ambitious for myself, not him. I wanted an academic career; I wanted to write. And I wanted to raise my kids too. In the 1950s, that was unheard of. A married woman stayed home and made cookies. A "career woman" did not marry, and certainly did not have children!

With three children to feed and keep clean, no time for myself, and no car in which to get away from the house, I fell into a state of listlessness. I couldn't read. I could barely walk to the store to buy groceries. I couldn't sleep, though I felt exhausted. I'd stopped resisting El's accusations. I was a whore. I couldn't do anything without him. My mother's words came back to me: "Nobody likes a smart woman." She was forever telling my sister and me that we would never get a man because we were too smart.

One day, after weeks of listlessness, I started thinking of ways to kill myself. What stopped me? Who would take care of my sweet children? I could not leave them in the clutches of my mother and stepfather. El could not manage on his own. My mother-in-law would turn them into Catholics, make them forget their half-Jewish mother. El came home and found me sitting in a chair staring at nothing. "What's wrong?" he asked. I burst into tears. "Please, Bobbie, tell me."

"I want to go home," I said.

El showed his compassionate side and said, "We're getting out of here."

A week later, we were on our way back to New York after four years of exile (for me) in New Hampshire. El had had a fight with his father and quit his job. We had no money, only hope and three children.

El got work building dorms at the college we had left. He took classes at night. I took classes in the daytime, getting my reluctant mother to babysit. Eric, my stepfather, worked as a proofreader. My mother's chronic leg ulcers were still unhealed. She sat on a chair, her legs raised on another, peeling vegetables or doing other sit-down chores. She read to the children. And she hated El as much as ever.

Finally, we earned our bachelor's degrees and found teaching jobs. Jobs were plentiful, and salaries were rising rapidly. This was the beginning of a new life for El and me and our children. I had had another child, finishing my ten weeks of practice teaching with a big belly. The principal of the Campus School where I had gone as a child said, "You must have unlimited energy output!" I was part of that generation of "Super Moms" who raised kids and held jobs at the same time. I wanted to write. It took another twenty years to fulfill my goals.

My independence was an economic fact, and it was becoming an emotional one as well, a situation that cut even more deeply into El's self-esteem as a man who was supposed to support his wife. The old values were dying fast, along with the old social and economic definitions of a man, a woman, and marriage.

We lived a little more peacefully nonetheless. El could no longer bully me, as I fought back and stood up for myself. He seemed to be slowly giving up, and getting more depressed. Drugs were coming into use to treat mental illnesses. I read everything I could to see how I could understand El—and myself. When the *Diagnostic and Statistical Manual of Mental Disorders, Fourth Edition* (DSM-IV) came out in 1994, a year after El died, I browsed through it looking up symptoms of various mental illnesses. El had been depressed, I could see. He had not been schizophrenic. The description of the behavior of a person with a condition called borderline personality disorder struck me as very close to El's symptoms and behavior. *That's just like El*, I thought again and again. This, of course, was an idle speculation, like matching the daily horoscope to one's real life, but this profile had scientific rigor, and I couldn't hurt El by doing it, now that he was dead.

The DSM-IV notes a familiar pattern of borderline personality "about five times more common among first-degree biological relatives ... than the general population." The pattern of behavior includes "undermining [himself] at the moment a goal is about to be realized [El had dropped out of three graduate programs despite straight A's]; "destroying a good relationship" just as it stabilizes; and some "psychotic-like symptoms such as hallucinations, body-image distortions, ideas of reference and hypnagogic phenomena [El and I would have had a good relationship, but for his temper and abuse of me with it; he was obsessed with his lower jaw, which he thought made him ugly; and he hallucinated that I was standing over him while he lay on the couch, calling his name while I was at work (American Psychiatric Association, 1994, 650–54).)

The chief personality markers of the borderline are listed in the DSM-IV as follows:

- Alternating extremes of idealization and devaluation in interpersonal relationships [El alternately called me a whore, a genius, and the only woman who understood him];

- Identity disturbance ... persistently unstable self-image or sense of self [El constantly asked me and the doctor to tell him who he was and what he should do; thinking of himself alternately as a moron and undiscovered genius];

- Intense episodic dysphoria, irritability, or anxiety [!];

- Chronic feelings of emptiness [El could not entertain himself, needing constant company. He went to diners when I wasn't home to avoid being alone];

- Inappropriate intense anger or difficulty controlling anger (e.g., frequent displays of temper, constant anger, recurrent physical fights) [all typical of El, though in his later years, he threatened only physical fights];

- Stress-related paranoid ideation [El thought that anyone who cared about him was really against him, like the doctor and me, especially].
  (American Psychiatric Association, 1994, 650–54)

Our therapist had labeled El's behavior as "El schizophrenia," since, in his opinion, mental illness was highly individualized. The borderline personality diagnosis was not then very common, but it seems a cousin to more severe schizophrenia. In 1999, a study by the National Alliance on Mental Illness (NAMI) reported that "there is mounting evidence that smoking is a form of self-medication for individuals with schizophrenia ... Nicotine is known to affect receptors for many brain transmitters" (Ross and Sperling 1999).Furthermore, this report states that "smoking decreases side effects of antipsychotic medications such as stiffness and tremors" (Ross and Sperling 1999).

These reports reinforced my perception of El as an addict, someone who needs a drug or drugs to function and cope with the everyday world. Adding nicotine to the list of preferred drugs made sense to me. Addiction is a major human problem that eludes explanation and defies solution. Some people drink alcohol, smoke tobacco, and try pot and other soft drugs without becoming addicted. Others are hooked from the first sip or sniff: "In a study on smoking cessation, smokers with no history of psychiatric illness were able to stop smoking for more than a year ... [but] among those with a lifetime history of major depression, less that 14 percent of smokers were able to stop ... Studies of smokers with schizophrenia reveal that smoking can transiently improve specific brain functioning" (Ross and Sperling 1999).

Is addiction genetic? Why could El stop drinking but never give up smoking? I could not stop thinking of these conundrums as long as El was alive, and for several years after he died.

One theory put forth that intrigued me was a genetic one called "genograms." In their book *Genograms in Family Assessment*, Monica McGoldrick and Randy Gerson presented a study of family patterns. Specifically, this book spells out remarkable success paired with severe failure, including addictions, in some famous families, including the Adamses of New England. John Adams and John Quincy Adams—from whom El's father was distantly descended—were members of several generations of siblings who either achieve great success or who failed or died from addictions. John Adams had two alcoholic brothers; his son John Quincy Adams had an alcoholic brother and one who committed suicide. Charles Francis Adams I, son of John Quincy, and Henry Brooks Adams, son of Charles Francis I, were matched with two eccentric brothers and the suicide of a spouse.

To assuage the grief and pain I felt concerning El's Jekyll-Hyde behavior, I call these examples to mind. Was it my fault that El was so unhappy? Was it his poverty-stricken and harsh upbringing? Was it in the family genes? I prefer to think that genetics had a lot to do with his incorrigible temper. I grieve for El, sorry that he died so young with such a strong body. I am angry that he caused his own death by smoking. I feel frustrated that I could not stop him from smoking or make him happy.

Tobacco helped El control whatever terrible feelings he had. The soothing effects of nicotine on schizophrenics suggests that nicotine could be used someday to help the mentally ill, without the side effects of drugs like Trilafon. Drug companies are trying to develop medications for schizophrenia that would stimulate the nicotinic receptors. Such a drug would be long lasting, unlike the nicotine from a cigarette, the effects of which last only minutes.

El exhibited symptoms of depression and anxiety as long as I knew him. He learned to use tobacco to ease the effects of a mental illness that was never clearly diagnosed. Nicotine acted like an antidepressant such as Prozac—not available until his last years of life—as well as a tranquilizer like Valium. El simply smoked every waking moment, for whatever effect he needed.

Tobacco was identified as an addictive drug less than two decades ago by C. Everett Koop, the surgeon general of the United States. Yet, nicotine addiction is still not generally recognized as a "disease." It isn't even considered an evil drug, like heroin, cocaine, and marijuana, or considered as dangerous as alcohol. It isn't illegal. It isn't tied to the committing of crimes. Yet it kills more victims than any other drug.

Until he got cancer, El's health problems were mental, not physical. Nicotine was the medium, the snake that delivered the poison into his healthy, powerful body. It destroyed it.

Chapter IV

GROWING UP, GROWING DOWN, 1932–1950

The funniest thing I did before I reached school age was pinch a little person's bottom. This particular little person—midget as we used to say before we became politically correct—was standing near me, wearing a tuxedo, and, as he was my size, I thought we were equals. So I pinched his small bottom. He yelped, his eyes bugging out. He couldn't believe a little girl in pigtails had assaulted him. My parents were somewhat embarrassed, but, after all, it was my father who had been pinching my bottom since I was old enough to scream. He always laughed. It was supposed to be funny.

"You must have had a difficult childhood," curious friends often remark. "Somewhat," I usually answer. Whenever I try to explain how I was raised, my friends react with looks ranging from horror to disbelief. The second funniest thing I did was in second grade. Miss Halpern, aka "Miss Hairpin," was teaching us a civics lesson on voting. President Roosevelt had been elected to his first term the year I was born, and eight years later, I considered him eternal and perfect. Hairpin asked us to raise our hands if our parents voted for Republicans. Hands flew up. And whose parents voted for Democrats. The rest of the class raised hands. My hands stayed in my lap, as I smiled smugly.

"Barbara, dear, why didn't you raise your hand? Don't you know if your parents voted Republican or Democrat?" asked Hairpin, her false teeth slipping slightly.

"Oh, yes, Miss Halpern, I know. We're Communists! Daddy voted for Earl Browder."

Miss Halpern's face turned white. She held her hand to her flat chest. "Oh, my poor dear." When I told my mother after school, and she told Daddy that night, they were afraid we would have to move. Miss Halpern did not turn us in, but ever after, she treated me as if I were an orphan.

My childhood was a riches to rags melodrama. Still, it wasn't all that bad, and I had a pretty good life despite minor hardships—certainly nothing at all bad by current standards. I had a father, sort of, for a while; and I had a mother, now and then. We moved a lot, but I was, basically, a tough city kid.

My birth certificate says of my parentage, "Father—David Block, artist, age 20; Mother—Helen Taxter Block, housewife, age 20." They married when they were both nineteen. When I was in grade school, Daddy was an art director, creating ads for big accounts like Schenley's Whiskey and Coty's perfumes. Mommy and I met him every Friday night in his office in Rockefeller Center. I could see the ice skating rink below from his window. He had a big, slanting easel full of his latest drawings and boxes of wonderful hard pastels. He always had a yellow pencil behind his ear. He tried to teach me how to use the "lucy," a prism used to copy an image, though I found it difficult to focus and draw the image I saw at the same time. I always had a full supply of new hard pastel crayons and drawing paper at home.

After Daddy had washed the charcoal from his hands and rolled down his white shirtsleeves, we would go to a favorite midtown restaurant, walking down steps into a noisy, packed bar full of advertising writers and artists. We had lobsters. I drank a lot of Coca-Cola, from which I am still not weaned. Or lobster, either.

Daddy wanted to be a famous artist. He painted a portrait of our maid, Minerva, her beautiful ebony face and stern smile. It hung in our living room, and it was the object of admiration by his Communist friend—the fact that she was black, not our maid. When Minerva got married to Mr. Pinckney and moved to North Carolina, Daddy gave her the portrait as a wedding present. I missed Minerva more than I missed my dog Dopey, who died giving birth to six pups named after the other Seven Dwarfs. I kept Grumpy, but he was an ugly tan color and had a disposition suited to his name.

Daddy taught me the basics of drawing and painting, setting me up with my own easel and oil paints next to his. We sketched portraits of my friends with soft pencils in big, rough-papered art books. He taught me to shoot a .22 rifle. I was left-handed and outshot him and his drinking buddies, most of whom were drunk. On long trips to the Cape, or short trips to Jones Beach or the movies, Daddy talked to me, telling me about the stars and planets. We listened to mysteries on the radio. Daddy usually drove the car, but Mommy (everyone said) was a better driver. The back of Daddy's neck turned red when Mommy corrected his driving. He answered every question with an expert's analysis of why the sky was blue, why he didn't believe in God, and why James Joyce was a genius. At dinner, he spoke French to me, *"Passez-moi du sel et du poivre, s'il vous plaît."*

My mother cooked fantastic meals of roast lamb, roast chicken, pot roast, apple pie, applesauce, roasted potatoes, glazed carrots. "Isn't this the best pot roast you've ever had?" Mom would ask. Daddy would nod, picking at the gourmet dishes. His mother, Grandma Abbie, couldn't boil noodles. I had a small appetite, ate small portions. Mommy thought I was too skinny. The doctor couldn't find anything wrong, but in those days, doctors believed that cutting out the tonsils would improve a child's appetite. When my sore throat healed, I still didn't eat much. Mommy bought me beautiful clothes, admired by my teachers, especially Miss Halpern. She made me stand in front of the class to show off my Scottish tartan skirt and matching hat. I thought my parents were the most beautiful parents in the world, that my mother was the best cook in the world, and my father the smartest person in the whole wide world.

One day, my mother gave me a book in which there were illustrations of the insides of a woman's belly. Rubbing her fat belly, she said she was having a baby, in June. I shrugged. But I was not happy about losing my only child status. My friend Ginny's baby brother stank of sour milk and poop, and she had to babysit after school.

Without my approval, my sister Judy arrived in summer 1941. My Jewish grandparents, Abbie and Earl, my uncle Billy, and my aunt Bea—my father's brother and sister—cooed over the pretty baby with big brown eyes and brown curly hair. I was ignored, no longer the precious only grandchild. Judy had taken my place.

I tried not to care. I had my own bedroom. I had bunk beds and slept alternately on the top, then the bottom. My sister slept in a crib in my parents' big bedroom and cried all night. My father came home late at night. "Can't you shut up the brat?"

My father and mother argued a lot about where to live, now that they had two kids. Daddy wanted to live in Manhattan: the center of the universe. My mother wanted to live in the "country" for the fresh air and natural beauty. Moving to Queens, as we did, pleased nobody. An "outer borough" of New York City, it might as well have been East Nowhere. I liked the country where we spent summer vacations—a small Hudson Valley town. It was ninety miles from Manhattan, reachable by bus (a three-hour ride with a lot of local stops) or by car. We stayed at a boarding house called "The Farm" with my father's Communist friends and families. The pond, made by a cement dam on which we often sat, smelled of fish. Water snakes circled the shore. I learned to swim when I jumped off the diving board and my cork water vest came off. Unaware of its loss, I dog-paddled to the ladder as my nude mother was about to dive in and save me. Women and little kids swam nude from noon to three in the afternoon. Men and older boys swam in the morning and late afternoons, also nude. The big boys, of course, spied on the women from the reeds.

Friends of my father eventually bought or built houses in this town. Daddy decided to build us a house. I watched it go up, like a dream atop bedrock that had to be dynamited for the cellar. We moved in and left the city behind—all except Daddy, who commuted to work, leaving on Monday morning, returning on Friday night.

The house was built on three acres of woods. We had a stream, frogs, orange salamanders, and snakes. The living room was wainscoted in knotty pine. There was a large stone fireplace. The walls were covered in sienna wallpaper with silver foxes. My sister had her own bedroom, next to the nanny, Celie, a toothless, country illiterate white woman, nothing like my beloved Minerva. I had a big bedroom to myself again, with my bunk beds; three piles of comic books—*Wonder Woman, Donald Duck*, and *Superman*; a collection of scrapbooks—airplanes, movie stars, and Disney's *Fantasia*. I had a worktable with chairs where I could sit and draw pictures. I made an Indian village with construction paper teepees and plaster models of warriors, Indian princesses, and a chief. I made model airplanes of balsa wood covered with tissue paper.

I loved my new school, the Campus School whose teachers came from the New York State Teachers' College in the town. My teachers wanted to skip me a grade. But I already had friends in the fourth grade. So they let me do independent projects while the rest of the class had spelling tests and reading lessons. I was the only Jew (half-Jewish, to be exact, but this upstate village did not make fine distinctions outside of Protestant Christianity). I was unaware that there *was* a difference. The teachers regarded me as the resident genius. My best friends were Dutch Reformed Protestants, which meant that they weren't Catholics. Daddy said Catholics were the dumbest of all. The Campus School, adjoining the college, was more like a private school than a public school. Our classes were invited to art shows, where I saw some Hudson River School paintings for the first time. My father's interests in art were mainly modern, and excluded such "sentimental" art. Best of all, I heard Eleanor Roosevelt speak. She lived in Hyde Park, on the other side of the Hudson River, and came often to promote savings bonds and refugee relief during World War II. Eleanor Roosevelt was my role model, a rare example of a successful, outspoken woman. I loved her funny, squeaky voice and messy hair. I thought of her as my ideal woman—smart, kind, and independent.

My mother, though she loved the country, missed shopping in city markets. She drove a new Plymouth convertible into town to the library every week for more books. She filled up the fridge with meat from an Italian butcher who didn't know how to carve a carcass, and gave her—for free—the filet mignon, having previously fed it to the dogs. My father brought friends home on weekends. Mom cooked. Everybody drank and talked about art and Marxism. I sat at their feet, listening. During the week, I loved being in school and brought my friends home to play. One of my girlfriends, Gerry, taught me that I had a third "hole" and helped me find it with her finger. I did not miss the city. My mother, however, seemed lost, had no friends. We took walks on the three acres and picked bittersweet. We both missed Daddy during the week. I came home from school to find her asleep in her bedroom. Under the blue silk duvet, she reeked of alcohol. Under the bed, the empty bottles told the truth: she had passed out. After a binge, she'd make my favorite meals and promise it wouldn't happen again. When it did, again and again, I took back the clay ashtray I'd made with my handprint in nursery school.

Six months after we'd settled into our new house, Daddy sold it. Sold everything: the furniture and the new Plymouth convertible. We were moving to California. Daddy said I could take one box of things— books, crayons, scrapbooks of fighter planes, but not my Indian village. I didn't want to go. "You'll meet movie stars, get autographs," Daddy said. My mother didn't say anything as she packed our clothes, her hair wrapped up in a scarf. No reason was given to me for this uprooting.

We left on the 20th Century Limited from Grand Central Station on a snowy night in March, two days before my eleventh birthday. The trip to Los Angeles would take three days and four nights. We had a drawing room with its own tiny bathroom. Racing through the snowy night, we arrived in Chicago where we changed to the Super Chief. It stopped in the middle of the Great Plains, where a troop train was connected onto the rear carrying soldiers on their way to the Pacific Theatre of the war. The troops took over our dining car, so we had no food until we reached LA. The porter got milk for Judy's bottle. When the train stopped at a station, Daddy ran and got oranges, candy bars, and sodas. My mother ran out of diapers for Judy and used her sanitary napkins. Hollywood, here we come.

Uncle Billy had moved to Hollywood a few months earlier, trying to break into movies. He met us at the station. We took a taxi to the house he had rented for us, a two-story, ugly house, with greasy, ugly furniture. Daddy thought he'd get a job with Disney, but he had to settle for a low-paying job at an ad agency after Disney turned him down. My mother cooked for all of us: Uncle Billy and his sister, Aunt Bea, who had followed us; Billy's chorus girl girlfriend Dotty; me; Judy; and Daddy. It was like a boarding house, only Mom didn't make a dime. Her only pleasure was shopping in the farmer's market. Billy got into the Pasadena Playhouse acting program. Bea quickly got a job as a bookkeeper. Helium-filled balloons loomed over the entire California coast, tethered to earth. They were supposed to confuse Japanese aircraft from trying to bomb us. I hated the Mitsubishi Zero fighter planes, squat and ugly. I liked the sleek American P-40 and British Spitfire. I saw only American planes speeding low to the ground, up and down the coast, not any Japanese planes. Adding to anxiety, temblors (small earthquakes) shook the dishes in the cupboard every day.

World War II roared on in Europe and the Pacific. I missed New York and my friends three thousand miles away. I finished fifth grade with a mean teacher, an older man whose military classification was 4F, and fifty kids crammed into a room meant for thirty. I hated school for the first and only time in my life. We spent a long hot summer in LA. I even hated the beach at Santa Monica, the sand dark and gritty, the Pacific Ocean gray, cold, and full of Japanese subs.

And suddenly, seven months after we'd moved west, in October, we headed back East, to New York. "Hurray!" I yelled, doing handstands on the filthy couch in our ugly house. Even seven months had been too long. The reason I was given for the return East was that Daddy wasn't making enough money.

Because of a raging polio epidemic in Chicago, my mother delayed leaving in September. The epidemic continued, however, so she planned a return route south of Chicago. We were driving back in a beat-up jalopy, only four of us: my mother, my aunt Bea, Judy, and me—female vagabonds without a man in sight to help. Billy had sold his Broadway musical records to buy a one-way bus ticket back to New York; he had flunked as an actor. My father had to "take care of business" in LA. He would fly back to New York later.

My mother and Bea planned to share the driving, but Bea kept falling asleep at the wheel, so Mom did all the driving. She had once dreamed of being a long-distance truck driver. The decrepit Chevy was unreliable, and gas rationing made us fraught with terror every time the tank read empty. I sat in back, crowded in with luggage, choking with a cold, soothed with a box of Kleenex and bottles of warm Coke. Judy cried nonstop, passed from Bea's lap to mine and back. Then she held her breath for an eternity, until she turned blue. My mother, frantic with too much responsibility, grabbed my bottle of Coke and threw the fizzy drink into Judy's face. Judy froze. She never held her breath again.

Despite the discomfort, I was just happy to be going "home." And, despite the hazards and inconveniences caused by World War II, I loved traveling.

We left Hollywood on a hot October morning, and headed into the Mojave Desert. The heat rose like waves above the endless sand. Halfway across, the jalopy ground to a halt. It would not move. We got out and sat on the running board, my mother shading her eyes looking up and down the empty road. After an hour, a car stopped. A man got out wearing a fedora and suit. He inspected our car briefly and said the brakes had "frozen" in the 110-degree heat. When the sun went down, he said, they would cool off and the car would move. He tipped his hat and drove off. As the red sun dropped over the Pacific, the dry desert air cooled quickly. In the dusk, we drove out of the desert and into the Sierras. We spent the lovely cool night in a motel in Lone Pine, among fragrant pines.

The next day, we raced through Utah, stopping once to try the slot machines in a town with a wooden sidewalk. I lost all my nickels. With the six old cylinders clanking, the jalopy climbed the mountainous road into southern Wyoming, where we watched a Wild West rodeo parade beneath our hotel windows. In the morning, we coasted down the eastern slope of the Rockies, the engine turned off to save gas and coupons, and slid into the flat endless plains, the road a tunnel through fields of ten-foot corn. Omaha was crowded with WAACs at the training base, and a magnet for male soldiers. No rooms at the inn. On to Indianapolis, to a city hotel where my mother tried to buy a drink at the bar.

"Ladies Must Be Accompanied by a Male Escort," a sign said. A waiter seated us the dining room, at a table covered by a white cloth, where Mom could order a gin martini and Bea a scotch on the rocks.

Indiana was the most boring place we'd encountered, the heart of the Bible Belt, I learned. We were now stuck there for three days. The gas coupons allotted for our three-thousand-mile journey had run out, since coupons had lost value from five gallons each in California to three gallons each east of the Mississippi. From the hotel, my mother went to the rationing board every day to beg for enough gas coupons to get us to New York. It was mobbed with people trying to get coupons. On the third day, a man said he could help her. He took her to the manager, and she got enough coupons to make it to New York. She had dinner with the man, and didn't come back to our hotel until morning. I wondered why—but Mom didn't explain. We had the coupons, period.

We had spent two weeks on the road, and now were nearing the final eight-hundred-mile leg home—to New York—speeding down the new Pennsylvania Turnpike. And then into New Jersey. My heart lifted as I saw the gray haze and familiar profile, the Empire State Building, tallest building in the world! Through the Holland Tunnel, up the West Side Highway and cross town through Central Park, we pulled up in front of my grandmother Abbie's swank apartment building on the Upper East Side. The jalopy sighed, steaming its last breath. The doorman called for a tow truck. It died like a worn-out horse that had brought us to safety. Abbie buzzed us in.

Abbie and my grandfather Earl were Daddy's parents. Their apartment was on the ninth floor and had a balcony overlooking the East River. Bea soon found herself an apartment nearby and another bookkeeping job, and Uncle Billy moved in with a gay actor friend. We stayed at Abbie's for two weeks, when Mom found a one-bedroom apartment on Manhattan's Upper East Side—a slum in the middle of opulence.

Mom, Judy, and I moved into the dark, furnished apartment on Seventy-Second Street, between Madison and Park avenues. Our new "home" was swarming with cockroaches and bedbugs. Two living room windows looked out on luxury high-rises across the street that blocked the sun. But Daddy did not appear. Eavesdropping on my mother's phone calls, I figured out he was back in New York. Along with six million other people.

My mother took me to register at the local public school. The gates were locked. Kids screamed from barred windows. In that silk-stocking neighborhood, most of the children went to private schools, except for kids living in the tenements on Third Avenue under the El. My mother called my father. The next week, I was enrolled in the sixth grade at Walt Whitman, a progressive private school on Seventy-Eighth and Madison. I sewed the school emblem onto last year's winter coat, dark plaid with a raincoat lining. I had grown several inches. My arms stuck out of the sleeves like sticks.

In our dreary apartment, my mother drank herself into a stupor, rousing every few days to shop for food and cook. I still had not seen my father since we had returned from California, but now I knew he was paying the bills for us, at least. It was called *alimony*: Latin for *nourishment money*.

My mother had chronic phlebitis, and since Judy's birth, ulcers had oozed from both her ankles. Doctors at New York Hospital tried everything: the new sulfa drugs, patch skin grafts, skin grafts from one leg to the other ankle. Mom spent weeks at a time in the hospital. Aunt Bea or Uncle Billy came to babysit Judy.

Walt Whitman School was a heaven-haven. I loved learning about poetry and art, learning Spanish. There were six of us in the sixth grade, my five classmates from wealthy WASP families. They treated me as an equal, probably unaware of my half-Jewish heritage. I made one good friend, Jane. She invited me to her family's apartment nearby. Her parents were quiet, pale, polite, mousy. The walls, linens, and furniture were pale shades of ecru. I wasn't comfortable there, but neither could I invite Jane to my slum on Seventy-Second Street.

We studied electricity and even created some of our own with a sulfuric acid battery in a real lab. I loved our teacher, Mr. Buttinger, a Jewish refugee from Germany. We studied art at the Metropolitan Museum and read poetry with our class teacher, a kindly white-haired woman who invited us to her Park Avenue apartment, which was adorned with Chinese art. Walt Whitman's gym was a former ballroom. I excelled at the high jump and the sprint. On Halloween, we had a contest with a parade of homemade masks and costumes. I had no glue, no paints. Daddy used to keep me supplied with every imaginable art material. I took a grocery bag and cut out big ears from another one, found some string from a bakery box, and threaded the ears to the bag face. I did my best to draw in eyes, nose, and mouth with crayons, cutting holes for my eyes and mouth. The next day, my mask won second prize.

One dreary Saturday, Mom went out in a cab. I took Judy to the playground despite the threatening rain. At dusk, we walked home and I made supper; the only food left was peanut butter and stale bread. I killed roaches swarming in the breadbox. At eight o'clock, I read Judy stories and put her to bed. "Where's Mommy?" she asked, her big brown eyes wide with fear.

"At the doctor's," I said. I listened to my records: Arthur Rubenstein playing Chopin. I spent most of my allowance money on classical records.

The next morning, Mom still hadn't come home. I tried to hide my terror from Judy. We ate cold cereal. Finally, I called Grandma Abbie. "Mom isn't here. She didn't come home last night."

"Take a cab to my apartment."

"I don't have any money." Abbie said she'd leave money with her doorman to pay the cab fare. She had to get her hair done.

My hands shook as I dressed Judy, who looked more somber than usual. The phone rang—Mom! I hoped. The voice, however, wasn't hers. It was that of a woman I knew only by her odd name, Trixie. She said my mother had stayed at her place, in Greenwich Village. *Why didn't you call me last night!* I was fuming with rage. "When is she coming home?" I asked politely.

"I'll send her home in a cab as soon as she's awake."

You dumb bitch! I slammed the phone down. Rage and relief flooded my nerves. Mom was alive! I called Abbie.

"Never mind. Mom is on her way home."

It was nearly dark when my mother lurched out of a yellow cab. Judy and I had been watching from the window for hours. Mom had no idea how long she'd been away. Why didn't I have my father's phone number for emergencies? That long day and night without mother or father ended my childhood. I realized one can be an orphan with two living parents.

My mother broke down completely. A psychoanalyst now joined the horde of doctors at New York Hospital who were treating my mother's leg ulcers. My father footed the bills. Alimony. Child support. Doctors' bills. The "famous" psychoanalyst insisted Mom bring me to meet him. Rage had obliterated my misery. I would not let anyone hurt me any more. I was angry all the time. I learned not to tell anyone how I felt. I trusted no one.

This "famous" doctor sat behind a big desk, my mother and I facing him like errant pupils in front of the principal. Venetian blinds behind him (of course it was a "him") let the sun through the open slats, blinding me. All I could see of him were thick eyeglasses and a black suit. He asked me questions; I answered with the "right" answers (preparations for my doctoral orals decades later). Then he smiled. "You should listen to your daughter; she is very intelligent and mature for her age." I was supposed to be flattered. He couldn't have imagined what contempt I felt for his so-called expertise. Why did so many adults shirk their duties? Why were they so stupid?

In her state of emotional ruin, my mother could not take care of herself, let alone two children. Nonetheless, she did save me from the horrific public school. My father would not have gone to the trouble. If not for my mother, I would not have survived that roach-infested apartment. She also got my father to rent a three-quarter-size piano, knowing how much I missed playing the one he had sold—the piano he had bought for me when I began piano lessons at age six.

Mom did one more thing for me before she abandoned her role as my mother. She sent me to Charles of the Ritz to get my pigtails cut off and my thin, straight hair permed. I had no thought of becoming a woman. I walked down Madison Avenue with fifty dollars in my pocket. A pretty young woman met me and seated me in a chair, then turned it around and tipped me backwards. My neck rested on a basin, as if my head was being prepared for the chopping block. She washed my clean hair, rubbed it with a towel, then cut, cut, cut, thin strands falling on the pink plastic sheet covering me. The wet remaining straggles were put into big curlers. The hairdresser then brushed on a goo that smelled like poison gas, after which she covered my head in clear plastic.

It took hours before she unwrapped my head, took out the curlers, and washed out the stink. More curlers. Then she moved me to a chair under a giant steel blower and set the dial. The heat burned my neck; the chemicals burned my scalp. Three hours later, my hair dried and combed, she let me look in the mirror. Brown curls, short hair. Who was that in the mirror? I looked fifty years old. I looked like my grandmother Abbie—minus the bluing in her gray hair. Despite my best intentions, they were making me into a woman. I did not cry, but I wanted to kill the women who had done this to me.

One Saturday, Daddy showed up, climbing the stairs to our second-floor apartment. He took me to dinner at the Kavkaz, then to a Soviet film at the Stanley Theatre. He bought me an album of the Red Army

Chorus and a pin of a pretty Russian girl. He handed me a twenty and put me in a cab.

The next time I saw him, just before Christmas, my mother told him I was outgrowing my clothes. I needed a new winter coat, especially. Daddy took me to an expensive children's store near Central Park. The saleswoman, seeing a classic scenario of father-daughter bonding, said, "Oh, doesn't she look *darling!*" I was enveloped in a white fur coat I'd spotted. The price was outrageous, I knew. Daddy took out his wallet. He let me carry the big box with red ribbon to Rumpelmeyer's, a fancy soda shop. He bought me my favorite black-and-white soda, with a cloud of whipped cream. On Fifth Avenue, he put me into a cab and gave me a twenty. As I looked back, the cab turned back into a pumpkin and mice scurried ahead. My father disappeared into his forbidden palace.

"How will you ever keep it clean?" my mother said, shaking her head. I hugged the fake white fur, admiring the Russian embroidery trim and silver buttons. I refused to sew on the Walt Whitman school patch.

I sat by the cold ashes of our lives that night. I had the white coat, proving that my father was real and that I had once lived another life with him.

People usually lie when a family breaks up. My family—grandparents, uncle, aunt—said nothing. Mom said nothing. Daddy, of course, said not a word. The whole family pretended that nothing had changed. In the spring, I learned that Daddy was living with another woman. Bella. She had been the reason we had moved to California—to "get away" from her; she had also been the reason we came back from California—so he could live with her. Bella had worked in his office in Rockefeller Center. Bella was everything my mother was not: Jewish. Younger. She couldn't cook.

In June, when the term ended at Walt Whitman School, my mother asked me where I wanted to live. Whitman only went to the sixth grade, so I'd have to change schools anyway. We looked at an apartment in London Terrace. It had trees and grass in a central courtyard. It was a pretty apartment. But I did not want to live where you had to take an elevator to get in or out. Where you couldn't walk on the earth itself.

"Upstate," I said. "Let's go back there."

In July, Mom rented a house on a street next to the college, and we moved in with my Irish grandmother Nell. I hardly knew this Irish-Dutch side of me. "So, he left you for another Jew. Serves you right for marrying a kike." Nell was the first person who taught me I could be hated for being Jewish. She had one brown eye and one hazel eye, both of which ignored Judy and me. Uncle Edward, my mother's younger, somewhat mentally retarded brother, also lived with us. He repaired pinball machines for the local branch of the Mafia, his head shaking from a childhood bout of rheumatic fever.

In August, Daddy rented the Fo'c's'le for us, a big, airy house on Fire Island, off the coast of Long Island, but he wasn't coming with us. I loved taking the boat launch there from Babylon on the mainland. I loved picking wild blueberries by the quart. I bought my first bikini bathing suit, at thirteen, when I had barely enough breast buds to make it usable. Every day, I walked to the beach and bodysurfed the Atlantic rollers. Judy played in the sand, and Mom got brown as a pecan, her premature white hair wrapped in a pretty scarf.

And then Mom had to go back into New York Hospital. Uncle Billy, unemployed as usual, came to the island to babysit. He was a better parent than my parents, cooking, braiding Judy's hair, dressing her in pretty pinafores, and guarding me. When Mom came back to Fire Island at the end of August, Daddy came. A photo of us shows the next to last time we were together as a family. My father looks very angry; my mother looks very sick.

In September, I went back to my beloved Campus School, entering seventh grade as if I'd never been away for a year and a half. I walked Judy to the Campus Nursery School, and picked her up after school. I had my friends again. Mom bought an old upright piano, and I resumed lessons with Mrs. Upright (her real name). She played like an elephant, but let me choose what to practice: Chopin and Beethoven, which I got by mail order. She also guided me through the *Thompson Books, Grades II and III.*

My mother cooked and went shopping in Kingston and Poughkeepsie for food and clothes. She read books from the library. Her loneliness was beyond my range of vision, that of a self-centered teenager.

One day before Christmas, Grandpa Ed came home, raving with the DTs (delirium tremens—alcohol withdrawal). It was worse than anything that followed my mother's binges. I stayed in my room, huddled with my sister, as he roared and ranted downstairs. He sat in a flowered armchair covered with Nell's crocheted doilies. The fit lasted all night.

The next morning, I crept down the stairs. Grampa was snoring, my grandmother's eyeglasses hanging off his nose. That evening, he woke and was as jolly and cheerful as Santa Claus. He cooked himself a big meal of fried potatoes and runny eggs. "Let's get the tree!" he said.

My mother drove Ed, Judy, and me to the farm outside of town where they had fresh-cut trees. Lights were strung so we could walk amidst the fragrance of this temporary forest and examine the spruce and balsam trees. Ed shuffled through the rows and came to a well-rounded spruce, yanking it upright. It was a ten-footer, the most expensive size available. Mom paid for it. Ed helped the farmer tie it to the roof of our car.

In the back yard, I watched my grandfather saw off the bottom trunk, then fit the tree into a stand and screw the bolts into the trunk. He dragged it around front and into the living room, where he stood it in the corner we'd cleared. It was the biggest, fullest tree I'd ever seen. Daddy had always got a medium-sized tree, which we decorated according to Daddy's artistic demands: shiny balls of red, gold, silver, blue, and green spaced carefully, as were the strings of lights, everything balanced, and just enough tinsel to suggest icicles. My Jewish relatives came with heaps of presents, mostly for me, the only grandchild until Judy was born. It was my own Shirley Temple movie—the *Good Ship Lollipop*, with every toy a child could dream of.

Grandpa Ed's tree was a miracle of extravagance. He had saved rare ornaments from his childhood in Tarrytown, brought to the United States by a Dutch grandfather. These were old glass ornaments from Holland in faded rainbow colors and shapes of people. He also had tiny metal figurines of ice skaters, skiers, reindeer, people dressed in long coats and fancy hats. From another box, Ed withdrew a folding red fence, four inches high, long enough to encircle the tree at a three-foot distance from the trunk. He unrolled a package of cotton batting around the base of the tree to simulate snow. He inserted mirror lakes in cuts in the batting, put a triangular carton under the "snow" for a ski hill, then added tiny fake trees, a church, log cabins, and houses. Then he let me help put in the figurines.

After stringing the lights on the tree and through the tiny village, he plugged them in. It was the most beautiful town I had ever seen. I sat on the floor wishing I could live in this ideal village.

My mother cooked a twenty-pound turkey and made the stuffing and gravy from giblets and drippings. She made two pies—apple and pumpkin. Nell mashed the potatoes with half a pound of butter and a cup of milk. The table was set with Nell's newly finished crocheted tablecloth, two hundred circles in lacy ecru covered with clear plastic to save it from gravy spills.

I loved my mother's cooking, but my stomach shut down with excitement. My father was coming for Christmas!

"Daddy!" I screamed and ran to hug him.

"Hiya, kid." He carried a shopping bag of gifts and added them to the pile under the tree. My mother looked beautiful, her hair done up in nice rolls. She wore her red silk blouse (a former gift from my father) beneath her flowered apron. "Can we open the presents now?" I begged. Judy sat on the floor, looking up hopefully, but mystified. She barely remembered Daddy.

My father poured himself a stiff bourbon. "Okay." I restrained myself from tearing open my gifts, reading nametags and passing gifts to the recipients. The snow-covered scene under the tree was matched by the snowy streets outside our rented house.

Daddy gave me just what I wanted: *The Encyclopedia of Music and Musicians*. Mommy gave me a pretty sweater and plaid skirt. Judy played with her toy music box, holding a baby doll Aunt Bea had sent.

"Time to eat!" my mother called, wearing the pair of red satin slippers with gold embroidery Daddy had given her. I was sure they were getting back together.

Uncle Edward carved the turkey, his head shaking as he laughed. A jolly family scene, right out of Dickens.

After dinner, I sat on the floor next to Daddy, reading my new encyclopedia. Bing Crosby was singing "I'm Dreaming of a White Christmas" on the big floor radio. Judy fell asleep, and Mommy carried her upstairs to our bedroom. Judy and I slept in twin beds on rollers. I read her nursery rhymes and Lewis Carroll. "Read it again," she always said, afraid to go asleep.

'Twas brillig and the slithy toves
Did gyre and gimble in the wabe;
All mimsy were the borogoves,
And the mome raths outgrabe.
    (Carroll, 1959, 208)

Daddy took the ten o'clock bus back to the city that night. He did not come back again until the following summer when he returned to arrange the final details of the divorce. Since adultery was the only reason New York allowed for divorce, Daddy had asked his best friend/ drinking buddy Al to play the adulterer. He was letting my mother "win" the divorce. As the day dragged on and the whiskey and gin bottles emptied, my mother started crying. Then the screaming began.

"Bitch! You've got my money *and* the kids."

"Please, Dave, don't do this!"

"Stop it, Daddy! Stop it!" I cried, tugging at his hard arm.

Daddy, his face turning purple, swung his right arm and struck me across the face. The blow knocked me into the wall. I saw the cabbage roses on the wallpaper black out as I slid down. I had never been hit before. Not by Daddy. Not by anyone. When air suddenly pushed up from my lungs, I screamed like a banshee. "Shut up, brat!" he yelled. I ran upstairs. I thought my father was going to beat me to death. I lay on my bed, weeping, waiting for the end. No one came to comfort me.

The next morning, Daddy was gone. Mommy was still in bed, an empty gin bottle on the floor.

There was a sense of anticlimax after the divorce. The worst wasn't over, but I had hardened myself against my parents. I would take care of myself.

Doc Reid was often called in to treat my mother's alcoholic comas. He was a recovering alcoholic himself, with a game leg he got in the war. He finally persuaded Mom to join AA. I was relieved, hoping she would come to her senses and get a life.

After a few months of sobriety in AA, Mom started dating fellow members. Some of the men were nice. They came to pick her up, vying for her attention. Then Eric asked her out. He didn't have a car, so she picked him up for meetings. A month after they met, Eric moved in with us, sharing Mom's bedroom, cooking our meals, and cleaning the house. He was twice divorced and had three kids who had disowned him. The doctors said he'd die if he took another drink.

Eric had a large, bulbous head, smarmy manners, and a tic of apologizing. "I'm sorry," he'd say if the coffee wasn't warm enough, if it rained, if he didn't put enough milk in the mashed potatoes. "Heh-heh," he'd chuckle, winning a game of gin, "I'm sorry." But he took care of my mother, bringing her meals on a tray. They sat in her bedroom for hours, playing gin rummy, drinking pots of coffee, and smoking cigarettes.

Mom and Eric married on my fifteenth birthday. We went to dinner in the Old Fort to celebrate, and then they left, taking Judy, six years old. "You don't want to come with us," my mother said to me.

"No, I don't." I was going to finish high school, staying with Grandma Nell. Daddy would pay my room and board and my allowance. His check came every month in an envelope addressed to me in his artistic handwriting. The letters always said something like, "We are up to our ears in work. Love, Dave." Or, "Work is terrible. We're going broke. Love, Dave." Daddy did not want me to call him "Daddy" anymore.

The emptiness in the pit of my stomach was matched by the emptiness of Nell's house. I could take care of myself. I did my own laundry, cleaned my room, and was at the top of my class. My friends noticed nothing different, assuming my grandmother was a nice old lady. They had never known (I hoped) about my mother's alcoholism. They thought she was just "sick." We went to movies and basketball games and flirted with the boys. I had a steady boyfriend who didn't understand a thing about me. I played the piano. Betty Anne and my other friends went to church and youth fellowships. I was an atheist, like my parents. Once a month, I took the bus to visit my father and Bella in Manhattan.

At my high school graduation, I was valedictorian, beating out an English professor's son, John, by four-tenths of a point. John and his family were quite chagrined that their son, who had read *Beowulf* in the original Old English by the age of twelve, was only salutatorian. In this small, upstate New York town, a half-Jew, a *girl* from the city, had upset the norm, the assumed social superiority of the Protestant (mainly Huguenot) residents.

To my astonishment, my father came to my graduation, sitting in the front row with Bella. Of course, *he* had been valedictorian of Townsend

Harris High School at age fifteen. My mother and Eric, now living in Florida, sent a bouquet of yellow roses that stood on the stage next to the podium. I gave my speech on federal aid to education, which had not yet been put into action. The conservative principal had demanded that I choose another topic. "No," I'd said. John's salutatorian address was on the history of the Huguenots in our town. That pleased the principal and the audience much more. My father's famous grin told me how proud he was of my liberal topic.

The day after graduation, I had no place to live. Nell had given up the rented house (no more board money from my father) and moved next door to take care of an elderly retired professor. So, for the summer between high school and college, I stayed in my father's one-bedroom apartment in Queens, sharing a bedroom with my toddler half-sister, Robin. I didn't know anyone. My high school friends had scattered to various camps and relatives. My books, records, and winter clothes were stored in a shed at Daddy's summer cabin upstate. When I finally collected them at the end of the summer, they were half ruined, eaten by mildew.

I had been accepted to Cornell University, but my father refused to let me go with "that bunch of snobs." "You can go to Hunter and stay with us." My stepmother would not be thrilled to have the once-adored favorite daughter move in for four years.

I visited Mom and Eric in July. "You can stay with us and go to the college at Coral Gables!" I could see my future: Mom lying on the couch, her legs wrapped in bandages, her ulcers oozing, and me waiting on her. Eric washing dishes before anyone finished eating. Judy needing attention. Mom drunk. Eric drunk. Again. And me trying to study and enjoy college life. Symbolically, the week I stayed with them, a black spider scurried down the wall toward my bed. I knew when to get out. *Sauve qui peut!* Every man for himself.

Eschewing the proposals of both my parents, I chose to go to upstate New York State College down the street from where I had lived with my grandmother Nell. It was tuition free, and I had a state scholarship that paid for my books. My father would have to pay only my room and board. He ranted at what I was costing him. That year, he put in a swimming pool at their summer cabin. But I had my own home at last.

Chapter V

SEX EDUCATION WITH UNCLE BILLY, 1944

Billy emerged from the steaming bathroom with his Carmen Miranda face: purple eyeshadow, eyes ringed in kohl, inch-long false eyelashes, fire-engine-red lipstick on his fat lips, three-inch silver hoops dangling from the flowered turban wrapped around his wide head.

"Aye, aye, aye, aye!
Hey, Mamacita, dashupeta!
Mama y quiero, Mama—"

My uncle Billy sang in a full-throated, raspy falsetto, snapping his fingers, which were adorned with red-enameled nails. As teenagers, he and his cousin Jack developed an act to get on *Major Bowes' Amateur Hour*, a live radio program we listened to every Sunday. Jack danced and told jokes, while Billy impersonated Carmen Miranda, Bette Davis, Katherine Hepburn, and James Cagney—"All right, Louie, drop dat gun!"

Billy and Jack got an audition and were given a slot on an upcoming *Amateur Hour*. "It could lead to big things!" Billy said. The Sunday of their broadcast, my parents and I gathered at Grandma Abbie's. Billy was Abbie's third child, the baby of her family. I sat on the floor in front of the big radio. The deep-voiced announcer said, "And now, ladies and gentlemen, the *Major Bowes' Amateur Hour*!" The first performer was a thirteen-year-old soprano singing the "Bell Song" from *Lakme*; she was followed by a fifteen-year-old vibraphonist. Then came a ventriloquist (we had to imagine that the dummy looked like Charlie McCarthy), and then a juggler whose skill at tossing clubs we only could deduce from comments of "Wow! Wow! Wow!" from the audience. Major Bowes said, "Wasn't that something, ladies and gentlemen?"

Finally, Billy and Jack were announced: "And here are the Queens Cuzzins, Billy and Jack!" At first, I didn't recognize Billy's voice. Billy didn't sound like himself *or* Carmen Miranda. We knew what his costume looked like, and had seen his hand-and-hip wiggling and rumba steps in high heels. We could hear Jack's tap dancing. The audience barely clapped. Then Jack told a joke: "What do you think is under Miranda's turban?" he asked. No one answered. He laughed, "A bald head and a wig!" Major Bowes gave them the buzzer.

Jack eventually made it in the new television industry, producing sit-coms, working behind the camera, but Billy had nothing but his drag queen image. He hung around actors and dancers in New York, living at home with Abbie and his father, Earl, in their nice apartment overlooking the East River. Earl complained about his deadbeat son. My father, his older brother, called him Billy the Bum. So Billy went to Hollywood, borrowing the fare from his cornucopia—Mom. To everyone's amazement, he was accepted as an apprentice at the Pasadena Playhouse, the repertory theatre where many actors got their start. Billy landed a small part as a detective in *Arsenic and Old Lace*. We were also living in Hollywood at that time (in the middle of World War II), so we all went to see Billy make his debut. He was so bad, even I could tell.

After Billy sold his collections of Broadway musical records to buy a bus ticket back to New York, his mother, Abbie, let him sleep on the living room floor, not wanting him to ruin the red velvet sofa. We arrived back in New York soon after he did.

When Billy was in his twenties, he camped out at Abbie's on the living room floor. When we visited Abbie, we all stepped over Billy, who slept soundly through the afternoon. As dinner was served, my father would kick him and yell, "Wake up, you lazy bum!" I'm sure the screaming could be heard all the way out on the East River.

But I liked Uncle Billy. He took me out for ice cream and bought me pretty clothes for my birthday, charged to his mother's account at

Bloomie's. He told me my eyes were beautiful—deep set blue, with long lashes—and talked to me as if I were a grown-up. He never bossed me around, like Aunt Bea, his sister.

The summer I turned twelve, Daddy rented a house for Mommy, my sister Judy and me, on Fire Island. Daddy wasn't coming with us. Then, my mother's ulcers on her ankle burst open again, and she had to go back to New York Hospital for skin grafting and new drugs. She'd be hospitalized for at least a month. Since the rent on the Fire Island house, "The Fo'c's'le," was already paid for the summer, it was decided that Judy and I would stay there with a sitter-housekeeper: Billy. Billy, always unemployed, took the offer. He became our governess, cook, and housekeeper.

I was glad it was Billy and not Aunt Bea. She loved taking care of Judy and me, but she was very bossy, nervous, and clumsy, telling us what to do every minute, what to eat every meal, and what to say whenever. Her cooking was true to her schooling as a dietitian: healthy and tasteless. No salt … meat steamed till it was gray. The only dish she made that I loved was steak tartare: raw ground roundsteak, chopped onions, and raw egg. Like Billy, Aunt Bea was single. She hadn't married, but not by choice. She was, to put it cruelly, unattractive in looks and personality. Her fits of anger and jealousy, plus her buckteeth and acned skin, drove men away. Even Bea did not love herself; her parents ignored her, Billy taunted her, my father hardly knew she existed. She craved love, nonetheless, like any human being.

"Who do you love the most, Billy or me?" she demanded of me.

"The same," I answered with self-preservation in mind.

Billy, by contrast, was fun and funny. He'd burst into song on the street, "oooooooOOklahoma! Where the wind comes sweepin' down the plain …" hoping he'd be mistaken by passersby for Alfred Drake, the handsome baritone who sang it on stage. (Billy was short and nowhere near as handsome, to say nothing of his froggy voice for such a hope.) He'd praise a woman passing by for dressing well; he'd criticized another for dressing in bad taste. In Manhattan, luckily, such behaviors are tolerated or ignored. He loved dressing up Judy and me in pretty clothes. I trusted Billy. I knew he'd be there when I woke up in the morning. I knew he'd cook tasty meals and keep our clothes clean and ironed. Billy could braid my pigtails almost as well as Mom could.

That summer on Fire Island, while Billy babysat, was when my father decided to leave us and divorce my mother. I didn't know it then, however. It was also the summer I found the bloodstain in my white underpants and on the bed sheet. I couldn't figure out what it was at first. When Billy gathered up our clothes and sheets for laundering, he would discover the stains. I was embarrassed. Shocked and angry. I was a tomboy. I could outrun boys and body surf the waves as well as any of them. But my mother had warned me and had provided me with the necessary equipment for dealing with menstruation. I had never expected it so soon—if ever!

Billy kept house in The Fo'c's'le with Judy while I walked down the wooden boardwalk to the brilliant Atlantic Ocean to be with my friends on the beach. They were city kids, like me, whose parents had rented houses for the summer. There were handsome twin boys who came from Hungary, Stefan and Ivan. I was mad for dark-haired, dark-eyed Ivan. Stefan, light haired and pale eyed, pursued me when we played tag. Beverly, the only "island" kid, from Long Island, was pigtailed like me, and brown as a pecan, skinny and tough. Her father owned a boatyard and marina in Bay Shore, across the bay. Daddy came to visit one weekend to check up on Billy (and pay him). When he saw Beverly and me playing, he sketched Beverly. I burned with jealousy. He never sketched me.

One evening after dark, my friends and I gathered on the bayside dock, watching the ferries come in, unloading more summer guests. Jellyfish glowed in the undulating seawater. Gradually, we wandered off toward the ocean side, the surf getting louder as we approached. Fireflies glittered like stars among the blueberry bushes and scrub pines. We came to an empty lot, sandy and dark. It was our hide-and-seek fairyland.

"Here I come, ready or not!" yelled Ivan.

We scattered behind bushes, under small dunes. Ivan crept up on me, silently, pinning me to the ground, and lay on top of me. I was tingling all over. His dark eyes shone. I yielded to his power. But he sat up, letting me go. I was disappointed.

That fall, walking in Manhattan with my father after he bought me that white fluffy winter coat (compensation for his leaving me), I saw Ivan across the street with a tall, handsome aristocrat—his father, I assumed. We stared at each other. But we did not wave or say hello.

Near the end of the summer with Billy, I met Suzie, a buxom redhead sixteen years old. Her sudden friendship flattered me, a mere twelve-year-old with no breasts. She was staying in a small cottage up the same "street." No cars were allowed on Ocean Beach; there were only wooden walkways for pedestrians and beach carts. We walked barefoot toward her cottage talking about religion, politics, and boys. Suzie was mature for her age, she told me. Her parents lived somewhere distant, letting Suzie and her seventeen-year-old sister Ellen live alone on Fire Island. Suzie took me to meet Ellen. She was sitting on the screened porch wearing a black cocktail dress, black heels, and smoking a cigarette. Her lipstick left a red ring on the paper. Smoke rose up through her dark, curly hair. Suzie introduced me, "This is Barbara. She's very mature for her age." Ellen offered me a cigarette. I shook my head, pigtails flying from side to side, making me feel like a child. She patted the flowered cushion on the wicker sofa, and I sat down beside her. Suzie took a cigarette, puffing it inexpertly, and sat in a chair opposite.

Ellen was petite, like a Kewpie doll, in her black dress and red mouth. She drew on her cigarette, then said, "I just got back from my honeymoon. I'm not a virgin anymore." Her eyes bored into mine. Suzie giggled. Ellen said her husband, a sailor, had been shipped overseas. "I'll show you my trousseau." I didn't know what a trousseau was, but smiled knowingly. She led me inside the dark cottage and opened a large box. We sat on the couch as she drew out the items: a black silk nightgown with lace insets, lace panties that were no more than a two-inch strip, a black lace bra with cutouts for the nipples. The "trousseau" looked like something I had seen in a movie. I thought everything would be very uncomfortable to wear.

I got nervous, for some reason; I knew that Billy served dinner promptly at five. "I have to go home," I said, and left feeling as if I'd escaped something, but I didn't know what. I walked back to The Fo'c's'le in a dreamy daze. Suzie and Ellen reminded me of the Hansel and Gretel fairy tale, offering innocent me forbidden sweets like a pair of witches. I didn't tell Billy. The next day, I showered and waited for Suzie to pick me up to go to the beach. When it rained the following day, we spent the dark afternoon in the smoke-scented cottage, while Ellen and Suzie told me about men they had "known." I was spellbound.

A few days later, Suzie came to the screen door of The Fo'c's'le and asked me to have lunch with her on the dock; she'd pay. Billy was still in the shower. I yelled to him, telling him where I was going. "Just a sec!" he yelled back. I waited on the porch, swinging myself in the glider as Suzie stood outside the screen door. Billy came up to the door, dripping, a towel wrapped around his waist, and looked through the screen at Suzie. I saw immediately that he was angry. Billy could tongue lash better than anyone in the family, and no one ever dared contradict him when he was in that mood. No one except my father, that is, who hated his younger brother so much he could kill him with a paragraph of hundred-dollar epithets.

Billy eyed buxom Suzie in her low-cut halter-top and skin-tight white shorts. Her freckled skin was burnt lobster red. "You," he snarled. "I don't want you hanging around my niece. Get out, and don't let me see you near her again."

Suzie's mouth opened. It took her a minute to speak. "I—I didn't do anything wrong! Who do you think you are?" Her red face turned purple.

"Who said you did anything wrong? You got something to hide?"

Suzie stood defiantly, her arms crossed. "You're only her uncle. *You* can't tell me what to do!"

Billy grinned, dangerously. "Only her uncle? And what are you, her pimp? You're not fooling me, you bitch. You and your sister pick up sailors every night at the dock—the Bobbsey Twins of Ocean Beach. A buck a bang."

Suzie screamed. "You fag! You're not even a man!"

Billy pushed open the screen door and stood face to face with Suzie.

"Take a good look, you bitch," said Billy, whipping off his towel. "Take a good look at a man. You know a cock when you see one. You've fucked half the navy and the coast guard."

Suzie stepped back, stumbled, and burst into tears. She ran up the boardwalk, her red-gold ponytail waving like a horse's mane, back to the dark, parentless cottage. My parents weren't there either, but I had Uncle Billy.

Billy's last moment in the spotlight occurred in the 1960s because he happened to be a patient of a famous psychotherapist, Dr. Arnold Hutschnecker. According to columnists Drew Pearson and Jack Anderson, Vice President Richard Nixon had undergone psychotherapeutic treatments with Dr. Hutschnecker. Nixon's press secretary, Ron Ziegler, said it was "totally untrue." Other patients of the doctor said he was treating Nixon, but they were unwilling to be quoted. One patient, however, was willing: Uncle Billy. Drew Pearson wrote: "A patient, William Block, a commercial photographer, of 242 East 60th Street, New York, has authorized me to quote him as saying: 'I was a patient of Dr. Hutschnecker for four and a half years, during much of which time Vice President Nixon was also a patient.'"

The spotlight on Billy went out after his fifteen minutes of fame.

Billy had a few good jobs, one as senior art editor of *Redbook*. But he was unwilling or unable to keep regular working hours, arriving at the magazine at five in the afternoon as everyone else was leaving. He depended on his mother Abbie to support him until she died, and then on his sister Bea. He ended up on welfare, living with his sister Bea in her dark, one-bedroom apartment.

I saw Billy for the last time in 1971, a few months before he died of Hodgkin's lymphoma. He came to visit my husband and me upstate, sitting in our New England rocking chair, scratching his arms. "The itching is the worst part; there isn't any pain." He couldn't eat much. I drove him to the bus station. Aunt Bea picked him up and took him to her apartment in midtown Manhattan. He died at age fifty-five. My sister Judy was there. I wasn't told until his ashes were scattered—somewhere.

Chapter VI

DADDY: PRESENT ABSENCE, 1943–

There's an oil painting of me hanging in my living room, signed and dated, "A. Kaufmann, XII 1938." I am wearing my favorite royal blue dress with the embroidered Russian collar and placket, blue ribbons at the ends of my braids. I remember sitting still for two weeks, as if I were being punished, my hands curved in my lap, one atop the other, stiffly, in an artificial pose. My somber face is in three-quarters view, my eyes almost as blue as my dress. It's a fairly good likeness, judging by a photo of me in black and white at about the same age, except that my braids are pinned on top of my head in the photo. The artist, A. Kaufmann, had done my portrait in exchange for some advertising work my father had done for him. I don't think Kaufmann wanted to paint me any more than I wanted to sit still for two weeks.

A snapshot taken a few years later shows me sitting on my father's shoulder at Jones Beach, both of us grinning, next to my mother who looks about to cry. I remember how happy I was that day. My father is balancing me with one hand, looking like Atlas. (The gold statue of Atlas holding the hollow world still stands in front of the office building in Rockefeller Center where my father worked.) My hair is loose, shoulder-length, dark brown. My mother's shapely bare leg shows at the edge of the black-and-white photo.

In graduate school decades later, the famous poetry professor who read my first poems with reserved approval asked, "Are you Irish?"

"Half ... my mother."

"What's the other half?"

"German Jew."

"With that background, you could have been a drunken gambler instead of a smart poet."

My father's eyes were the color of a gray-green ocean (same as mine). Though he'd been born and raised in New York City, he sounded like a sophisticated college graduate, perhaps from Yale. He had refused, in fact, to go to college. His tenor voice produced clear, intellectual pronunciations of all the words in his large vocabulary, which he had acquired from reading Hemingway, Joyce, Odets, O'Hara, Robert Benchley, *The Daily Worker,* and *New Masses.* His knowledge ranged from astronomy to politics and from modern art to carpentry. His memory, which seemed infallible, I have inherited. (A good memory is the bane of friendships and marriage.)

Unlike my parents, I was born left-handed. In nursery school, the teacher tried to put the crayon in my right hand. Daddy took a day off from work to take me to the school in Greenwich Village, instead of Mom. "Barbara is left-handed," he said, "and she will draw with her left hand."

"Yes, Mr. Block," said the cowed teacher in flowered smock.

One summer morning, when I was six or seven, we got up very early—the sky over Manhattan was still dark gray. I was sleepy, but I didn't mind because we were going on a vacation far away. Mommy packed a lunch of chicken, potato salad, and fruit, and a thermos of coffee. She filled my lunch box thermos with chocolate milk. The trunk of our car was filled with suitcases; the backseat was mine, with the lunch and my comic books. Daddy pulled away from the curb just as the sun came up over Queens in a milky, hot sky.

We drove all day, stopping for lunch at a roadside rest area, and stopped twice more to pee and fill the car with gas. The sun was setting over the tower of Provincetown just as we arrived. Daddy got the keys from the real estate agent near the dock, then drove down a narrow, sandy street to a little cottage. I jumped out, smelling the salty air—even stronger than at Jones Beach—and the beach roses that grew along the white picket fence around "our" cottage. I wanted to move in and stay forever! I loved the sea. I loved lobster. Why did we have to go back to New York?

We unpacked quickly and put the leftover lunch stuff in the fridge, which was unplugged and warm. My mother plugged it in. I had my own small bedroom, with windows overlooking a sandy plot of grass, and my parents had the large bedroom on the other side, facing the west where they had a partial view of the dock and harbor.

The sun had set when we walked down to the dock and to the bar, which served seafood. My father said, "This is where Eugene O'Neill hung out. Where he started the Provincetown Playhouse." Eugene O'Neill was one of the names I had begun to save for future understanding, because my father thought they were important. We sat at the bar while Daddy and Mommy had drinks—manhattan for him, martini for her, a Coke with three cherries for me. After the second round, Daddy ordered three lobsters, and we moved to a table next to the bar, carrying our half-full drinks. After we gutted the lobsters to their red shells, Daddy went back to the bar to talk to a guy who'd known O'Neill. I played the pinball machine, and my mother had another martini.

I woke up, bouncing on my father's shoulder as he carried me back to the cottage.

We spent every day on the beach. I picked up shells, dug in wet sand following bubbles left by a clam. On the bay side, I stuck my toes in the icy, silent water, afraid to swim in it because of the horseshoe crabs guarding the beach like helmets of buried soldiers. On the ocean side, I ran into the surf at Race Point, lying on my back to watch seagulls hovering and diving for fish, turning and swimming toward the shore until I caught a wave that threw me onto the sand. My body turned light tan, my mother's body darker, a deep walnut. My father burned red on his nose and shoulders and skinny legs. He wore a tank top to protect his chest and back and rubbed white zinc onto his nose and the tops of his bony feet. We had a shore diet every night: lobster, oysters, clams, flounder—washed down with alcohol or Coke.

Waking one morning to darkness, rain dripping from the oak leaves onto the roof, I lay under the quilt, listening to the rain hissing down the gutter pipes. No beach or dune walking today. Then I heard a moan. It came from the living room. Putting on my moccasins, I tiptoed out of my bedroom. The air was musty and moldy, mingled with the strong tasty aroma of linseed oil and oil paints at my father's easel. My mother moaned again. She was lying on the bamboo-framed sofa with the pink flowered cushions. Footsteps on the screened porch; then someone knocked on the front door. My father came out of their bedroom and told me to get back to my room. I went, leaving the door open a crack and saw a man in a black suit carrying a black leather doctor's bag. I thought how strange it was to see anyone dressed in a black suit in Provincetown. I stared through a dirty screen clotted with dead insects, watching the rain dripping off the trees.

I dozed off, reading a comic book. My father's cursing, slamming pots on the stove in the tiny kitchen, woke me. I put on my corduroy pants and a cotton shirt, both the color of raw salmon, and went into the living room. The black-suited man was gone. My mother was asleep on the sofa. My father muttered loudly, "Where's the goddamned salt? How am I supposed to cook this chicken! Fuck!" A pot slammed in the sink and water splashed loudly. I didn't dare ask what was wrong.

I set the table for Daddy and me in the living room. We carried our plates to the table and Mommy's dinner on a tray. She shook her head. "I'm not hungry. Just coffee, if you don't mind." The tray slammed down on the table. Daddy came back with a percolator. "How the hell do you make coffee?"

The room was chilly. My mother snuggled under a quilt and went to sleep again. "What's wrong with Mommy?" I finally dared ask.

"She had a miscarriage; she has to stay in bed for a few days." Miscarriage was a new word. Did it mean Mommy lost a carriage? Daddy muttered to himself, "What the hell am I supposed to do? Take care of her, as well as the kid? When am I going to have time to paint? Some vacation!" He drew on a fresh Camel, sucking it like a straw in hot ash. Then he picked up a pile of bloody sheets and towels and took them out to the trash can.

When my mother woke up, it was dark, but it had stopped raining. She smiled at me and waved me over. I sat beside her, glad to feel her warm body beneath the covers. "You would have had a baby brother." Tears ran down her face into the salty cushions.

I was relieved that my mother was fine again. Relieved to know I was still the only child.

I began second grade in Queens. My mother hated Manhattan. We lived in a two-story, attached house with an alley and a row of garages in back. Playmates were plentiful and mostly Irish, ranging from big twelve-year-olds, to little kids like me, and dozens of babies in carriages. Three big Irish boys followed me home from school one day, pulled down my underpants and stuck me up on a tree limb for a good look.

Everyone went to Mass on Sundays, except us and two other families. My best friend Ginnie was a Quaker. Her older brother Alan said he was going to marry me when we grew up. Quakers were quiet and polite. My other friend Ushie, who wasn't really my friend because I was so jealous of her, spoke German and funny-sounding English. They were Jewish refugees, my mother said. Ushie was even more polite than Ginny's family and wore a pink satin bow in her dark hair. The Irish neighbors were all Catholics—and stupid, my father said. "All religions are bad ... the opiate of the people." I wondered if Quaker and Jewish were religions.

At Christmas, in public school, we sang carols, "Away in a Manger," "The First Noël," and "Silent Night." My classmates put up pastel-tinted paintings of the Baby Jesus and Mary and Joseph. I did not know what a manger was, or who these pretty people were with big shining circles over their heads. The Three Wise Men were another mystery, riding camels under the same big star. "It's the Star of Bethlehem," one of my Catholic classmates told me. "You're going to hell," she said, "because you aren't a Catholic."

On Christmas Eve, we set up a fragrant spruce tree in the stand we'd saved from the year before. We decorated it with the bulbs and lights and strands of tinsel. Abbie and Earl, my Jewish grandparents, and Uncle Bill and Aunt Bea, Daddy's siblings, came for Christmas Eve dinner—turkey and sweet potatoes, cranberry sauce, turnips beaten with butter, homemade apple and mince pies. As soon as the table was cleared, we sat in the living room and Daddy plugged in the tree lights. "Oh-oh, one string is out!" He had to replace each bulb, one by one, until he found the burnt-out culprit. Then all eight lights burst into glorious red, blue, white, green, and yellow again.

Abbie and Earl gave me everything I asked for, and my parents gave me the rest. They seemed to like Christmas more than Mom's Irish Catholic parents, whom we rarely saw. When I was born, we lived in

Inwood, near my Irish grandparents. When I was fifteen, I found out that Nell, my Irish grandmother, had had me secretly baptized in the Church of the Good Shepherd, to make sure I wouldn't go to hell. Had my father known, he might have abandoned me on the church steps. But I was "saved."

My father collected records of Benny Goodman, Louis Armstrong, Sydney Bechet, Billie Holliday, Artie Shaw. My mother loved Judy Garland. I loved Tommy Dorsey, Glenn Miller, and big bands. Daddy bought a new record player, the first one with an automatic turntable. I asked for piano lessons because Ushie could already play. Ushie seemed luckier than I was. Daddy bought me a spinet, and my mother found a nice piano teacher. I wanted to be a famous pianist, like Artur Rubenstein.

On the Fourth of July that year, Daddy drove to New Jersey and bought a box of fireworks where they were legal. I couldn't wait for it to get dark. We took folding chairs and the fireworks to the empty lot in front of our house. Daddy set up the rockets and lined up the Roman candles and a box of sparklers. We waited for the dark sky blue to fade to black. Then he handed me a sparkler, lighted it with a wooden match, and it burst into a spray of white sparks like a thousand fireflies. I held on tightly, watching it burn down to the red-hot wire core, inch by inch. Two inches from my hand, it fizzled out. The wire turned from red to gray. "Put it in the bucket!" my father commanded. I plunged it into the cold water where it sizzled, sending up a curl of steam.

My mother's eyes glistened, ice tinkling in her glass, as she held another sparkler.

When it finally got dark, Daddy squatted down beside me with a Roman candle and told me to hold it in both hands and point it at an angle. He grasped my arms and directed the tip of the candle toward a distant treetop above another row of houses. Then he struck a match and lit the tip of the Roman candle. I whirled it around and around in a circle until it seemed to be writhing in my hands like a snake. Suddenly it spurted and hissed and out shot a column of red-blue-gold-silver into the night sky and exploded into a multiflora rose flinging its petals everywhere.

I took another Roman candle and Daddy lit it. He guided my arms again, around and around, and out of the end burst another searing flame, jetting into the night, pulsing and bursting until the powder was spent. I had never felt anything so exciting, so powerful in my own hands. I never wanted it to stop. But it did. And my idyllic childhood ended six years later, my father disappearing from my life like a Roman candle.

We moved from Queens, to upstate New York, to California when my father left, and back to Manhattan, where, eventually, he re-appeared. My father no longer played the role of father, and had become a living ghost, his sparkle for me burned out, now spent to dazzle a new wife and their offspring.

The first cold winter without him, in a gloomy Manhattan apartment, I followed World War II on *PM* newspaper maps. On the Russian front, the Germans were holding Stalingrad under siege. The Americans were being slaughtered in the Battle of the Bulge. My father would occasionally show up and take me out on a "date" to see Russian movies, movies glorifying Stalin and the Soviet Union. Afterwards, I'd have nightmares about the "atrocities," a word I'd added to my vocabulary. A Nazi soldier tossed Russian babies into the air and caught them on his bayonet, or shot them in midair like ducks; a pregnant woman, naked, was locked in a barn and gave birth by herself in the straw and then the Nazis stabbed the newborn baby and drove the woman to a frozen river where they broke a hole and forced her into the icy water, holding her dead baby. In the darkness of my roach-ridden bedroom, I saw her face under the ice, staring. My father thought I should know such things.

On our dinner dates, I discussed the progress of the Soviet forces with my father, hoping it would impress him. I thought it would make him love me again, prove to him that I was just as Communist as he was, and as Bella, my stepmother, pretended to be.

My father had said, when he still loved me, that I could be anything I wanted, just like a boy. "Can I be a pilot and fly a P-40 or a P-38?"

"Absolutely!" he answered. I made model airplanes from balsa wood, covering them with tissue paper, and hung them in my bedroom. But they crashed, broken into splinters, when we moved to California.

At the Stanley Theatre, where we saw Russian movies, they sold things for Russian War Relief in the lobby. Daddy bought me a pin of a Russian girl in peasant costume. The next time, he bought me the album of the all-male Red Army Chorus singing Russian political and folk songs. And then he bought me a Russian book for my birthday, about Russian women pilots, *The Heroic Flight of the Rodina.*

The book is an heirloom from my lost childhood. On the cover is a painting of a white, twin-engine Soviet bomber, circles of speed whirling around the propellers against a cloudy sky. Inside the front and back cover are identical maps of the USSR, with Moscow marked by a red star, a red line blazing across the vast country marking the flight path from Moscow to Komsomolsk near the island of Sakhalin in the Pacific Ocean. The one hundred eight pages tell the supposedly true story of three Soviet women who "flew nonstop from Moscow to the Pacific, establishing the international women's straight and broken line distance record" (L. Bronfman and L. Khvat 1938, 7).

The three women became "heroes of the Soviet Union" in 1938, were given medals, and were granted 25,000 rubles each (L. Bronfman and L. Khvat 1938, 7). Photographs show them to be attractive young women in Soviet aviator uniforms, receiving flowers and cheers from welcoming crowds. A photo of Stalin in military dress is in the front. The last photo shows the women with Krushchev and another commissar. Their beautiful airplane on the front cover is called the *Rodina.*

I took this book with me when I married.

In 1995, my half-sister Maggi called from Nebraska, telling me our father had died, aged eighty-three. She asked if I'd come to the funeral. My other two half-sisters, who lived in New York, weren't coming. Bella had died a few years earlier. My sister Judy had had no contact with any of them. I said I couldn't make it. I had been mourning the loss of my father for four decades already.

The ex-Communist, die-hard New Yorker, my long-gone father, was buried in Omaha. He was really dead, the man whose sperm had brought me into life. Not a living ghost any more. Just a dead man.

Chapter VII

Part I: FALLING IN MARRIAGE

I started college at the State University at New Paltz, New York, in 1950. I was already engaged to Tommy, a college grad who was in the Marines' Officers Candidate School. I did not want to, or plan to, marry him. His ring on my finger disguised my true intentions to go for an advanced degree, in English, unlike my female classmates, many of whom attended college to get an Mrs., in preference to a BA or BS. Tommy's ring proved I wasn't just a "grind" but a "normal" woman who wanted a husband.

In my sophomore year, United Nations Day came on a glorious October weekend. My friend June had a serious crush on Ray, who had a Model A jalopy. As cars were rare on campus in the 1950s, she wangled an invitation from Ray to drive us to a nearby farm where United Nations Day was being celebrated. Frank, whose father owned the farm, had invited us. The United Nations was, to us, a symbol of liberal hope in the midst of the Eisenhower '50s with its conservative values, McCarthyism, and the Korean War. All male college students were exempted from the draft. Our classmates were having a good time in the "Fat Fifties." I belonged to a small band of liberal students, mainly vets from World War II like Ray and El, and a few women with budding feminist ideas. Frank, our host, was a rebel, a motorcycle-riding rebel.

On United Nations Day 1951, June hopped in the front seat beside Ray, and I crawled into the back seat with Aggie and El, a man I had casually met once before, when he was dating a friend of mine, Sonya. Aggie was thirty-three pretending to be twenty, with long, dyed black hair, an anorexic body, and the worst case of acne and boils I've ever seen on anyone. Aggie inserted herself between El and me. El smoked a cigarette and stared out the window.

We drove the fifteen miles to Frank's farm in silence, except for Aggie's endless chatter about herself. When we arrived, we piled out, exhilarated by the perfect fall day and the expanse of fields of corn and hay. Inside a long boardinghouse-style building, Frank's mother was preparing a huge lunch. She looked like a woman worn to death by toil. Frank's father barely spoke to anyone. Oddly, my father had known Fred's father in the '30s, when the farm had been one of the boardinghouses frequented by the city Communists for summer vacations. I had no memory of having been there.

June took photos that day, capturing the day El and I met and paired off as if we had planned it. The guys in her snapshots are clowning around—Ray, Frank, Phil, and Walter—acting like hillbillies in funny hats, pointing unloaded shotguns in the air. Aggie is squeezing into some shots to be included with the men.

June's photos did not capture the moments that bound El and me together for the rest of our lives: El and I talking about Beethoven and Robert Frost, Mozart and Hemingway, Chopin and T. S. Eliot … art and sex mingling in the first conversation, which would continue for forty-one years … desire in the dark, as some black-and-white film was rolling in the rec room … El chasing me down a long hill, and catching me, literally tackling me, gently. Nor did she click her camera as we lay in the long grass, El on top of me. I had run down that hill because I wanted El to chase me.

We were the only couple that linked up that day. June pined after Ray, a pacifist holding a shotgun. Ray was oblivious to June. Ray, the smartest male student I'd met until I met El, was dating a brainless, blue-eyed blonde whose only interest was marriage. I also had had a crush on Ray, but realized, after one date at the Greek diner, that he loved only politics and himself. Ray got a PhD in politics and became a labor leader in the South, as the civil rights movement began. He died in his forties, divorced.

Wandering through the acres of untended fields and clumps of hardwoods, El and I talked and talked, as though we'd always known each other. Now I thought *he* was the smartest man in college, not Ray.

In the evening, Frank's pregnant wife Sara, a thirty-two-year-old widow with two small, pretty daughters, and his haggard mother prepared a picnic of hot dogs, potato salad, potato chips, and sodas. Ten years younger than his wife, Frank had a cruel mouth and treated Sara and his mother like servants. Once, Frank had asked me out, taking me for a hair-raising ride on his motorcycle. The mountainous dirt road wound around tight curves up the eastern slope and descended rapidly down the western slope in a slalom zigzag. We skidded over the rock-strewn, dirt road, edging a cliff. When we got back to town, in one piece, I was furious with Frank, who was grinning like a sated crocodile. "Never again," I said. He just laughed.

Frank and I had similar backgrounds, which I thought would have made us friends. We had one Jewish parent each, and both our fathers were Communists, but it did nothing to draw us together. Frank wanted to scare me and get into my pants, but I felt only repugnance at his adolescent cruelty and contempt for women.

El sat down next to me on an old sofa as the film rolled and put his arm around me. Ignoring the old Soviet propaganda movie, we talked of Shakespeare, Beethoven, art. I felt complete freedom to speak my mind, without pretending to be dumb. Among my dorm mates, I imposed censorship on myself. They had pegged me as a "brain" for always reading, for being interested in literature and politics. I had to "play the game" of being one of the gals. I played softball and sang harmony to popular songs like "Mockingbird Hill." But I wouldn't join them in drinking green beer on St. Patrick's Day. I didn't drink any alcohol at all. I made them pay attention to reality, once, asking why only women had curfews and not men. "If I want sex, I can have it before 10:00 p.m.," I said, shocking them.

At the end of the day, we got back into Ray's car. El climbed over Aggie, pushing her aside to sit beside me. "Well!" said Aggie, a fifth wheel trying to insert herself between couples. When Aggie finished college, she got a teaching job upstate, had her acne treated, and married a one-legged taxi driver. Her skin was deeply scarred where the boils had been removed.

El had helped Ray put in a new engine in his old Model A Ford. Then El bought an old Chevy coupé he dubbed "Sweet William." His GI Bill allowance covered his room in Men's Hall, his books and registration fees, and a small stipend for food. It left very little for gas for "Sweet Willie." When his monthly check came in, El filled Willie's tank, but by mid month, he only could afford fifty cents' worth, just enough to drive us up the mountain to a secluded spot.

On Fridays, we went for spaghetti and meatballs at an Italian diner, going Dutch. On rare Sunday afternoons when I didn't have an essay to write, we drove to Emil's on the mountain road to Minnewaska and ate real ham sandwiches on German rye while Trudi, the waitress, in Tyrolean dress, waltzed and polka-ed with the German customers who fed nickels into the jukebox loaded with German music. One warm day, El cooked me hot dogs in a shady grove near a stream while cows munched nearby. He built a fire and found a piece of bedspring to use as a grill, toasting the rolls to perfection. He put our soda cans into the stream to cool. For dessert, he toasted marshmallows. Nobody had taken such good care of me since I was twelve. I'd been homeless for seven years when we met. El made me feel at home again. He *was* home.

During the Christmas break, I brought El to New York to meet my father. Daddy was impressed with El's construction-hard muscled body. El had acquired the chest and shoulders of a bodybuilder by lifting fifty-pound cinder blocks. Politically, El passed muster too: he was an anti-Eisenhower liberal Democrat. He loved classical music and good literature, which he'd discovered in the army and in college. El's tendencies were good enough for Daddy. My previous boyfriend, the Republican Tommy now at Camp Lejeune to become a Marine lieutenant, had not made a good impression at all. As we left, Daddy shook El's hand and said, "I like this one better than the other one." I was certain I'd found the right man.

In January, during the semester break, I took the train from New York to White River Junction, Vermont, on my way to meet El's family in New Hampshire. The scenery through Connecticut, Massachusetts, and Vermont was new to me and looked like Grandma Moses' paintings and Robert Frost's poems. The train was packed with skiers and skis. I wore a new ski suit, expecting cold weather, though I didn't know how to ski. At least I looked the part, like everyone else.

El picked me up at the station in his uncle Allan's car, which had a heater, unlike Sweet William. He was so nervous, his hands shook on the wheel. We drove across the Connecticut River into New Hampshire. It was only five miles to Lebanon where his family lived. Driving through the center of town, we circled the common, gracefully guarded by giant elms. There was a band shell in the middle. The town hall facing it was the only large brick building, save for a bank at right angles and the Mascoma Mills, a woolen mill where many of the French Canadians worked. "Frogs," "Canucks," "Frenchies," El said they were called. But a bricklayer friend of his was called Frenchy out of friendly respect: bricklayers were a cut above mill workers.

El drove out of town to Heater Road and steered up a steep driveway with a ditch on one side and a bank that dropped off on the other. His father's car, a Nash they dubbed the "bathtub" because of its shape, sat in the driveway. Reat was El's father—a name I'd never heard. It was short for Aretus, which I'd never heard of either. His actual first name was Fred, but nobody ever called him that. Just Reat.

The one-floor house with gray asphalt siding posing as stone was cut into the bank. One side sat precariously atop a deep cellar made of cement blocks. A flight of cement steps led up to the door in the middle. I saw faces peering through the curtained windows, hands wiping circles in the condensation for better viewing. It was ten below zero outside. We climbed the uneven steps—El warned me that one was two inches taller than the others—and stepped into the kitchen. Heat blasted my face from an oil stove. It was 90 degrees inside.

Lined up across the room behind a long Formica table were five of El's younger siblings in perfect descending order: Roger, Jane, Jimmy, Judy, and Bobby. Five pairs of innocent brown and blue eyes studied me as if I was from a foreign country. Like wild deer, they seemed ready to bolt from an unknown intruder. If they were shocked by me, I was astounded by them. The Adamses seemed like a lost tribe in a remote forest. I felt like an explorer breaking into their hidden world. El, the oldest, was the only one to have left his village to explore the modern world. Fred, the second youngest, was already married and the father of a three-year-old girl. Rita, at seventeen, was pregnant and had been forced to marry the father, a mean-tempered, Napoleon-sized Frenchman who worked in the mill. Bobby, the baby, was just seven. The smell of the kerosene stove permeated the overheated air.

El's mother "Mame" said, "Sit down! You must be frozen! Let me get you something to eat!" I got used to hearing her say this every day, and of being fed a substantial, delicious meal cooked on the stygian oil stove. She bustled about, a big-boned Irishwoman with lush thick hair the color of charcoal. Her club-heeled shoes thumped back and forth from stove to table, fridge to table. We dove into the hot food. Everyone watched me eat—as if I had never eaten such food. And I hadn't. Reat sat at the head, red faced from working outdoors and from a daily bottle of straight rye, washed down with beer. He grinned wryly, "You look like you could use some fat on you—you ain't but skin and bones." Roger smiled shyly at me, a sweet-tempered twenty-two-year-old about to leave for basic training in the marines. It was peacetime, but it was also his only chance to make a living doing something other than bricklaying. He'd been a dunce in school, like Fred who'd never learned to read. El told me how his father tried to make Fred learn. "Read, goddamn it!" Reat would say, smacking Fred upside the head. Fred's wife Thelma got him through high school, doing all his homework. El was regarded with awe, the only one to attend college.

After we'd eaten, Mary (I hated calling her Mame) cleared away the dishes and served instant coffee and a big cake with gooey icing made from a mix. The three youngest took big slices of the cake. I shook my head. El lit a cigarette and started talking, between deep drags, about college, about me. "The smahtest girl they ever seen there," he said proudly. "She can drive the cah as good as me." Mary and the two girls looked at me in disbelief. No woman in the entire clan had a driver's license. The faces around the table glowed with rosy health and excitement. El kept them spellbound, reading them his story, "The Welfarers," about their freeloading relatives. They laughed and smacked the table with their hands.

Reat got up periodically to read the outdoor thermometer, which was nailed to the window frame outside. "Twenty-two below"; "twenty-eight below"; "thirty below." I didn't know such temperatures occurred in the United States! These below-zero temperatures were typical, I was told. The snowdrifts along the roads were six to eight feet high. The sky, as night fell, was a crystalline lapis lazuli with stars like diamonds. I'd never breathed such clear air, scented with pine and innocence.

If the Adamses seemed like a lost tribe to me, I was in reality a lost child looking for a home. I thought I'd found it at last. The sky above was a motherly shawl, the oil stove a womb serving up heat and food. I hadn't felt so warm and so comfortable since I had sat beside Daddy in our house in New Paltz, warmed by the blaze in the fireplace.

By ten o'clock, my eyes were drooping. The day-long ride on the train, the evening warmth and food, the bitter chill held at bay.

"C'mon, Little Squaw. Let's get you to bed," said El, picking me up and carrying me into a back bedroom.

"Land sakes! Don't call her that! She ain't no Indian," said Mame (a family nickname for Mary, one I detested).

Off the kitchen were two bedrooms, a pantry, a bathroom, and a doorway leading into the living room. Off the living room was a third bedroom that, as esteemed guest, I was given all to myself. Jimmy and Bobby, Judy and Jane all slept in one bedroom and Reat and Mary in the other. El slept on the sofa in the living room.

The chill struck me as I entered the icy bedroom, the thirty-below winter seeping through the uninsulated thin walls and floor over the cement basement. The oil stove in the kitchen, I discovered, was the only heat in the house. The living room had a fireplace Reat had built, but the rickety house has settled and pulled away from the chimney, leaving a dangerous gap.

The double bed I had all to myself was piled high with blankets and comforters. The sheets smelled sweetly of fresh air. Mary filled two hot water bottles and put them in between the sheets before I got in.

Everyone said goodnight and went to their rooms, after taking turns in the bathroom that had only cold running water. El sneaked in and kissed me goodnight. When I shut the door behind him, I felt as if I were standing in a meat locker—I could see my breath. I climbed quickly under the quilts, grateful for the hot water bottles. I fell asleep immediately.

Suddenly I woke to complete silence, except for a distant snore. I was shaking with cold. The hot water bottles were icy. I looked at my watch: two in the morning. I'd have to spend another four or five hours in this refrigerated room before anyone got up and I could go into the warm kitchen. I jiggled my legs and rubbed my arms, trying to stir up circulation. I put on thick socks and my robe. Freezing. Sleep was impossible. I crept out to the bathroom and then paused in the kitchen to snuggle up beside the oil stove, which had been banked low for the night. It gave off a feeble semblance of heat. I crawled back into the gelid sheets. The night was endless. I wondered how people could live like this, without central heat. I thought of homesteaders in cabins with the wind blowing through, of water freezing in a bucket inside the cabin. People could freeze to death right in bed, I realized.

Dawn came thankfully. I heard someone stirring. My door opened, and El said, "Jesus Christ, Bobbie! You must be frozen!" his breath making a cloud as he spoke. He bundled me up, quilt and all, carried me into the living room, and put me on the sofa. Then he got firewood and built a roaring fire in the fireplace. "Dad should have fixed the chimney, but I can't wait." As the flames built up, I crawled over and sat in a chair as close as I could. It was ten o'clock before I stopped shaking. "Nobody ever sleeps in that icebox alone. Fred, Rog, and I used to sleep together and keep each other warm. Ma should have known better," he said with some embarrassment. Privacy had its drawbacks, I'd learned. I did not take a bath until late in the day, after Mary had heated up cauldrons of water and poured them into the tub. The steam filled the bathroom like a heavenly benediction.

Mary was large boned, and stronger than a lot of men. She had lived under even more primitive conditions most of her life. The house on Heater Road was a big step up, despite its lack of heat and hot water. She and Reat, growing up in the Depression, had been forced to drop out of high school to help support their families. Mary raised her younger siblings when her mother became ill. Reat became a bricklayer and helped support his family when his mother came down with tuberculosis. Not having enough money to send her to a sanatorium, El's Grandmother May and Grandfather Sammit lived in a tent on their farm all winter. It would cure or kill her. It didn't kill her. Reat and Mary married young and had El seven months afterwards. They lived in a crude handmade shack on the farm, without a road, without a well or pump. They had to carry water down from the farmhouse. "The Shack," as El called it, was made of slats Reat had foraged. It had no siding. The flooring consisted of open slats, and the only furniture was handmade beds with rusted springs. All of this poverty took place only five miles from Dartmouth College in Hanover, where the educated privileged knew nothing of these Adamses.

A few days later, El drove me back to New York. The temperature warmed as we drove south, reaching the twenties as we cruised down the Hudson Valley. It seemed almost tropical at thirty as he pulled up to my dorm. "I guess you'll never want anything to do with me, now that you've seen my folks," he said sadly. I caressed his cheek with my warm hand.

"Don't be silly. I think they're strong people. I love you." He held me tight. I felt his strength and his heart beating through our thick winter clothes.

As the spring semester of our sophomore year progressed, El worked tirelessly in the bio lab making slides for cytology. He had had developed a hypothesis that bacteria thrived under low barometric pressure and went dormant under high pressure. In his physics class, whose professor he hated, he had begun to develop a plan for unlimited energy—"a gravity machine" run only by the force of gravity. I admired his knowledge of science and his curiosity that led to his devotion to lab work. But El wanted to be a writer, as I did.

After he would drop me at my dorm before curfew, I thought El went back to his dorm. But I found out he would go to the Tavern, the local gin mill, and have several beers. Then he'd stay up to write until dawn. I wondered why he never got up for early classes. In the evening, he'd be wide awake, reading me his stories, wooing me with satires and political diatribes. A piece he wrote opposing capital punishment was published in the college newspaper. It drew praise from all our liberal friends and from liberal faculty members. Even a conservative professor stopped El to tell him how much he admired his writing. This professor, the father of my best friend in high school, admired me but did not like El. My advisor, a professor of speech, warned me not to marry El. "You're too much alike," he said. I was furious at his poking into my private life. El had his supporters on the faculty, however. One was his cytology professor; another was my favorite professor, Lou Salkever.

One Saturday, my geology professor arranged a field trip to study the rock formations of the Catskills. Seven of us signed up. Professor Ordway would pick us up at five in the morning. I waited on the front steps of the main building, the whole college still asleep. I was groggy from lack of coffee, as the cafeteria hadn't even opened yet. Stan, the campus security guard, saw me and came over, asking what I was doing up so early. He grinned in sympathy and said, "Come with me." I followed him inside the empty building and into the sacrosanct faculty lounge. He made me a cup of instant coffee, and one for himself. With my head cleared, I thanked Stan and went back outside to wait for the geology professor. We spent a pleasant spring day climbing ancient rocks and chipping off shards. Dr. Ordway studied our samples, describing the characteristics and naming the types: Glenerie limestone, Hudson River shale, Precambrian, Ordovician; and the trilobite fossils imbedded in Cambrian. We ate a bag lunch the college had supplied, then drove home, sleepy and satisfied with ourselves. It was six o'clock when I got back to my room in the dorm.

I called El from the pay phone in the hall, the only phone on our floor beside the one in the resident advisor's office. One of El's roommates answered, so I left a message for him to call me. I went to supper in the dining hall, then rushed back to my room, waiting for El's call. At ten-thirty, a dorm-mate knocked on my door. "Phone for you." I ran down the hall.

"Hi! Where've you been?" I said. There was only the sound of deep breathing. "El?"

Then a low gutteral voice I barely recognized came over the wire. "Did you have a good time with Stan?"

"El, what's the matter with you? You don't sound like yourself." My heart was racing.

"Stan said he had a 'good time' with my girlfriend this morning," El growled. Then he hung up.

I couldn't take this in. *Stan?* The dumb security guard with missing front teeth? I lay awake all night. I didn't understand what was wrong with El or why he was angry.

The next day, El came to my dorm, all apologies. He hung his head. "I don't know what came over me," he said. His thick hair was wild, and he kept running his hand through it. His eyes glittered, narrowed.

We went to the coffee shop where I kept questioning him, cajoling, trying to figure out how his mind worked. It took till evening for him to appear somewhat normal. "I just went crazy when Stan said you and he had coffee together. I wanted to kill him." It didn't make sense to me. But I was relieved that El seemed his old self again. I was shaken by the transformation from a gentle, thoughtful man into an irrational madman crazed with jealousy. What had I done?

I buried the doubts that sprung up on that crucial day. In those dark days of the '50s, a movie like *Splendor in the Grass* illustrated how repressed women were. Considered "promiscuous" if she had sex before marriage, a woman was denied the pleasures of womanhood, though any man was supposed to be sexually experienced before marriage. An unmarried woman could not be fitted for a diaphragm by any doctor. Any boy or man could get "rubbers," keeping them in their wallets in case they "got lucky." I had assumed that El, as an army vet, was sexually experienced. I had slept with a boyfriend in high school, feeling great shame, telling no one. A few college girls entered into "sudden" marriages and left school. But El had very little sexual experience, the first with a prostitute when he was in the army. So the first time El and I made love, or tried to, he was impotent. He shook all over. The second time, he pinned me to the ground and practically raped me.

El told me that his first girlfriend in New Hampshire thought having sex once a month was more than enough. I told him about Tommy, my unwanted fiancé. How glad I was to be rid of him. I felt nothing for any man but El. My heart *and* mind felt love, not just my body. El believed that loving him was exclusive: I should not care about anyone or anything else.

By April, however, I was sure I wanted to marry El. My father's complaints about my college expenses were becoming unbearable. I still had two years to go, unless I could manage to put myself through summer school again. Every check Daddy wrote included a savage letter in which he ranted about the seventy-six-dollar registration fee, the four-hundred-dollar room and board each term, the burden, and my selfishness. He implied I was a spendthrift, a wastrel, using up his money for a frivolous four-year vacation. He had never gone to college, never wanted to, though he had graduated valedictorian of Townsend Harris High School—one of the most competitive schools in New

York—at age fourteen (my sister says fifteen; my aunt says thirteen). Daddy had worked, climbing up the ladder like Horatio Alger to a top position in advertising. Nothing I said placated him. He wanted me *out.* Out of his checkbook as well as his house, his new life with Bella and Robin, the first of my three half sisters.

I couldn't bear the thought of a whole summer alone in college. My mood sank as April advanced and the valley grew fragrant with lilacs and new grass. The apple orchards surrounding the town burst into sweet pink bloom. I wanted—I didn't know what. To study forever, to become a professor of English. To write stories and poems. To marry El and have six children. To prove to Daddy that I was still his smart little girl. To prove to him that I wasn't selfish, as both my parents said I was. Once, when I ate the last chocolate in a box of Fanny Farmer candies, my mother went crazy. "You selfish girl!" she shrieked. She harangued me until Daddy got home and she told him. "You selfish girl!" they both yelled. "You selfish girl! You selfish girl!"

My friend June and I talked over our futures. She had gotten nowhere with Ray, but had found a nice boyfriend—dull, bland, and sexless, like herself. June looked like an old maid at eighteen—hair in a tight roll, no makeup (even nice girls were then wearing lipstick, mascara, powder, rouge), and convent-style pastel skirts and white blouses. Saddle shoes and socks.

Another problem arrived without warning: my mother and stepfather were moving back to New York immediately. Eric had not been able to earn a living in Florida, and my mother hated living there. I had written to tell her that El and I were planning to marry in June. The timing of Mom's return was no accident. They arrived in late April and moved into a trailer next to a cheap motel. My trailer-trash Mom was in my own backyard.

I brought El to meet Mom and Eric. She sat, as always, on the sofa with her bandaged legs resting on the coffee table. Her skin was like tanned leather, her hair totally white, tied back with a pretty scarf. She looked like an Indian queen in exile, holding court. My mother's haughtiness, when she was sober, struck me not as bravado in the face of my father's rejection and her consequent poverty, but as a righteous sense of entitlement. Mom ruled a little kingdom of loyal subjects from her sofa: Eric, Judy, and me, if she could coax me back into her power.

A queen bee with two drones and no hive. El lit up a cigarette and began to rub his hands rhythmically. He kneaded his hands, constantly wringing them, when he talked to anyone. I sometimes put my hand over his to stop him. He'd pause, not looking at anyone, and resume the wringing as soon as I took my hand away. It struck me as odd, but it didn't seem to signify anything but an absentminded habit. El never looked directly at people when in conversation, but somewhere off in the distance. His talk was intelligent, but one sided.

Mom took one look at El: hatred at first sight. Eric made the usual pot of strong coffee and served it in mugs, along with pastries from an Italian bakery. "Sorry," he said. "It's all we could afford." Judy was already enrolled in the local public school. Eric had gotten a steady job at Western Printing as a proofreader. Judy would graduate as valedictorian—as I had, and our father had.

"El is very strange," said my mother after they had been introduced. I burned with fury, wanting to scream, "And you're perfect? A perfect, normal mother?" My mother recognized El as a rival, one whose needs I would serve instead of hers. They both wanted me to take care of them—and no one else.

Despite Mom's hostility toward El, despite my father's wishing I'd drop dead, and despite having no money—or perhaps because of—El and I decided to get married at the end of the semester, right after finals. My faculty friends did not want me to leave college. Dr. Gene Link, our sociology professor, offered me a teaching fellowship in sociology. I didn't want to become a sociologist, but I was tempted by the offer of money for schooling. I wanted to be an English professor but did not have the means to pursue that goal alone. My father would not support me, I knew. Going to college part-time wasn't an option then. If I stayed in college, I'd have to take two years of dull education courses and endure a ten-week stint of practice teaching at the Campus School, without pay.

But I was too exhausted from the emotional struggle. I couldn't deal with my mother or beg for every nickel of college costs from my father. I wanted someone to take care of me, to cradle me and not make any demands. I couldn't sleep. Food wouldn't stay down. I lost weight, dropping from a hundred five to a hundred pounds. I studied. Slept with El and prayed for the end.

I finished my exams in a blaze of As and turned down Dr. Link's assistantship. El got As in cytology and embryology and Fs in physics and statistics. He could have dropped these two courses, but was too proud to admit he couldn't handle them. He'd never taken any math courses, not even in high school. Unable to understand the advanced physics and statistics textbooks, he spent his time dreaming up his "gravity machine." He said the professors hated him. I told him to ask for their help, but El was too proud, believing he could understand the textbooks on his own. I had begged him to drop the classes. He had glowered. And he failed the finals. I was my father's child, a born student, and could not fathom such illogical behavior. My mother had dropped out of high school, though she'd been an A student. As an adult, she would never consider taking courses to finish the diploma. El and my mother shared self-destructive pride.

The night before we were married, El called his mother, ensuring she wouldn't have time to come to our wedding, bringing a dozen other relatives. I had written to my father a week earlier that I was leaving college (much to his joy) and was marrying El. Bella replied with a happy note offering to buy our "linens." We didn't have a pot to piss in. I never answered. Pride.

But I couldn't keep Mom away. Mim, my romantic roommate, made the occasion a happy one, calling all my friends. I had asked her to be my maid of honor, and El had asked Ray to be his best man. At the last minute, I discovered that we couldn't be married in a civil ceremony at city hall because I was only nineteen. New York civil marriage law required the bride to be twenty-one. Dr. Link came to the rescue. He was an ordained minister as well as a professor, and agreed to marry us, delighted to officiate. "No religion or mention of God," I requested. Dr. Link wrote us a simple ceremony, leaving out God and gods.

On Friday, June 6, 1952, it rained, a pleasant series of showers that cleared by six in the evening. El and I arrived at the Links' house at seven as the sun was setting over Mohonk Mountain. Dr. Link's wife, who also had her doctorate, had made punch and a cake for the reception. I wore a white skirt I'd bought a few days earlier, with my only white sweater, and the single pearl necklace my grandmother Abbie had given me for my sixteenth birthday. I carried a small bouquet of flowers my friends had bought. Lou Salkever, my "adoptive" professor father, sat in a corner easy chair, a grinning Buddha blessing us. My friends Mim, June, Nancy, and Rita circled around. Eric Polisar, the dreamboat professor of history and our friend, stood in a corner, arms folded, with an approving smile. Dr. Link stood in front of El and me and read the special service he'd handwritten on cream-colored folded stationery. I did not look at Mom and Eric. My nine-year-old sister Judy looked curious, puzzled by the ceremony. El slipped the Woolworth's ring on my left hand. We were married.

The ring turned black within a few months. I still have it in a jewelry box. El bought me a gold wedding band a few years later, which I lost in the ocean off Cape Cod a year after he died.

After the ceremony, Mom and Eric took us to the Greek diner where Tommy's father was still a waiter. I wasn't hungry, too excited to eat, and ordered a ham sandwich and Coke. Mom and Eric and El ordered big diner dinners. Judy ordered a hamburger. The waitress brought coffee and Coke, and my sandwich. "The dinners will be right out," she said. El reached over and took a bite of my sandwich. "Hey! That's my sandwich!" We all laughed. Ha, ha, ha. I had a moment's foreboding. "I never thought El would get married!" El's mother had said to me when we first met. After El and I went back to New York, Jane, El's sister, told me Mary said, "What does she want with *him?*"

In the motel that night, which Mom and Eric had paid for, El discovered a large pimple on his penis. And my period had come a week early. We laughed and laughed and laughed. Then the bed frame collapsed onto the floor. We laughed so hard we couldn't make love. Fools in love. There'd be plenty of other nights ahead.

The next morning, we packed our things into poor old Sweet William and headed for New Hampshire as Mr. and Mrs. Elwood Adams.

Part II: FROST, 1952–1957

I had never seen so much snow. Drifts so high you couldn't see the road outside our apartment, our old station wagon buried in snow to the roof. Inside was warm enough; we had central oil heat—better than our first furnished apartment with an oil stove for heat between the kitchen and bedrooms. We bought a crib for our first child, Steve, born in April 1953, ten months after we'd married. In 1954, we bought a second crib for Amy, born sixteen months later. Anne, born in 1956, came twenty-three months after Amy. I watched a lot of snow and read library books.

It was like living inside a glass paperweight, snow falling every time it jiggled. I was reading *War and Peace* for the first time. There wasn't any construction work in winter, so El slept. When he woke up, I'd make a fresh pot of coffee. He'd sit and smoke. After he showered, and the snow let up, he'd go out and start digging out the station wagon.

A pot of New England baked beans was bubbling in the gas oven, the aroma of salt pork, brown sugar, onion, and molasses filling the dry air of our small house on the edge of town. Snow covered the back yard and part of the front porch. When El cleared off the sidewalk and porch, I dressed Amy and Steve in snowsuits and boots and took them out to play. Amy stood, crying. It was ten below zero. Steve listlessly tried making a snowman, but there wasn't a clear enough space to build it on the deep snow. They came back inside in less than fifteen minutes.

El started up the station wagon, letting the engine and heater warm up. He came in to warm up, then drove off. He went to fetch milk and bread. When he did not come home after an hour, I knew he had gone to his mother's house, leaving us alone all day. Brothers and uncles showed up at that house as they dug out of the snow. They talked around the kitchen table. El and his father played cribbage sometimes. The men bragged about how many deer they'd killed, how many birds they'd shot. His mother talked about who was sick and who had died. They all drank instant coffee until early darkness fell, then someone would drive to the store and bring back six-packs.

When El got home, he had had more than a few. The children were in bed, and I was watching out the window for his headlights. I had already eaten a hot dog and a small dish of beans.

"El, please don't leave me alone so long," I asked.

"Oh, we got to talking." And he fell into bed, asleep in minutes. I lay awake for hours, wishing I was back in New York.

There was no break in this routine until April, when construction finally resumed just as unemployment insurance ran out. I read books all day, which I'd checked out of the town library—classics and new fiction—until I had read everything on the shelves. As soon as I read about a new book in *The New York Times* Book Review, I'd wait for the library to get a copy. A new book about Loeb and Leopold, the young thrill murderers, fascinated me with its analysis of their psychopathology. I read parts aloud to El. It was the one way I could get his attention, outside of the bedroom.

On summer weekends, El and I took the children swimming at Storrs Pond in Hanover, bringing a picnic. We went to county fairs to watch oxen pulls and sulky races, and bought homemade jams and pies. We went to Mascoma Lake with El's brothers and sisters for cookouts. I brought my own potato salad, winning my mother-in-law's rare praise. But I would not go swimming; Mascoma Lake was full of leeches. "Just shake a little salt on them," said my sister-in-law Thelma. "Don't be such a sissy," she said laughing and holding a saltshaker in one hand and a lit cigarette in the other. Sometimes she scorched a leech on her leg with the cigarette. Salt or fire, the leech squirmed, shriveled, and died.

When we had a little extra money, I bought a used sewing machine for twenty-five dollars, a pedal machine converted to electric. I bought patterns in Woolworth's and taught myself to make clothes for myself and my children. I mended El's jeans and shortened the hems. Never again would Mary be able to embarrass me. When we first arrived in Lebanon, the seam on El's jeans had pulled apart. In front of a kitchen full of relatives, Mary insisted El take off his pants so she could sew them up. I was furious, and El was ashamed.

Without a car, I was literally trapped while El was at work. I could not go anywhere except on foot, pushing a carriage with Steve and Amy, and soon, Anne. The walk into town, or "upstreet," over rough sidewalks and through the noxious air of the tannery took about half an hour. When I made it to the center of town, I sat under the trees on the common while the children slept or played in a sandbox. At the library, I returned books and took out more, piling them into the carriage. At the grocery, I bought a bag of meat, vegetables, and milk, squeezing them in alongside babies and books.

On a Sunday, if El was working overtime, I would walk into town to the drug store, buy the children ice cream cones, and treat myself to a black-and-white soda. The clerk did not know how to make one, so

I explained: chocolate syrup, a touch of cream, and soda water, topped with vanilla ice cream. The best treat, however, was the Sunday *New York Times*. I piled it into the carriage and hurried home to read the Book Review, Arts & Leisure, and the Magazine. Oh, how it made me envious to know what I was missing: Dylan Thomas was giving a poetry reading at the 92nd Street Y; a new play by Tennessee Williams! Oh, how I longed to be there!

In the fall, El was rarely home. Construction speeded up before the winter shutdown. He'd start work at six in the morning and wouldn't stop until dark, working with lights. El came home exhausted, ate a big supper, showered, and fell into bed. The only pleasure we had was seeing the famous New England fall, more brilliant in person than glossy calendar photos and sentimental poems. The air was pure blue, crisp, and fragrant with burning leaves before the first snow. When El had a day off, we spent it at Allan's, or at Mary's. The men talked of the impending deer season with excitement. The women talked of waxing linoleum floors and whose baby was due next. I was silent. Allan coaxed El to go hunting along with him and Doc H from Boston. El could shoot better than Allan, his kill being credited to Doc who showed them off back in Boston.

The only intellectual stimulation to be had, aside from my weekly *New York Times*, was Dartmouth College, five miles away in Hanover. Only men attended this Ivy League college, but I was drawn to its music series and lectures, open to "outsiders." It was proof that there was a life outside of the Adams clan, outside of cooking, babies, hunting, sex, and never enough money.

Before my first child was born, I had applied for a job there, as secretary to two professors. After all, I thought, I was a college girl. But my typing was so bad and my secretarial skills so wanting that the tweedy, pipe-smoking professors could barely contain their laughter. I wasn't a cute young college girl any more.

One day, I read in the local paper that Robert Frost was giving a reading at Dartmouth.

"El, Robert Frost! We have to go!"

It was free. And open to the public—the poor, the illiterate, and even women. I dressed up in a skirt and sweater, feeling like a coed again (*coed* dates me, a term now considered politically incorrect). El wore a jacket and tie. The auditorium in Baker Hall was full to overflowing, students sitting in the aisles and at the foot of the stage. El and I luckily got seats in the middle. It felt so good to be in a college again, among people who cared about poetry.

Robert Frost walked out, slightly stooped, smiling wryly, and carrying a book. He waited for the thunderous applause to die down, then put the book on the lectern. His white thatch of hair hung over his craggy face, his startling blue eyes visible even at a distance. "'Two Tramps in Mud Time,'" he intoned, then recited this poem from memory. He never opened the book of his poems. Poem after poem, he recited from memory. "I can't read very well, you see," he said, laughing. His eyesight was failing, but his memory was better than anyone else's in that room.

Pausing to drink a glass of water, he looked up at us, "You know, they kicked me out of here." Laughter. "I'm not a good example for you to follow." Louder laughter.

"Now, what do you want to hear?"

"'Stopping by Woods'!" "'Birches'!" "'Fire and Ice'!"

"'The Hill Wife,'" one of my favorites.

It was nearly eleven o'clock when Frost stopped reading. He looked tired, but happy. He thrived on adulation. On the twenty-minute drive back to Lebanon, I floated on a sea of words. We stopped at Mary's to pick up our sleeping children. Mary said she'd read a poem by Robert Frost in grade school.

"Why would anyone want to listen to poetry?" Reat said, laughing.

We got back into our station wagon, babies nestled in my arms. I looked up at the stars in the clear New Hampshire air. El had wooed me, reciting "Stopping By Woods on a Snowy Evening." I was breathing in the air of Frost. But I knew I *had* to get back to New York, out of the cruel reality of Frost's world. Out of a home where poetry was less important than waxing the linoleum floor.

Chapter VIII

UNCLE ALLAN AND THE ADAMS "BOYS"

I saw the Adams family farm for the first and last time just before Grammie May sold it to a developer in Hanover. El drove me to Etna, the tiny hamlet where El had ridden on horseback to a one-room schoolhouse. On the long drive from New York in El's ancient car, Sweet William, he prepared me with legendary stories about his grandfather Sammit and his biblical temper. Until his dying day, Sammit called his four sons "the boys." When summoned by Sammit, the "boys" would drop everything, leaving their own families to their own devices, and wait on his needs.

"Here we are," said El. He turned up a steep dirt road, rutted and bumpy with big rocks, and pulled up next to the collapsing porch of an old New England farmhouse, weathered gray, with a few remaining flecks of white paint. Our footsteps made hollow sounds on the shaky porch. Through the glass-paned front door, we entered the nineteenth century.

The sweet aroma of wood smoke filled the dry air; the darkened wood floors creaked under out boots. Grammie May, a spindly old woman in a neat, flowered dress with hand-crocheted lace collar, jumped up and greeted us laughing, as if we were the tag line of a joke. She hugged and kissed us, her soft, wrinkled skin fragrant with talcum powder as it brushed my cheeks, her clear blue eyes twinkling among wrinkles radiating from the corners. I took a seat on the dark velvet sofa decorated with lace doilies, and saw El's stories come to life: Georgia's piano, May's rolls baking in the wood stove, Sammit slapping the baby El in his high chair for bad manners. I imagined I could even see shards of a broken plate imbedded in the floor. "This plate is cracked, May. Can't you give me a whole one?" he had said sweetly, flinging the cracked plate to the floor. An upright piano stood in the corner of the living room, on its top sepia photos of a pretty woman in a high-necked lace dress—Georgia, a foster daughter who had died at nineteen in the influenza epidemic of 1918. And another photo of Sammit and the "boys" lined up like logs, some taller than others, all thin. There was one of May in front of a one-room school with four little pupils; Grammie had been a teacher before she married Sammit at eighteen.

I can never resist a piano. I went over and ran my fingers over the yellowed keys in an arpeggio. Before I could play a second one on the badly out-of-tune piano, El shouted, "Don't!" I stopped, shocked. May sat with her lips pursed, her hands clenched. Since Georgia's death, he told me later, no one was allowed to touch that piano. Georgia had played it, singing for Sammit and the "boys." It struck me as silly and selfish, especially as no one else in the entire family could play. Only El had a taste for classical music. The rest of his family listened to country music and went to barn dances for fiddle music.

Growing up, the four boys had enough food to eat from the farm and illegal hunting. But their education had been thwarted by the Depression. Ben and Reat, the two eldest, had been forced to quit school to help on the farm. Bob, the next to youngest, helped as best he could, but he was not bright, unlike his father and brothers. Allan, the youngest, was the only one to finish high school. There was only a five-year difference between Allan and El, his favorite nephew. El regarded Allan as his best friend for that reason, and Allan treated El as his sidekick.

The boys were equally used to New England winters, using an axe to chop firewood for the woodstove in the kitchen, and to break the six-inch layer of ice on top of the rain barrel. They carried ice water in buckets to fill kettles and tubs. What didn't kill them made them strong. May made the best Parker House rolls anyone had ever tasted, but El, who spent much of his childhood with his beloved grandparents, said she only cooked when she felt like it. When the mood hit her, she would fire up the wood stove and commence to cook and bake all day— preparing a huge feast of roast venison, mashed potatoes, greens cooked in lard, squash soup, apple and lemon pies, and the famous Parker House rolls—a recipe she took to her grave. As the food disappeared over the succeeding days, famine would creep back, until the mood to cook a feast struck her again. I imagine stoking a woodstove was a big reason to put off cooking until the cupboard was almost bare.

There were no electric poles, no wires leading from the main road through Etna up to the farmhouse, a mile up the rutted, dirt road. There was a well, and a pump handle. Looking out the frosted, large-paned window, I imagined where the tent must have been staked next to the porch, and reminded of when May got sick with TB. Sammit had put up an old army tent with the "boys," so he and May could sleep outdoors in below zero New Hampshire winters. The doctors were amazed, when, the next spring, they found May cured.

When we left, Grammie gave me another firm hug, gazing into my eyes, "You're a smart one." She gave me a bag of rolls and another of sugar cookies she'd baked. Apparently, she had forgiven me for playing Georgia's piano.

The year after El and I married, Grammie May taught herself to type on a new portable bought for her by Mr. Pitkin (I never knew his first name, and Grammie always called him "Mr. Pitkin"), a retired engineer she married when she was ninety and he ninety-three. They bought a white frame house on the main road, at the foot of the homestead, with central heating and in good repair. "It's the Laura Bridgman house," Grammie May said, proudly.

"Who was Laura Bridgman?" I asked.

"She taught Annie Sullivan, who was nearly blind, to read and write. Laura developed the techniques for teaching deaf-mutes. And Annie Sullivan became the famous teacher of Helen Keller." I was impressed. So much history in microscopic Etna.

We drove on to Allan's dairy farm, on another deeply rutted dirt road, closer to Hanover. Sweet William got stuck in the gooey mud, two feet deep. I sat in the car, trapped, surrounded by a river of mud.

El slogged through it on foot and got Allan, who came back with his tractor and pulled the old car out.

Allan had bought his farm at the beginning of World War II, to stay out of the army. He hated farm work, but it kept him out of military service. His herd of Holsteins lived luxuriously in a cow barn made of concrete blocks with a new roof—better accommodations than the ramshackle farmhouse he and his family lived in. It reminded me of a story, "The Revolt of Mother," by Mary Wilkins Freeman, in which the farm mother moves her entire family into the spanking new barn when her husband refuses to build them a new house.

Wearing wellies, El and I waded behind Allan through knee-deep manure and mud to watch him and his grizzled farmhands hook up the milking machines to one bellowing Holstein after another. I was given a lesson in dairy farming: "Holsteins give more milk than other breeds, but have the lowest butterfat content. The milk is so thin it's blue." Clouds of bluebottle flies that bred in manure piles continually tormented the cows' eyes, rears, and teats. The sad-eyed beasts were trapped in stanchions, swatting helplessly with their tails. Allan went down the rows, spanking each cow fondly on the rump, one after another. I liked Allan, despite his reputation for slyness, because he was El's only real friend in the family. Allan stood six feet two inches, and had the craggy handsomeness of pure Yankee, with Grammie May's sharp blue eyes. His thick, sandy hair was rarely washed or combed.

Out of loneliness, El and I spent nearly every weekend at Allan's in the first years of our marriage. Doris, his half–French Canadian wife, looked like a child beside Allan. She was barely four feet eleven, and a terrible cook, but she had a cheerful disposition, bordering on madness. She never complained about the hardships of her life or Allan's endless schemes that kept them on the verge of bankruptcy.

The farm kitchen was immense—twenty feet long, fifteen feet wide—the sink and cabinets built to Brobdingnagian proportions. Little Doris scurried around on the cracked linoleum, from the sink that came up to her chest, to the giant fridge on one wall, to the woodstove on the opposite, preparing fried steak and boiled vegetables, laughing merrily. She had to stand on a footstool to reach a hand pump in the sink to fill a pot with ice-cold water. Then she had to carry it to the stove where she'd open the burner and throw in another chunk of wood from the woodpile on the floor. "Allan, you'll have to chop some more wood," she said, laughing. "The pile won't last till breakfast." She stood on a stepladder to bring down dishes, then she carried them to the big, round oak table on the opposite side of the room. This is where we sat—Allan, El, and I, their daughter Sandy curled up on my lap sucking her thumb. I was spellbound by Doris's skill and strength, and what could be called "pluck," if it weren't so down-putting. Being married to Allan, a genuine New England Adams, filled Doris with so much pride that she didn't seem to notice the drudgery and poverty. When they ran out of money and were close to losing the farm, Doris got a job as a lab tech at Mary Hitchcock Hospital. She had on-the-job training, and came home spouting the medical vocabulary with pride. She called the doctors by their first names—Rob, Bill, Joseph—as if they were her equals.

Allan always made the coffee, filling an enamel pot from the pump in the sink, then throwing a cup of ground coffee on top of the icy water and setting the pot on the roaring wood stove. Doris brought mugs and spoons and sugar, and opened a can of evaporated milk with a beer can opener—"the church key," Allan called it. Sandy grabbed the can of milk and drank down half of it. Doris kept up a nonstop monologue about her new job at the hospital lab. "Rob said he'd never seen such a rash …" and she'd rattle off the name some rare disease.

I liked Doris and Allan. They were the only members of El's family who treated me like a part of the family, not as an alien city girl.

As part of the ritual of joining his family, El had to take me to see his other uncles, Ben and Bob; that is, to let the uncles see *me*. Ben, the oldest of Sammit's boys, trained English setters as hunting dogs, keeping them in kennels in back of his house. In hunting season, he guided wealthy Boston doctors to shoot grouse, partridge, and woodcock; later, to shoot deer. Ben also made a decent living as a master carpenter and had built his own rustic house. It was small, made of dark wood, and looked more like a hunting camp than a house for a family—which it was in actuality. His wife Hattie, I was warned by Allan, was "mad as a hatter." Ben had once been El's mentor, encouraging him to go to college when he got out of the army. Ben's daughter Esther, already in college, helped El fill out the application to the University of New

Hampshire. When El was accepted, majoring in English, Ben sniffed and said, "English is for fags."

Hattie and Ben sat in the small living room. She didn't look or sound crazy to me; she seemed to be an ordinary housewife in an ugly housedress, with gray hair and colorless eyes.

Ben, his thin black hair slicked back, studied me from a leather chair. He had a mean face. Dressed in a flannel shirt and puffing on a pipe, he quizzed me on my studies, where I came from, what I wanted to do. I answered politely, with gritted teeth, as little as possible. "I'd like to teach English." My instincts told me I couldn't trust him; he was an overbearing bully who treated his dogs with more affection and kindness than he treated his wife. His children, Esther and Don, had escaped—Esther to college and then a teaching job in New York State, and Don to the army and alcohol. The Adams family had a ratio of about one alcoholic for every three people.

Last among Sammit's boys in terms of status was Uncle Bob. He was an ordinary man, an ordinary farmer. His dairy farm was a mile closer to Etna than Allan's, on the same road. The fields around his house were snow covered, but looked well tended compared with Allan's. From the outside, the house looked sturdy and neat, and the concrete block barn was solid and clean. He strode out to greet us, his face an exact copy of his mother May's. Same white, wrinkled skin, same blue eyes, only his lacked the spark of wit and intelligence that brightened his mother's. He took us first to the barn to show us his team of prize-winning oxen. "Yup, won at the Canaan fair three years runnin', the ox-pull." He mentioned some unbelievable amount of dead weight—huge concrete blocks—the oxen had dragged across the fairgrounds.

"Come in and meet Ruth," Bob said. We entered the nice house, and my eyes grew wide in shock: there wasn't a single interior wall, just studs and open spaces where walls might eventually be. The studs were dark, having aged during their wait for walls. Kitchen sink, stove, and fridge were ranged along one bare wall—no interior wallboard, just the outer siding—under windows facing the barn. In what might have been a dining room or living room, there was a stuffed chair where Ruth sat, sorting laundry, a pile of clothes four feet high on the floor in front of her. Ruth had blue eyes, faded like washed silk, and pale, nearly colorless hair. She smiled vacantly. She continued to smile as Bob and El talked about oxen. I heard sounds like mice and realized there were children somewhere; I could see an occasional towhead, a blue eye peeking from behind a stud. The children were never called out, never introduced. Ruth said nothing. I wondered how the family had decided that Hattie was crazy. Ruth seemed catatonic. Yet she lived to ninety-seven, sharp as a needle, and her children did well, one going to college.

"Bob isn't very smart," said El as we drove away.

"What's wrong with Ruth?" I asked. El shrugged. He'd never noticed anything unusual about her. Because Bob was kind, unlike Ben, Reat, and Allan, I guess they considered him stupid.

If I'd wanted to get far away from my defunct parents, New Hampshire was only four hundred miles in actual distance, but it might as well have been Pluto. I had plunged backward into the 1930s Depression and its victims, and headlong into a different culture, a colder climate, into fresh air and fresh water and few modern conveniences. I acquired a new vocabulary: Holstein, Jersey, Guernsey, hybrid Brahma, heifer, freshening, shoat, partridge, ruffed grouse, pheasant, woodcock, quail. And then there were twelve-gauge, .410, over-and-under, double-barreled shotgun, 30-ought deer rifle—an arsenal particularized to kill anything from the tiny woodcock to a twelve-point buck to a four-hundred-pound black bear.

Allan gave El one of his .410 shotguns to go bird hunting. On fall weekends, El and I walked into his beloved New England woods at its most beautiful season. He recited Frost's poem, "Birches," and walked quietly as an Indian. "Hark!" he whispered. "It's a ruffed grouse! Hear the whirr?" Bam! The bird was knocked out of the air as it took off, the whirring the giveaway. The setter, released from point by Allan's whistle, yelped and ran to pick up the dead bird, gently, by its limp neck. El showed me how to hold the lightweight .410 shotgun against my left shoulder. "Squeeze and hold it tight to your shoulder. The recoil won't hurt you then." I fired at a tree, leaving it pockmarked with buckshot. My shoulder felt the buck, but it didn't snap as I hugged it tightly. One shot at a tree was enough to end my hunting career, however. It seemed cruel, unless you were really hungry and needed the meat for dinner.

As a teenager, El was a dead shot, killing birds when he went hunting with Ben and Allan and Doc, a famous cardiologist from Boston. Doc couldn't hit the side of a barn, so it was El's job to down the birds Doc would take back to Boston in triumph. But in November, when deer season arrived and Ben and Allan went wild with excitement, El made excuses not to go. By the time we married, he couldn't bear killing an animal. El's change of heart was blamed on me—a city girl who didn't know what a real man was. The Adams code of maleness did not include eyeglasses, "fag" dress shirts and suits, and reading books. The fact that El, who'd worn glasses since first grade, read books for pleasure as well as learning was a big black mark against his manhood in the Adams' canon. No Adams could call himself a man unless he killed his own meat and had a freezer full of venison he'd shot himself. Not one man who married El's sisters was considered a "real" man.

One day, we visited Allan. Robert, Doris's younger brother was there. Robert, Allan said, had just come home from the war in Korea, and had been given a medical discharge. "Robert's got the jungle rot," Allan said, laughing. "His feet are rotten." We looked into the small bedroom off the unheated living room to meet Robert. He lay on a narrow bed, his bare, yellow feet sticking out from a faded quilt. He opened one eye, his face yellow from jaundice. He was the most wretched-looking man I had ever seen still alive. Allan laughed. "Ain't he a sight?"

Worse still, as a man, was Doris's father. He was a "white" man who had married a Canuck. He was barely five feet tall, toothless. When Allan had picked up El and me on my first visit to meet El's family, Allan said he'd have to drop us off at Mame's. "Gotta take the car, El. You know my father-in-law? He tried to kill hisself." Allan chuckled. "He ain't but farty-eight years old." I stifled a laugh at the New England accent. El asked what had happened. "Oh, tried to tie his neck to the rafters. Couldn't even make a knot. He's gonna make it, though. He's in Mary Hitchcock. Got one of them smart Jewish doctors." My face burned. El looked at me sideways.

"Um, Bobbie's half-Jewish, you know," El said. Allan looked stunned, his eyes wide in his long face, turning red.

"Well, gee, I *didn't* know. Anyway, she can't help it."

The current crop of Adams men had obviously never met a woman like me before—uppity, able to drive a car, cook, *and* read books, *and* half-Jewish. I hadn't met any men like them before, for sure. Shortly after I arrived in Lebanon, they discovered that I could drive. "No. You ain't got no license!" said one of them.

Mary was unconvinced I could drive a car: "No woman drives." I was breaking some unwritten rule. They really didn't believe me. One day, in the kitchen crowded as usual with Adamses of every age and relation, Roger asked me, "Hey, Bahb, can you drive me overstreet to get some beer and milk? You can drive my cah." Unaware that this was a test, I took his keys, climbed into his car, and backed out of the alpine driveway, El staring jealously out the window. When we got back with the beer and milk, Mary declared, "My land! You ain't supposed to drive without a license!" The entire clan stared at me wide eyed. I took out my wallet and showed them my driver's license from New York. "I got this when I was eighteen." El crushed an empty beer can in his hands.

My negative view of the Adams men was tempered somewhat by their gift for story telling. They mythologized themselves and their deeds, exaggerating and embellishing with the skill of Homer. It was an oral tribal history. One story Allan told I will never forget: it was a tale of murder, plain and simple. The victim was Clint, Ben's father-in-law.

Ben, Reat's older brother, had to take Clint to the State Farm—the old people's home. Reat and Allan volunteered to drive Clint there, as Ben had a broken ankle. A week earlier, Clint had had a severe heart attack and was told not to drink anymore if he wanted to live. He was scared into sobriety, but he was too weak to take care of himself. His daughter Hattie, Ben's wife, refused to have anything to do with her stepfather. He'd abused her, according to Allan, who just laughed at the idea. So the State Farm in Littleton, on the Canadian border, was the only option.

Reat and Allan set out in the dead of winter for the long drive north. It grew dark as they slid along the icy roads of northern New Hampshire on bald tires. The heater did not work, and the windows iced up. They were chilled to the bone, the sick old man shivering under a moth-eaten buffalo robe in the backseat. Reat stopped for a break on the winding country road in the midst of a silent, snowy forest. There were no other cars. Not a house in sight. Allan got out and tried scraping the ice off the windshield with his gloved hands. Reat laughed and pulled out a fifth of liquor from under the seat, took a healthy swig, and handed it to Allan. Reat took the bottle back and turned to Clint. "Have one—it'll do you good, warm you up." The old man stretched out a bony hand, but he couldn't move his frozen fingers. Reat held the bottle to Clint's lips and poured. The old man gasped and coughed, but Clint's eyes lit up.

They drove on a little way, then stopped again and had another round of slugs from the bottle, until it was empty. They all felt much warmer. The old man leaned back in the icy car and fell asleep, snoring loudly. "He'll freeze if we don't get him moving some," Allan said. So Allan and Reat dragged Clint out of the car and walked him around in the snow hoping to wake him, but he was out cold. They threw him in back again, covering him with the buffalo robe, and finally made it to the state home at midnight. Reeking of alcohol, they carried Clint inside and put him in a chair in the waiting room. A night nurse came, raised Clint's eyelids, and felt for a pulse. "This man is dead!" she said.

"Saved the state some money!" said Reat laughing. "He don't have to live on welfare."

Everyone laughed at the punch line, one of Reat's favorites. The Adams philosophy avowed that it was better to let the old man die happily drunk than let him endure the indignity of living off the state. They just supplied the poison.

El could repeat the family tales verbatim, but he was also deeply ashamed of his family's code of ethics he'd had to accept as a child in order to survive. He tore himself in half—defending his family and trying to educate them on the one hand, while hating their ignorance and amorality on the other. "You're not like them," I insisted. "You can't help them. You can only help yourself." El thought he *could* teach them, show them how to change, but they didn't see any need; they were having a good time.

As alien as I felt, I sensed I had some things in common with the Adamses: I was a rebel and an outcast. Poverty had made them outcasts; my parents had made me persona non grata. They were strong in body and as a clan. My strength lay in intangibles—intellect and education—abstractions denied to them and therefore distrusted. I entered into their life in every way I could, without disowning my own values. In truth, I found these self-sufficient survivors of the Depression powerfully attractive.

Allan continued to be our best ally, and, at times, my worst nightmare. When I was pregnant with my first child, Allan invited El and me to go ice fishing on Lake Fairlee in Vermont. Vermont struck me as somehow more "civilized" than New Hampshire, so I agreed, warily. The day we went, it was fifteen to twenty degrees below zero. The ice was two feet thick.

We arrived at Lake Fairlee in Allan's car with the heater on full blast. I was in the back seat with Doris and three-year-old Sandy; we felt no heat. Allan parked the car at the edge of the big lake where several other ice fishermen had parked. He and El took out the fishing gear and started walking out onto the frozen lake. Allan yelled back, "Come on out when we've set up."

Shivering in heavy winter clothes and boots, we got out of the car, which was only faintly warmer that the great outdoors. Hundreds of ice fishermen were huddled around holes they'd drilled in the ice. Some had put up rough shacks, and built small wood fires atop the thick ice to thaw out frozen fingers. Allan waved. His spot had no tent, no shelter. The wind cut into us three females as we shuffled across the frozen lake. Allan used a manual hole-driller to grind out a fishing port about a foot wide. When it broke through, the water gushed up, blue-green, and froze on the surface. El and Allan dropped a long line into the hole. There were a dozen baited hooks on one end, and a flag at the top, which would tip when there was a bite. All over the lake, flags stuck up, then tipped, as a bass or lake trout grabbed the bait.

Sandy, sucking her thumb through her mitten, screamed, "Goddammit, Allan. I'm freezing to death!" Doris, shivering, laughed. She, Sandy, and I walked back across the ice to the car. My feet hurt with cold, as if someone were squeezing my toes with pliers. Opening the car door, my numb fingers couldn't grasp the handle. Doris turned on the engine. The heater slowly warmed up. Whatever warmth came through did not penetrate my frozen bones, my icy blood.

After that ice fishing adventure, whenever Allan suggested a day seeking nature's bounty, I stayed home. My romantic view of Robert Frost's New England died of a chill that permeated my body, heart, and soul.

PHOTOS

*El's grandfather, George "Sammit" Adams, El, about
two years old: Etna NH, circa 1928*

*El's parents, Fred Aretus "Reat" Adams and Mary
Fields Adams: Lebanon NH, circa 1955*

El, school photo, two years before his death: Newburgh NY, 1991

*Three generations of Helens: my great-grandmother, Helen Dunn;
my grandmother Helen Dunn Taxter; and my mother, Helen Taxter
Block. Me, Barbara Helen Block: Yonkers NY, circa 1934*

*My youthful parents with Grandma Abbie, David Block
and Helen Taxter: Rockaway Beach NY, 1930s*

My mother and me: Manhattan NY, 1932

Grandma Abbie and my mother, circa 1930

*The last photo of my family before the divorce : Daddy, sister
Judy, Mom (home from the hospital), Grandma Abbie, me, and
my best friend Betty Anne Will: Fire Island NY, 1943*

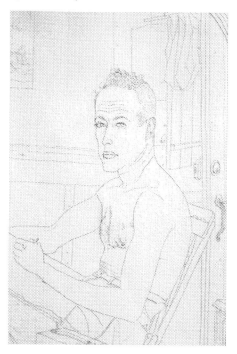

My father's self-portrait: Provincetown MA, 1944

My father and me, my high school graduation: New Paltz NY, 1950

My mother, Helen, and stepfather, Eric Tyler: Newburgh NY, 1970s

Dr. Louis Salkever, shortly before his death: Philadelphia PA, 1994

Uncle Billy, publicity shot: New York NY, 1960s

Uncle Billy, on stage at Oriental Theatre, circa 1941?

A photo El took of me: Newburgh NY, 1980s

El, making our stone patio: 1970s

Chapter IX

A HOME, AFTER ALL, 1957–1966

In 1957, after five years, we left New Hampshire with a sigh of relief. We arrived back in the middle of the Hudson Valley with three small children and no place to live. My mother said we could stay with her. She and Eric and Judy lived in an upstairs apartment in a large old house, ten miles from the college town we had left when we were married five years earlier. El would look for construction work, which was about to shut down for the winter months. He collected unemployment insurance, our only income.

My mother and Eric treated us like dumb immigrants. I guess we were, in a way. We had not planned our life very well so far. I heard them whispering, loudly, about El, a "shiftless good-for-nothing." I had to eat my anger. Who else would help us? I soon realized I was pregnant again, and wept silently. Under the circumstances, there was nothing I could do. Abortion was illegal in the 1950s, so I accepted another life to be, vowing, this time, that my fourth child—and last—would be a New Yorker. El, however, demanded sex every night, rain or shine, in illness and in health.

When construction work started up again, El and I rented a nice old stone house a few miles away, in Highland. We had privacy again, and I began to feel more hopeful. El's mood, however, was unpredictable. He got angry with or without provocation. He would stop at a tavern after work, drinking beer and smoking. I would eat supper, put the kids to bed. When he finally came home, drunk and covered in mortar dust, he didn't care that his supper was cold. I was just glad he came home safe. I said nothing.

One morning, when our old Ford station wagon wouldn't start, El picked up a fifty-pound cement block and threw it at the disobedient car. The block left a deep dent in the front passenger door. The "woody" wagon was our only means of transportation. Every car we'd had so far had been old and already worn out when we got it. El spent entire weekends trying to get a car to run again, replacing spark plugs, water pumps, and tires … changing the oil. All the while spewing out curses. He was perpetually angry. Perpetually tired.

In New Hampshire, it had been even worse. Winters were colder and longer, and old cars with six-volt batteries never started without a jump start. El would search for used parts and do his own repairs. While he worked on our frozen car in his mother's driveway, his bare fingers frozen, his parents, brothers, and uncles watched from inside the warm kitchen, laughing as El threw tools and cursed. When he came inside to warm himself with coffee, Reat would snicker, "Got her going yet?" None of them offered to help. They just lounged around, drinking coffee and eating Mame's nonstop banquet. Without money or a place to live, we had escaped the clan and returned to New York. It took enormous effort and fortitude. Both families thought we were crazy and would end up on welfare. Or, they hoped, divorced. El's mother never stopped telling him to come back, "Lots of work up heah," she'd write, or say on the phone. I remember her words when she first saw me, "What does she want with *him*?" My mother despised El; he despised her. Electric daggers filled the air when they had to speak to each other. I had to tune them all out.

In New York, El joined the local bricklayer's union and, in the '50s boom times, worked from six in the morning until seven at night for high wages. I took care of our small children, cleaned, did laundry, and then went to college, taking day classes. My mother babysat, lavishing attention on her favorites, the boys, and ignoring the girls. El took classes in evenings and on Saturdays. At one point, he was laying brick on a new college building, then dashing into the men's locker room, showering, donning clean clothes, and going to classes.

We needed more money to pay for doctors' bills and car insurance. El went to the bank and asked for a loan; we had no assets, so he had to have a cosigner. We asked Eric to cosign the loan. (My mother and I, as married women without outside income, couldn't sign for a loan or have a credit card in our own name.) Eric refused, sniffing. This was a man who had ended up in the gutter once, and nearly died of acute alcoholism. I couldn't believe it. My mother was stony faced and did not coax Eric. I was stricken with terror that we'd have to go back to El's family, begging. Then El went to see our friend and professor, Lou Salkever. Lou was a kind, brilliant, fat Buddha, a professor of economics, who had taken us under his wing. Without hesitation, Lou cosigned the loan. Lou was more of a father to me than my actual, absent father.

We finished the classwork, and then had to do ten weeks of student teaching, five days a week. I got up before the children woke, prepared lunches, and got myself dressed for teaching. When my mother came, I kissed my babies good-bye and drove my mother's car to the Campus School. The school day ran from eight to three-thirty, and there were after-hours conferences with my mentor teacher. I got back home by five in time to make dinner, do the dishes, bathe the children, read to them, and then lay out clothes for the next day. By midterm, I was so exhausted I got sick. Walking down the corridor in school, I felt lightheaded, as if I were floating three feet above the floor. The school nurse said I had temperature of 104. I drove myself to the doctor on the way home. "Walking pneumonia," said the doctor. "Bed rest and antibiotics." I slept for three days while El stayed home and took care of the kids.

And then, finally, we were done. Another June, nine years late. The naysayers—El's family and mine—couldn't believe that we had finally earned bachelor's degrees. For our graduation, El's mother mustered a horde of El's siblings and arrived on our doorstep, uninvited. They slept on the floor, in sleeping bags, and on the sofa. At the ceremony, El and I marched side by side in cap and gown, applauded by Lou and his sweet wife Edna. My mother, Eric, Judy, and our children watched from the sidelines, waving. As I passed her, my mother leaned over and yelled, "Hiya, Smarty Pants!" I was valedictorian. Again. My father wasn't there. Lou Salkever had seen to it that I was valedictorian; my GPA was 3.9.

We got teaching jobs immediately in Milton, the heart of the apple-growing region in the heart of the Hudson Valley. My first contract was for a combined fourth and fifth grade with handpicked students. El was assigned a fifth grade in another school. Later, he switched to special education for mentally and emotionally challenged students, a growing field of education. Another teacher, Linda, had urged him to try it. El was especially gifted in working with these disabled students.

We rented an old farmhouse in the same town. It was small, with two big bedrooms and two closet-sized ones upstairs. Downstairs, there was a dining room and a living room with old pine flooring, knotty pine walls, and a stone fireplace. There was one bathroom downstairs for the six of us. The kitchen overlooked the orchard, and the back door opened onto a stone terrace with a low stone wall. A gigantic catalpa tree gave shade and dropped leathery pods every fall. We had an Italian plum tree in the backyard. It seemed to me too good to be true: a fairy-tale house.

The day we moved in during a thunderstorm, a white ball of shivering dog curled up on the front porch. We looked for her owner, but no one claimed her. Migrant workers from the south often discarded pets before heading back home. Thus, Sniffy joined our family, named by our older daughter Amy because the dog was forever sneezing.

Our landlord Fritz was a winemaker who lived in Brooklyn during the week and sometimes stayed in the small cottage in back on weekends. He rented the little cottage for a month in summer to a red-cheeked young choral singer, Daniel, who practiced scales we could hear as we ate supper. We invited him to dinner. Daniel told us he was engaged, and that his fiancée would be spending the following weekend with him. "But there won't be any funny business going on, I assure you," he said, blushing. He and his fiancée, a soprano, actually practiced singing all weekend.

On my birthday, after the first winter in that house, El bought me the best birthday gift he ever gave me in our married life. He and the children waited for me to come home from grocery shopping, told me to close my eyes, and led me into the dining room. "Open!" they yelled, pulling a blanket off a lovely new spinet piano. I had not had a piano for a long, long time. For years, I had "practiced" by strumming my fingers on a table. I had saved all my music—Beethoven, Chopin,

Mozart ... books of folk music. For the first time, I could play for El and our children: "Sweet Betsy From Pike," "Red River Valley," "My Darlin' Clementine," and all the folk songs in my *Fireside Book*. They sang along, El with his sweet, high tenor voice. I resumed practicing Chopin, Beethoven, and Mozart.

The apple orchards were rented to the Italian farmer across the road. Every fall, southern black migrant workers arrived in the valley by the hundreds, to pick the ripe fruit. Fritz said we could pick as many apples as we wanted. Eden was our backyard.

The farmhouse was the first real home I'd had since I was twelve, the first real home for El and me since we'd married. We bought new beds for everyone. An elderly teacher about to retire gave us a cherry dining table. We bought maple chairs and a wringer washing machine—on credit—so we wouldn't have to spend every Saturday afternoon in the Laundromat. The washing machine had to be rolled up to the kitchen sink and filled through a rubber hose attached to the faucet; it was emptied down the sink drain by the same hose. I ran the wet clothes through the electric-powered wringer, then hung them on the line in the backyard to dry. Our sheets and clothes smelled of fresh air. I longed for the day when we could afford an automatic washer and dryer, recently invented but still far beyond our means.

We liked our teaching jobs and made friends with Linda, El's colleague, whose husband was one of the wealthiest apple growers in the region. Jim was also the current president of the school board. Most of the residents in Milton were of Italian descent, with a smattering of Irish, and a few early English families like Jim's who had settled the region. During the height of the harvest season, September to November, our classes swelled by a third with black migrant children from Florida, the Carolinas, and Georgia. Most of them could not read or write, did not know where they'd been born or when, and some could not even write their own names. By the time they learned, the apples were picked and they headed south for citrus farms.

El and I became good friends with Linda and Jim. They got us to join the Unitarian Church, the same church we'd belonged to in New Hampshire. I wanted our children to belong somewhere in society, if not to the religious spectrum. I did not believe in God or Jesus;

neither did El. The Unitarians we met were a motley mixture of mixed marriages, mostly atheists like us.

Fritz offered us the old farmhouse for a good price. We thought about buying it, but it needed major repairs—new furnace, new kitchen, another bathroom, and remodeling of the tiny upstairs bedrooms, not to mention roofing. It had no driveway. I wanted to move to a nearby small city with a more balanced mix of Protestants, Catholics, and Jews. I did not want my kids growing up to think that everyone was Catholic, and never meeting any Jewish people at all. So we thanked Fritz, but said no.

As our economic circumstances improved, we had time to breathe a bit. Time to look ahead and see what the future held. El and I worked in different schools. I got home as fast as I could, to be there when the children's bus arrived. El went to a diner with Linda and sometimes other teachers to drink coffee and talk about work. Oftentimes, after supper, El went out to a tavern, where he sat drinking beer. He was moody, and would not talk to me. We began to fight continually about his family and mine. Every time we visited his family, he'd have an anxiety attack. He'd had his first attack shortly after our first child was born in New Hampshire. Clutching his chest, he'd gasped, "I'm dying! I can't breathe—I'm having a heart attack!" His pulse was racing. I didn't know what to do, sitting with him until his breathing slowed and pulse returned to normal. I insisted he go to see the doctor the next day.

"There's nothing wrong with your heart," said the doctor. "You had an anxiety attack." He referred El to a psychiatrist at Mary Hitchcock Hospital in Hanover. We could barely afford one psychiatric visit, let alone extended therapy. The psychiatrist, a woman, said El didn't need extended treatment (she'd sized up our income), blaming the anxiety attack on our marriage—his snotty New Yorker wife taking advantage of a poor bricklayer (so El reported afterwards). He had told her about Rick, his professor friend who had grown up in the same town, and was on sabbatical. El visited Rick every weekend; El begged him to take care of me when El took a job out of town for three weeks. Depressed and lonely, I fell for Rick. I wanted affection and warmth. Rick soothed me, wanting sex. I felt ashamed. El found out, of course, and told his mother. She said I was no good; she'd always known it. Then he nearly strangled me. After that, he went to Rick's house. "I coldcocked the sonofabitch," he told me.

Every time we fought, El threw Rick in my face, calling me a whore. I thought we'd left that all behind when we moved back to New York. But El never let me forget, calling me a whore every time he got into a black mood, which was often.

One day, I noticed a bald spot on top of my head, a round bare spot like a mini-Cromwellian haircut. My hair was falling out in clumps. I thought I'd caught ringworm from one of the children in my class. The dermatologist studied the bald patches under an ultraviolet light. "It's definitely not ringworm."

"What is it?" I asked.

"Alopecia," he replied.

"What's that?"

"Nothing serious. Are you under any particular stress, dear?" he asked, patting my shoulder. So it was all in my head. "The hair will eventually grow back of its own accord," the doctor reassured me.

At the same time my hair was falling out, I broke out in a bright red rash and had a slight fever. German measles was running through the schools like a grassfire. I was glad to take a week off from teaching, staying home to rest and catch up on reading. I was very tired and slept a lot. On the second day at home, as I was ironing El's shirts, my stomach suddenly cramped so severely I ran to the bathroom thinking it was diarrhea. The pain was intense and terrible, but as I strained on the toilet, what I saw in the bowl wasn't feces. It was bright red blood. And then a huge clot shot out of me. I felt faint. As soon as I could get up, I grabbed a towel and stuffed it between my legs and called El at work. He got home in fifteen minutes. I had bled through three more towels. El wrapped me in a blanket and drove me to the emergency room in Poughkeepsie. "You're okay. You lost a little blood," said the ER doctor. "You've had a miscarriage. The fetus has already been expelled." I thought of the clot I'd flushed down the toilet. I hadn't even known I was pregnant.

German measles apparently had caused the miscarriage—thankfully. Had the child survived, it might have been blind or mentally disabled from German measles. I stayed overnight in the hospital, for observation. El said Linda had taken our children home with her. She washed the bloody blankets and towels. They should have been thrown out, as the stains were indelible. When El drove me home the next day, he looked sheepish. "I'm sorry," he said. "It's all my fault." I couldn't understand what he meant.

"Why?" I asked.

"I've been having an affair with Linda," he confessed. I sucked in air, stunned. My body had known, reacted with baldness, before my mind grasped the truth.

The fairy tale was over. My hair grew back. I forgave El. But I never forgave Linda. A few years later, Linda's husband left her for his male lover. El had never forgiven Rick either, who was, we learned, a notorious womanizer and seducer of his female students.

We settled into a quieter time, looking for our own house. I had not given up my dream of teaching college and writing. El continued to write his "pieces," reading them to me in the middle of the night. It never occurred to him that he could have waited until daylight.

I was ready to leave this "storybook," narrow-minded, small town— and Linda. Shortly before we moved, a large family of rats infested our house—Fritz's house—in the orchard. We set traps baited with cheese and stale bananas. In the morning, the bait would be gone, the traps sprung, but no dead rats. "I'll get the bastards," El vowed, his hunting upbringing rising to the fore. He got our son's BB gun and sat by the cellar door. The kids and I went to bed. I fell asleep. El sat in the dark, staring at the crack beneath the door, moonlight shining across the pine floor. Suddenly, I was awakened by a loud *pop*! I ran downstairs. El was holding up the corpse of a fat rat by its tail. He'd shot her through the head. "There's more where she came from," he said grimly. We set out rat poison and more traps in the cellar. In the next three days, we caught and killed eight more rats, a whole nest of rat babies. They were perhaps symbols of the dangers we faced if we stayed in this house.

Our last summer in the house, there was a drought and a heat wave. Fritz, spending the weekend in his cottage, watered his acres of lawn until the well ran dry. We had no water for cooking, drinking, or bathing. It was hot, crackling dry. We went out for supper at Howard Johnson's. At bedtime, we couldn't brush our teeth or flush the toilet.

As the kids settled down to bed, El marched out the kitchen door and strode toward Fritz's cottage, his fists clenched. For once, I hoped that he would "coldcock the sonofabitch." I went upstairs to the kids, who all snuggled in one big bed while I read another chapter of *The Wind in the Willows*, their favorite, using a hammy British accent they loved. When I finished, the boys went to their own beds and the girls curled up on either side. I went downstairs to wait for El. I played the piano, read a mystery, and finally went to bed.

In the morning, El's side of the bed was empty. I ran downstairs—El wasn't anywhere. I looked outside—our car was parked where we'd left it the day before. I was terrified, wondering if I should call the police—maybe he and Fritz had killed each other! Or one had killed the other and was burying him at this very moment. I ran outside in my nightgown and slippers. The kids' tricycles, bikes, doll carriages, balls, and bats lay strewn about, looking perfectly normal. My heart pounded. How would I raise four kids alone?

I went back into the kitchen and made a pot of coffee with a trickle of water before I called for help. A thought crossed my mind: maybe I should call Linda, just to rule out that possibility. Just as I took a sip of coffee, the kitchen door opened and El staggered in, reeking of wine.

"Where have you been? Are you all right?" I poured him a cup of coffee; his hand wobbled unsteadily as he lifted it to his lips.

"I've been at Fritz's. We're good buddies." Then he stumbled upstairs and fell into bed. We still had only a trickle of water.

As he slept it off, I took the kids to a diner for breakfast and took our clothes to the Laundromat. When we got back with the clean laundry, the kids ran off to read new comic books. More water began to trickle out of the faucet. El had shaved and looked as if he'd never a drop taken.

"What happened?" I asked as we finished unloading the car.

"I went to Fritz's, ready to coldcock the sonofabitch. I told him he didn't give a fuck about our kids, running the well dry. Fritz yelled back, 'Get out of my house! And take those brats with you. It's *my* water and I can do what I want with it!'

"I said, 'You care more about your goddamn grass than you do about my kids!' We kept yelling for quite awhile. 'I do care about your *kinder*,' Fritz said. Then he looked sad, and I don't know why, he brought out a gallon of his homemade wine to give me a taste—sickening sweet stuff. I drank some, to be polite. I hated it. We sat there all night while he told me his life story, his childhood in Austria."

El paused for another cup of coffee. "The truth is, Fritz is half-Jewish. His mother. When I told him you were half-Jewish, he suddenly changed his tune. 'My mother died in the camps; my own Christian father had turned her in.' Fritz escaped from Austria, over the Alps, just in time."

El took a deep drag on his cigarette, "And he loves our kids—says he's never met nicer, better behaved kids than ours. He's sorry for running out the water, won't do it again. And he gave me this, for the kids." El held out a check for one hundred dollars. That month, Fritz also refused to let us pay the rent.

Leaving the little house in the orchard, we moved into our own newly built house in August of 1966. It had seven and a half rooms, two and a half baths, and half an acre of our own land. We had town water and our own lawn. El eventually built a fireplace and chimney. My piano fit nicely in the large downstairs family room. The children grew up here, and finished school in this small city on the Hudson River, with a diverse population of Catholics, Protestants, Jews, Hispanics, and blacks.

A few years after El died, our youngest child, Sam, came to visit. He wanted to see the little farmhouse he remembered, where he'd fallen out of the plum tree and broken his collarbone. We drove north about fifteen miles, up the familiar steep hill, and came to the stone wall that fronted the old house. But we could hardly see it; it was completely overgrown with brush and brambles. We parked up the hill, and then clawed through the prickly tangle to get to the door. Windows were smashed, the front door stood open. Animals had taken over, building smelly nests, eating whatever they thought edible—woodwork, plaster, wallpaper paste. Birds swooped in and out the gable windows. "I wonder how much they want for it?" Sam said.

"You'd have to tear it down," I said. "It's beyond repair, dear. Let it go."

As we got ready to leave, a neighbor working in her yard recognized me. "Hi, Barb! How ya doin'?" I asked about Fritz. "Oh, Fritz died years ago, and his daughter didn't want the place. She let it fall apart," said Dolly. "We tried to buy the land several times, but she won't let it go. Nobody farms the orchards anymore." The house had been the site of a new beginning for El and me. Now it was a ruin returning to earth. The brambles had it.

Chapter X

WHY AM I A POET?

A poet is born, not made, they say; it's in the poet's nature to write poems. But how do you know you're a "born" poet? You have to have the "voice," but, like an opera singer's, it has to be trained. My education in poetry was scant until I was in my thirties. In addition to just being born one, a life lived must also have to have something to do with becoming a poet.

"You have the right background to be a poet," said a Pulitzer Prize-winning poet (who had become my lover). I guess he meant I had a good education and bad parents. His background was also "right" by this measure. That mix of poetic nature and nurture can add up to madness as well.

All poets are mad, it has long been believed. In the ancient world, poets were "divinely inspired," blessed by the gods, and not governed by reason. Because they were, by nature, irrational, they would not be governable. In *The Republic, Book X*, Plato therefore banished poets from his ideal Republic as irrational and ungovernable:

> There is an ancient quarrel between philosophy and
> poetry ... lyric poets
> Are not in their right mind when they are composing
> their beautiful strains.
>
> (Kaplan 1953, 14, 16)

Wordsworth, thinking of "that marvelous boy," Thomas Chatterton, wrote of him in "Resolution and Independence." Chatterton, who had committed suicide at seventeen, led Wordsworth to conclude that all poets ended in madness:

> We poets in our youth begin in gladness;
> But thereof come in the end despondency and madness.

(Wordsworth 1807, 138)

In a speech on his seventieth birthday, in 1926, Freud credited the discovery of the unconscious to "the poets and philosophers before me"(Trilling 1950, 678). Ever since, psychiatrists and psychologists have devoted numerous studies to the exploration of the unconscious mind, in the never-ending search for the causes and sources of mental illness. "Mad" poets have proved fertile ground for many psychogical studies.

In her 1993 study, *Touched With Fire,* Kay Redfield Jamison, a psychiatrist who herself suffers from manic depression, compiled a list of eighty-three poets in the last two hundred fifty years who could be considered "mad." Jamieson categorizes them as having committed suicide, attempted suicide, or been put in an asylum or psychiatric hospital, and identifies specific mental illnesses: "cyclothymia [a milder form of bipolar illness], major depression, and manic-depressive illness [bipolar illness]" (Jamison, 1993, 267). Twenty of these poets were suicides, twelve attempted suicide, and twenty-nine were put in institutions (overlap categories in some cases). Some are important contemporary poets: Hart Crane, Randall Jarrell, Robert Lowell, Sylvia Plath, Theodore Roethke, Delmore Schwartz, John Berryman, and Anne Sexton. I admired these poets, and found in their work the impetus for my own.

How did I fit in? Was I mad? Does madness make a poet? I have been treated for depression on and off most of my life, and take an anti-depressant. A diagnosis of depression and treatment, however, will not make me or anyone a poet.

I questioned myself, What stimulates poetry? Nature, books, family, society? How can you separate which aspects of your life compel you to write?

My first word was "tree." My mother had parked my carriage under a tree in Inwood Park when I looked up and began naming the world. My mother herself spoke very little; my father talked a lot.

In my childhood, I absorbed books—*Black Beauty, Heidi, The Blue Fairy Book, The Red Fairy Book,* and *The Green Fairy Book.* The stories took me to another world. I was one of the twelve dancing princesses. I was Rose Red, competing with my sister Rose White for the Bear Prince. The pale face always wins.

Longfellow's "Evangeline" was assigned in seventh grade. The story was sad, but the narrative poem was very long and boring. It didn't rhyme but had this bumpety-bumpety meter:

> This is the forest primeval, with the murmuring pines
> and hemlocks
> Bearded with moss, and in garments green, indistinct
> in twilight …
>
> (Longfellow, 1998,162).

In eighth grade, Miss Kelly, who seemed more modern than the other teachers, taught us a poem by Robert Frost, "Birches," reading it with tears in her eyes. I thought Miss Kelly was pretty, and very smart, so I forgave her for saying that "Birches" was a "nature poem." I wanted to believe her, but I did not agree. She made Frost's mystifying poem sound like a greeting card with a pretty picture of trees. How did I know that at the age of twelve?

I wanted to know about the boy who has to fetch the cows, swinging birches coming and going to the barn. Now he's an old man and can't swing birches any more. The poem didn't jingle or rhyme. Something about it was different from telling a story, a beat underlying the seeming prose. I did not understand what it was. Neither did Miss Kelly.

In high school, the teachers caught up with poetry so that it made more sense. Miss Sheerin had us read Shakespeare—*Julius Caesar* and *Macbeth.* The plays were written in iambic pentameter, "blank verse," said Miss Sheerin, beating out the rhythm on her desk. She underlined allusions, metaphors, symbols, explained paradox, irony, and soliloquy. I was studying Latin, where I finally learned grammar, and read Caesar's own words. I was fascinated with ancient Rome. Everyone had to memorize a soliloquy. I chose Lady Macbeth's "Out, damned spot!"

Reciting it, I felt as guilty as she, understanding the power and magic of poetry in mere words.

Miss Genove, an enthusiastic first-time teacher, opened a whole new universe to me, filling the blackboard with an outline of English literature, from Beowulf to Chaucer, to the King James Bible, to Shakespeare, to Milton and the Romantic poets. I copied it word for word, determined to read them all.

My classmates and I were all romantics, teenagers in love with love. Hormones bubbled through us as we read the romantic poets: Shelley, Byron, Coleridge, Keats, and Wordsworth. I don't think we understood much of what we were reading, but we became so infatuated with handsome, crippled Byron and his romantic life that we competed to write our term paper on him. Miss Genove put the poets' names in a hat. I drew Shelley (some lucky C-student drew Byron) and threw myself into his poetry and biography. His life was as romantic as Byron's: elopement with Mary Wollstonecraft, the author of *Frankenstein*, drowning at sea in a homemade boat, his friends burning his corpse on the shore of the Ligurian Sea, then snatching Shelley's heart out of the coals to preserve it "forever."

Shelley said, "Poets are the unacknowledged legislators of the world" (Kaplan 1955, 374). Wow. That was a different from saying they were mad, and banishing them from the Republic. I tried to memorize the twenty-one stanzas of "To a Skylark," but settled for fragments:

> Hail to thee, blithe Spirit!
> Bird thou never wert—
> That from Heaven, or near it,
> Pourest thy full heart
> In profuse strains of unpremediated art ...
> (Shelley, 2000, 767)

"To a Skylark" sang, it made no sense, and I loved it. Shelley taught me that a poet wrote what a bird could sing: "Such harmonious madness" (Shelley 2000, 767).

In my senior year, I knew I wanted to be a writer. My English teachers encouraged me to apply to Cornell and Radcliffe. But my father would not support me, though I had a small scholarship. I was valedictorian; my teachers were shocked when I said I was going to the

State University college in New Paltz—just a few streets away from my high school. It had a weak program in English, but I thought I could transfer after two years. And I could read everything on my own.

By the end of my second year of college, I was feeling terrible, sad, and lethargic. I thought about disappearing into nothingness, about killing myself—drowning in the muddy Wallkill River. My father wrote complaining letters about my expenses, and barely endured my presence when I had to stay with him and my stepmother during vacations.

And that is when my life began as another person I met El and let my former self go into hibernation, in a cold climate.

Poetry disappeared from my life for the next fifteen years. I loved my babies, learned how to cook and to sew, and played the perfect wife and mother as Plath described in "The Applicant":

> A living doll, everywhere you look.
> It can sew, it can cook,
> It can talk, talk, talk.
> (Plath, 1961,5)

Living in New Hampshire for five years taught me how to appreciate what I'd left in New York: not my parents, certainly. But I wanted to regain my identity as a woman who had goals other than marriage and child-rearing; who had ambitions, the same ambitions I had as a teenager: to become a professor of English and a writer.

Returing to New York was only the first step. For the next decade, we both taught elementary school. In summers, El built fireplaces. The only poetry I had time for was reading Mother Goose and Lewis Carroll to our children. We both got tenure—secure for life. Despite our well-earned security and comfort, I felt worse and worse. I could barely get out of bed in the morning, waking with a lump in my throat. I cried on the way to work and went on automatic pilot to get through teaching. One day, looking out my classroom window at the Hudson River, I saw

> The river stands still,
> Reflecting the hill
> No motion,
> Perpetual emotion.

I wrote it down, then copied it in my secret journal that evening. I had never written anything like it before, wasn't even sure if it was a poem.

I cried whenever I was alone—in the small bathroom, if I couldn't find any privacy. I went to work, I smiled, I cooked dinner and helped my children with their homework. I played the piano and we sang songs together. Even El joined in the singing, with a smooth tenor voice. I was a tenured teacher, certified from kindergarten to grade twelve. We had bought our own house. We drove a new car instead of a battered used one. A real suburban middle-class family. Settled. Miserable.

I had to write, I had to try again. I wanted to be a poet.

With El's support and his double career as tenured teacher and bricklayer, I was able to resign my teaching job. I took out my teachers' pension money, using it to cover expenses for a master's degree in English.

The first course I took was modern poetry, with a brilliant, sadistic professor. We read T. S. Eliot, Dylan Thomas, W. B. Yeats, W. H. Auden, Wallace Stevens, W. C. Williams, Theodore Roethke, and—yes—Robert Frost. "After Apple-Picking." Professor G knew a lot more about poetry than Miss Kelly.

"Do you think this is a 'nature poem'?" he asked the class.

A boy raised his hand. "Yeah. It's got apples and trees."

"You're even dumber than you look," smiled Prof. G. "It's about sex, something a boy of your age should know all about. Take off your hat!"

The boy blushed, removing his cap.

Prof. G itemized "two-pointed ladder," "a barrel I didn't fill," "the scent of apples," "ten thousand thousand fruit to touch."

"He's a man, with a *penis*, people. It has *two* functions: urination and sexual intercourse. Women are apples, scented, they are ripe for the picking, in the thousands. But now he's tired, and can't get it up anymore."

We were flabbergasted. I saw exactly what he meant, and had missed it completely. Poetry was sex. Poetry was saying one thing and meaning another at the same time.

Every week, we had to write a paper. Every week, the glowering professor sifted through the pile of papers, casting each one aside as "dreck." Then he came to mine. The professor's black eyes pinned me to the student chair as he scanned the first page. "Well, someone who can actually write intelligible, intelligent English," he said. I was flattered, scared. I ate up his praise. Several students dropped the class.

On my own, I discovered Sylvia Plath in *The New Yorker*. Plath's poems spoke to me, *for* me. I felt as if I had written them. When her book of poems, *Ariel*, was published posthumously in 1962, Plath became a force to be reckoned with. *The Bell Jar*, Plath's autobiographical novel, put her at the top of the best-seller list. Poetry and feminism joined forces, moving in on male-dominated academia, demanding entrance into the old boys' poetry club.

One male professor, I'd heard, had ridiculed Plath as a crazy woman; no wonder she killed herself. Her poetry was incomprehensible ravings. It was no wonder that a handsome poet like Ted Hughes had dumped this ugly woman, he joked. Male students had joined in the laughter, I was told.

Women poets were so rare then, so unheard of, that it was believed that women were not capable of being poets. Who were the women poets before Plath? I had never heard of Sappho, the woman who invented lyric poetry in the seventh century BCE. In grade school, Emily Dickinson was taught as a "children's" poet: "a narrow fellow in the grass," and "I like to see it lap the miles" as fun riddles. "Tell all the Truth/But tell it Slant"—was not taught (Dickinson 1961, 229, 149, 248). The first American woman poet, Ann Bradstreet, had disappeared from American memory and books.

When I completed the MA, I taught part-time at several local colleges simultaneously, as the market for full-time college English teachers had completely dried up. I decided I needed a PhD if I was to get a full-time job. I also needed to know more if I was going to write better poems.

My whole life changed when I was accepted into the doctoral program at New York University in 1972. My first class was with M. L. Rosenthal, one of the top poetry critics. It was held in the evening, so I could teach and do housework during the day.

The classroom was in an old building facing Washington Square. It was a large lecture room with a wooden platform and lectern in front facing fifteen tiers of attached wooden theatre seats, ten to a row. The upper back rows and middle rows were already taken, so I had to find an empty seat four rows from the front. As I sat down, the entire row of rickety seats squeaked and tilted. I counted at least ninety more students, all of whom seemed self-confident as they talked and laughed.

Exactly at six o'clock, M. L. Rosenthal rolled in on short legs, his gray hair bristling on the sides, absent on top. He wore a dark gray suit, patterned tie, and a gray shirt. His bushy eyebrows beetled above black eyes. I held my breath, hoping I would not make a fool of myself in front of this renowned professor. Silence. The windows over the square darkened.

Suddenly, the row of seats I was in cracked and fell backwards, sending me sprawling.

"Are you all right?" asked Professor Rosenthal. "Do you need help?"

A man in the row behind helped lift up the seat as I struggled to my feet.

"No, no. I'm fine," I said, sweating in the overheated room.

"You're sure you don't need a nurse?"

The thought of being treated by someone in a white coat terrified me. "I'm fine, really."

I moved to the row ahead, even closer to the professor. This was not the sort of attention I had hoped for.

Rosenthal opened the book on the lectern and began talking. I soon forgot my embarrassment and learned more about poetry in one class that I had in all my life. Three hours later, I got my car out of the garage and headed home on the FDR Drive, drunk on poetry.

My first paper was on Plath's view of women in the poems "The Applicant" and "Lesbos." I got an A-. Then I dared to answer Rosenthal's questions in class.

"What drives a poet to write?" I raised my hand.

"I always thought that poetry was driven by the writer's inner conflicts."

Rosenthal nodded. "I agree, Ms. Adams."

He knew my name! At the end of the term, after another A paper, I screwed up my courage and asked if he would read my poems. Rosenthal took the small folder. The following week, he returned them, with succinct marginal comments that became my first guidelines to editing my poems. I felt I had made the right decision at last: to be a poet.

Rosenthal became my mentor, directing my dissertation on Laura Riding, a topic he proposed. I'd never heard of this American poet. Only one prior critical study was in the library catalogue. Riding's poetry was very abstruse—abstract and unemotional—and mostly unavailable and out of print. The New York University Loeb Library didn't have any of her poetry, but I found a copy of her *Selected Poems* in the Strand Bookstore. My daughter Annie, a student in Cornell, was working in the graduate library where she discovered that Riding had donated her works, published and unpublished.

I spent a weekend in Ithaca, taking notes, and then found a copy of *The Collected Poems,* four hundred pages, in the open stacks. I wasn't allowed to check it out, so I made a photocopy, one page at a time, on a slow copy machine. A red-faced, older man in a straw hat stood next to me, waiting for the copier. We struck up a conversation. I told him about my dissertation topic, and, proudly, of my mentor Rosenthal.

"That SOB!" he shouted, his face getting redder.

The famous poet A. R. Ammons obviously did not like whatever Rosenthal had written about his poetry.

I found Riding's address and began a correspondence. She wrote lengthy typed letters on thin paper with handwritten additions circling the margins. Eventually, she invited me to visit her in Florida. Rosenthal was amazed. "Nobody has ever been able to get along with her. Be careful of that buzz-saw," he said. He was only half joking.

I stayed in a bug-ridden motel near Riding's house in Wabasso, Florida. Riding had given me a can of bug spray to control giant flying cockroaches. The window air conditioner roared like a B-29, but did nothing to cool the tiny room.

Riding lived in a house of weathered cypress, without electricity. It was shaded by trees and cooled by breezes blowing through open windows. For three days, I sat with her at a handmade cypress table, talking and taking notes. She fed me lunch of poached chicken breasts and garden tomatoes in olive oil, prepared by a woman who came in every day.

Riding walked with a slight limp, the result of a broken back when she had jumped out a fifth-floor window fifty years earlier. Her white hair was held back by a black ribbon, her face unchanged from the strong features shown in photos taken in the 1930s. I avoided any mention of her one-time partner Robert Graves.

Graves and Riding met in London in 1925, when Graves, already a famous poet, invited Riding, an unknown American poet to visit him after reading her poems in *The Fugitive,* a prestigious poetry magazine. Riding, who was born Laura Reichenthal, had married Louis Gottschalk, a college professor she studied under at Cornell, and published her first poems under the jaw-breaking name, Laura Reichenthal Gottschalk. She wisely changed her name to Laura Riding, left Gottschalk, and sailed for London. She moved in with Graves and his family on their houseboat docked on the Thames. In short time, she and Graves founded the hand-operated Seizin Press, publishing their own poetry. A year or so later, Graves's wife, the eccentric Nancy Nicholson, left him with their four children. Riding and Graves returned the children to their mother's care, and left London. After drifting around Europe, they settled on Majorca, an idyllic island off Spain. Graves supported his family, Riding, and himself by writing novels. The *I, Claudius* series became best sellers, Graves's very successful memoir of World War I, *Goodbye to All That,* published in 1929, was originally dedicated to Riding. After they parted, he deleted the dedication (Adams 1990, 1–24).

Driven from their home on Majorca by the outbreak of the Spanish Civil War in 1936, Riding and Graves took refuge in the United States and were invited to stay with Schuyler Jackson, an occasional poetry critic for *Time Magazine,* at his gentleman's farm in Pennsylvania. After thirteen years together, Graves and Riding came to a parting of the ways, developing new relationships. Graves paired off with Beryl Hodge, the wife of his good friend Alan Hodge, and Riding and Schuyler Jackson formed a strong bond based on their belief in a kind of witchcraft, accusing Jackson's wife Kit of being a witch. Kit ended up in an asylum for awhile. Then Jackson left her and his four children, moving to Wabasso, Florida with Riding (Matthews 1977, 207–208;

211–212). Graves and Beryl Hodge married and went back to Majorca when World War II ended. I met Laura (Riding) Jackson in 1980, in Wabasso. Jackson had died in 1968. Graves and Beryl were living on Majorca, where they remained until they died some years later. (Adams 1990, 1-24).

By 1977, when I began the dissertation on Laura Riding, she had dropped into obscurity. She did not write new poems. Further, she disallowed publication of any of her poems in anthologies, magazines, and the like, and refused most interviews (Riding and Graves 1928, 159–76). But she wrote megillah-length letters to every journal, magazine, book, and scholar who dared mention her name in connection with Graves. Any scholar, including me, who wanted to write about Laura Riding, quickly learned never to mention the name Robert Graves. The gist of these letters is that Riding considered herself deserving of the fame and fortune granted to her former lover and co-writer. *She,* not he, was the superior poet. (Adams 1990, 1–114).

We got along very well during my three-day stay, I never mentioned Robert Graves.

In the evening, Riding lit oil lamps with neatly trimmed wicks. She allowed me to take photos of her house, but not of her. One wall held a complete set of the *Oxford English Dictionary* in a long niche. Outside was an open-air building where Riding and her husband, Schuyler Jackson, had crated and shipped citrus fruit for a living. Two heavy steel safes stood along one wall in the sitting area. Riding said she kept all her unpublished work there.

When I had finished taking notes, Riding agreed to let me write up the interview, but I had to mail it to her for clearance, one question at a time. It would take longer than the gestation period of an elephant! She liked me well enough to ask me to be one of her literary executors. I looked at the safes, realized the enormous task of sifting and editing. I had my own writing, not just a dissertation on Riding.

On my last afternoon in Wabasso, I drove Laura and myself to a nearby beach. She sat on a bench as I swam. "You watch her, now," she commanded the lifeguard.

The interview never got published. Riding cut me out of her circle after another executor bad-mouthed me. A peculiar retired military man, perhaps CIA, visited me after I had been shopping at the West

Point PX. I had invited him, as he wanted to hear about my interview with Laura. I had to leave the house before his scheduled arrival, so I left the door unlocked for him, trusting that I'd be back shortly. When I returned, I found him snooping in my notes. This man had an office in the basement of his Westchester mansion that contained files of unpublished writing. He was very jealous that Laura had let me interview her, I realized.

My dissertation became a book published in 1990, *The Enemy Self: Poetry and Criticism of Laura Riding*. Rosenthal was proud, and I was too, after all that hard work. I learned a lot about writing poetry by analyzing Riding's. Her husband, Schuyler Jackson, persuaded her to renounce poetry as not useful in the impending war between fascism and democracy. Instead, Jackson and Riding collaborated on an interminable behemoth, *The Dictionary of Meaning*, never published.

Riding made Jamison's list of "mad" poets for having attempted suicide. Her one-time partner, Robert Graves, also made it for being committed to Craiglockhart in Scotland, the first psychiatric hospital for war veterans, opened after World War I.

In the same year I began studying at New York University, my first poem was accepted for publication. "I'll take this poem—but only the first page, if you agree," wrote the editor who had drawn flowers along the margin. Who was he to cut off half *my* poem? I fumed.

"Okay," I wrote back. Half a poem published is better than none.

Menke Katz, the editor, continued to accept my poems, without surgery. We became friends. He invited me to visit him and his wife Rivke in his little house near Ellenville. Rivke, a schoolteacher, supported the family and did all the work, and Menke did all the talking and writing. His poetry was published in many languages, including Hebrew and Aramaic. He had spent time among the mystic Sufis in Israel.

I invited Menke and Rivke to visit El and me in our Hudson River town. Rivke drove them to our house. After dinner, we drank wine, sitting by a fire in our downstairs room. El wasn't exactly happy with Menke's friendship with me, or with my nascent success as a poet. Menke was egotistical, loud, and nutty, but he was the first editor to accept me as a poet.

On his third or fourth glass of white wine, Menke admired the fireplace. I saw my chance to please El. "El built the fireplace, out of stones from our backyard." El smiled, looking down at his hands.

Menke jumped up and ran his hand over the huge gray stones. "It's a work of art!" he declared. "Eli, you are a poet in stone! L'chaim!" He clinked glasses with El and downed another glass of wine.

After Menke and Rivke had gone home, El, aka "Eli," said, "'Poet in stone,' my ass."

But Menke had a point: poems and stones share a sense of immortality. Which lasts longer, a poem carved in stone, or the stone?

Two years after I completed the PhD, I finally nailed down a full-time, tenure-track job at a university in New York City. My first book of poems, *Hapax Legomena*, a title that I thought clever but puzzled readers, was published a few years later. I started giving readings, the first one in Chumley's, a former speakeasy in Greenwich Village. El, my children, and my Aunt Bea came. I looked exactly like a suburban housewife, out of place, in the "cool" village scene.

In my exurban small city on the Hudson, my friends bought my book. At parties, I was now introduced as "a poet." Few, if any, read any poetry.

After El died, I wrote about him ... our life together. Being a poet did not ease the pain of losing him. I drove to the cemetery often in the first year of widowhood. I had chosen a double grave for El and me, in New Paltz:

Facing Mohonk Mountain
Where we first made love, vowing
Casually, "Forever."

I took my grief along and started out on a single voyage, devoting myself to writing, giving readings, and going to writers' conferences and workshops.

Writers' workshops were no substitute for a long marriage. But at least I got out of my own skin and traveled to Italy, Mexico, and Ireland. Measuring my work against that of others boosted my confidence.

I found several poetry reading venues in the mid-Hudson Valley, reading my poems in town halls, pubs, and colleges in the area. These readings gave me a connection to other people who wrote poetry. Though their work was often amateurish and unsophisticated, their enthusiasm for poetry more than made up for their style. They accepted me, and I accepted them as poets. They knew me only as a fellow poet, not El's widow.

My second book of poems, *The Ordinary Living*, came out eleven years after El's death. The simple title was inspired by a poem written by Marie Howe, "What the Living Do."

A third book of poems is ready.

I still don't know why I am a poet. Steve, my oldest son, once said, "I'd like to think that your poetry comes from your Irish half."

If there is a genetic factor for being a poet, the Irish, "a nation of poets and priests" is a probable source. My German Jewish half seems to govern my intellectual life. The emotional poet and the rational intellectual are often at cross-purposes, but instead of a war in the blood, they joined forces to make me a writer. Whatever one inherits can be a curse or a blessing. Not that one has a choice in the matter.

An Irish saying sticks in my head: "'Tis death to love a poet, to marry a poet, to be a poet."

Chapter XI

SPELLMAN TWO

After twenty-five years of marriage, a crisis loomed. I was growing out of the role of housewife, moving up from the limited career track of elementary school teacher, and entering an academic profession with greater status than my husband's. I no longer took El's temper tantrums quietly, and had begun fighting back. Our college-age children were unlucky witnesses to our increasingly angry battles.

El was furious that I would no longer proofread and type his stories; I was in the doctoral program at NYU and had my own writing and typing to do. He could type them himself, cursing at his typos and mistakes in grammar and spelling, using bottle after bottle of Wite-Out. I cooked the meals, did the laundry, and shopped. El had always shared the housework, cleaning the bathroom, vacuuming, and doing dishes. We still enjoyed Friday nights together, eating out without the children. Every Saturday, we went to family therapy, battling for the chance to speak to the besieged psychiatrist. The atmosphere at home was electric with anger.

I seemed to be living with two opposite husbands: one, the kindly, loving helpmate; and the other an abusive prison guard afraid I'd escape. El could not bear losing control of me, of my being out of his sight. He accused me of infidelity every time I went to classes at NYU, and continued the accusations when I became a teaching assistant. Two days a week, I was in the city, breathing free. The rest of the week, I had to defend my right to live my own life, to go to classes, and to work.

I came to dread "family" therapy. Our psychotherapist couldn't really handle two such volatile people. I had to struggle for his attention. He had silly rules that drove me mad: whoever spoke first, El or me, got the session. And we had to begin the session with any dreams we'd had. Gr-r-r! Each session was a lesson in extreme frustration, El using his temper to control it. Nonetheless, I was creating a new identity for myself. When my first poems were published, El said to me, in a jealous rage, "You couldn't have written these without me!" I tried to hide everything I wrote in my unlocked filing cabinet, but I soon realized El was reading everything in my files when I was in the city.

My classes at NYU ended at nine in the evening. It took an hour and a half to drive home in good weather. El waited at the kitchen table, smoking like a dragon and drinking coffee, refusing to speak to me when I got home. When he finally spoke, after I'd gone to bed, he said he knew I was sleeping with someone. I grew weary of his paranoid torment, and began to think seriously of divorce. I hoped to wait until I finished the PhD, when I could get a full-time job. My parents' divorce made me hesitate; I worried about its effect on my kids. I was also afraid El might kill himself—or me.

I might as well be hanged for a sheep as a lamb: I fell in love with another man. I felt happy and ecstatic, ashamed and depressed. I didn't know what I wanted: to leave El, but not my kids; or to start a new life with "Ian." My lover, a well-known poet, had been married twice before. I wanted to live with Ian, but I had no intention of marrying him. I'd already fallen into that trap. My loyalties split: old me against new me. I needed to confide in our therapist, but he had another unbreakable rule: he would not listen to one spouse unless in the other's presence. What a joke our "therapy" had become! I had no one to confide in.

One night, driving home from the city, I was so depressed I stopped and called our therapist from a public pay phone on the Palisades Parkway (no cell phones in those days). The operator, unbeknown to me, called my home to confirm the reverse charges. I poured out my story to the therapist. He said he'd keep my confidence. He lied.

When I got home, El was in a fuming rage. He'd gotten the operator's call. "Whore!" he said in front of the children, "Get out!" I stood my ground. "Then I'm leaving." Instead of packing, El ranted at me all night. I didn't get any sleep. It was his favorite way of punishing me. Then he went to bed at dawn and slept like a baby.

We barely spoke for weeks. I avoided confrontation as much as possible. El continued his nightly inquisition as soon as I'd fallen asleep, waking me with a flick of the light. The therapist was nearly useless. "She comes home every night," was all he said to El. El insisted I tell him who it was. "Nobody you know." He wouldn't let up. "A poet who gave a reading at NYU," I finally revealed.

I couldn't tell El how much I cherished the memory of meeting Ian. The affair began, like many affairs, with one glance. That El had been present when I first saw Ian, and he me.

It was a spring evening in New York City. As president of the NYU Graduate English organization that had invited Ian to read his poetry, I was supposed to introduce him. But we were very late; El had insisted on coming with me, deliberately stalling until I thought we'd miss the reading altogether. After the reading, I went up to Ian to apologize for being late. I had been too late to introduce him. Ian's eyes locked on mine. He signed his book for me, asking for my full name. A few days later, I got a phone call. "Thank God it's you!" he exclaimed. "I've called every Adams in the state. And I've finally found you!" I shook with joy, just hearing his deep voice. We began meeting in the city for lunch. One day, when there were no classes, I told El I had to go in for exams. Then I drove to Ian's home on Long Island. It was the first time we made love, on a freezing day in January. Afterward, we walked along the icy shore of Long Island Sound. I wasn't at all cold. We came back to his house and Ian made hot whiskeys and broiled lamb chops. And I went home to El.

El kept up his campaign to punish me, waking up the children to tell them about their "whore mother." Ashamed and depressed, I did not know what to do. I wouldn't leave the children with El; I wouldn't leave our house. And I couldn't give up Ian. One night, as we sat down to dinner, El was dishing plates of my homemade spaghetti sauce and pasta, keeping up a bitter fusillade. When he passed my plate to me, I smashed it on the floor (shades of Sammit!). It felt very satisfying. The plate smashed, splattering red sauce everywhere like blood. Then I walked out of the house and got into my car—it was *my* car; I had paid for it, with my salary. I drove aimlessly for an hour, cooling off.

When I got back, the house was silent, the kids staying away from the battle in their rooms. The mess had been cleaned up. (The kids told me the next day El had cleaned it up.) El did not wake me that night. Things could not go on this way much longer. Something had to give.

At work and among friends, El had been considered gentle and mild by everyone who knew him. But at work, he was falling apart. He ignored the students. He couldn't teach. The students began to laugh and run riot. El ceased to exert any control over his class. Parents complained to the principal, Ron, who began watching El closely, walking into El's classroom unannounced, finding the students in chaos and El nowhere to be seen. He was outside, smoking, leaving the students without supervision. Ron, a strict disciplinarian, despised any sign of weakness in a man. He wanted to get rid of El, and put him on notice: get control of yourself and the class, or you'll be suspended. El had tenure, so it would have been very difficult to fire him outright. Instead, Ron made him miserable, sitting in his class every day, watching his every move, pressuring him to resign. El ignored these warnings. His clothes were messy, stained with coffee and cigarette burns. He forgot to zip up his fly—I had to remind him as he left for work. His thick hair was wild and uncombed as he ran his nicotine-stained fingers through it constantly.

Finally, Ron called El in, along with the assistant superintendent of schools, a kind man, and the union representative, a friend of El's. They offered El sick leave with full pay. El had accumulated three months of unused sick days and was eligible for another six months of paid leave from the union's sick bank. The "sick bank" consisted of sick days contributed by teachers—one a month—from which they could draw for catastrophic illness. El's illness had clearly become catastrophic—for himself, our marriage, and our children. He accepted the offer. He really had no choice.

For the first month of paid leave, El sat at our kitchen table smoking cigarettes and drinking coffee. I went to my teaching assistant's job at NYU, and tried to work on my dissertation. The kids were struggling with high school SATs and college entrance exams, three of them honor students. El spoke to no one for weeks. Stalemated in therapy, one day El surprised both the therapist and me. "I want to go into the hospital," he said. The doctor looked stunned.

"Why?" he asked.

"I can't stand it."

"*What* can't you stand?" asked the doctor. El shook his head, staring at the floor and wringing his hands.

St. Francis Hospital was the only hospital in the area with a psychiatric ward. I had mixed feelings about El's wanting to be hospitalized. On one hand, I thought he was trying to arouse sympathy and punish me in a public way; on the other, I was relieved that he'd be out of the house and not my responsibility. The doctor called St. Francis Hospital, making arrangements for El's immediate admission. When he hung up, he looked at El with some irritation. "You'll be admitted to Spellman Two, the locked ward. I'm not sending you for a vacation in a 'country club' to be coddled." The so-called "country club" was Spellman One, an open ward, for "spoiled" patients. With such an attitude, it's a wonder anyone got better in either ward.

I didn't think El was ill enough for Spellman Two, meant for patients who were helpless, murderous, or suicidal. The doctor was clearly unsympathetic with El's wish to be hospitalized, thinking it was a ploy to get sympathy. The doctor also felt professionally embarrassed, having treated El for so many years, and apparently failing to help him. Instead of getting better, El had gotten worse. Was it my fault? For refusing to take El's verbal abuse? The doctor's fault? He clearly was out of his depth.

We left the doctor's office and went home. El packed an overnight bag, including a carton of cigarettes. I told the children, "Your father is going into the hospital—he's not really sick; that is, he'll be in the mental health ward." What a confusion of words, I thought. No one really believes there is such a thing as "mental illness." They would prefer, perhaps, to blame odd behavior on a germ or a witch's spell. I was ashamed, I admit, realizing how much El reminded me of my mother who always found ways to punish me for not taking care of her. Both El and my mother wanted me to devote myself to taking care of them. My mother claimed to hate being in hospitals, but she also loved the attention of big shot doctors while I kept vigil at her bedside. When my sister grew up, she took over many visits to Mom. We had to go to Mom's bedside as often as we could, our lives coming in second. In hospital, my mother was the star. El and my mother tried to make me feel guilty, and succeeded. I was supposed to shoulder the burden of their problems and their care. Much of their sickness, however, was the result of their own behavior.

A voluntary hospital stay in the psych ward was limited to three weeks, after which the patient would be released or admitted to another, long-term facility, depending on the doctors' evaluation. At the insistence of our psychotherapist, I had to go to the hospital every day. Stupidly, I thought then and still do, Dr. W insisted on continuing "joint therapy" which was obviously not working. These sessions were futile and frustrating. El barely answered the doctor's "interrogation," only staring or shaking his head. And the doctor would not allow me to speak! I thought El would make progress if the doctor saw him alone. Or let me speak!

So every day, for two weeks, I drove twenty-five miles to St. Francis Hospital, and checked into Spellman Two through a locked glass door embedded with wire mesh. Then I waited alone in a small, beige room at a conference table with six or seven chairs around it. At one o'clock, our doctor arrived, unlocking all the doors with a key—one of about fifteen other keys attached to a chain, like a medieval jailer. El then came in, led by a nurse, and sat down opposite me. The doctor sat between us and began his interrogation instantly. "Why can't you teach?" he asked.

"I don't know," El said, shrugging and taking a drag on a cigarette.

"What happens in the classroom?" the doctor persisted.

"The kids go wild, throw things, and call me names."

"Why can't you make them behave, sit down, and be quiet?" The doctor, educated in a strict *gymnasium* in Germany before fleeing the Nazis, did not understand American schools and lax American standards of discipline. El couldn't answer, wouldn't answer. The doctor kept firing the same questions, over and over. El sat in hostile silence, filling the room with hopelessness and cigarette smoke.

For the entire forty-five minute session, I listened. Not once did the doctor address me or ask me what I thought. If I tried to explain the peculiar combination of will, authority, and wits it took to maintain control over a classroom of energetic ten-year-olds, he ignored me. I thought the doctor's method was ridiculous, and was getting us nowhere. He never discussed anything in our marriage or in El's behavior, only

El's failure to control the classroom. I endured two weeks of this absurd one-way conversation like a walk-on character with no speaking part in a Beckett play. I had no choice except to do as the doctor said. I knew El needed help, and this was all we had. The antipsychotic medication, Trilafon, did very little but take the edge off El's temper.

On weekends, when no "therapy" was scheduled, I visited El at dinnertime. El's enjoyment of food had not waned, his nervous breakdown notwithstanding (for lack of a better term, "nervous breakdown" is as close as any that can describe this frequent human occurrence). Dinner was the big meal of the day, and a high point for most of the patients, bored out of their skulls with hospital routine. We sat in a big recreation room with the other patients and psychiatric aides, everyone serving himself or herself from a buffet. "They make you serve yourself here," El said with a pout. "You'd think they'd serve you—it's a hospital, after all." But he filled his plate with the nourishing food, its flavor spicier than food served in the other wards to stimulate the interest of the psych patients. El's pleasure in eating good food came a close second to his pleasure in smoking cigarettes. Nearly all the psych patients chain-smoked.

After dinner, we played gin rummy, but El played so indifferently, I kept winning. He couldn't focus enough to play Scrabble. El almost always beat me at Scrabble. I updated him on the kids, but he wasn't interested. He stared ahead or at the floor, as was his wont most of his life outside the hospital. He complained that the nurses never let him alone during the day. "They make me get out of bed and stay up, stay awake *all day*. I never get enough rest here." The complaint was so similar to my mother's complaint about hospitals that I nearly laughed. El said he tried sneaking back to bed, but a nurse came and found him and made him get up again. They wouldn't let him shower before bed, as he usually did at home. "They say the shower is stimulating, keeps you awake," he said. Most psychiatric patients either have chronic insomnia or want to sleep all the time.

When I ran out of neutral things to say to El, I studied some of the other patients. They watched TV, read magazines, played solitaire, and talked with aides. When dinner was announced, they stopped whatever they were doing and hurried to get on the buffet line first. They all loved to eat as much as El did, except for the anorexic girl who had to be led to the table by an aide who filled a plate for her. El ate big portions of stewed beef, noodles, and carrots. He poured a glass of milk and took two slices of bread and butter. I sat and watched him savor every bite, wiping up the gravy with the bread. Dessert was canned fruit and a piece of cake. When the meal was over, El lit another cigarette and wished out loud for a cup of coffee. No stimulants allowed, however. Too many insomniacs. Too many medications in the patients' systems.

El described some of the patients he'd talked to in the dayroom or listened to in group therapy. A plain young woman was trying to decide if she was a lesbian; a housewife had attempted suicide but had been talked out of jumping off the Mid-Hudson Bridge by her priest and a local police officer; a young man heard voices; a woman couldn't stop crying, though she had nothing to cry about, they said. All the patients looked sad, nervous, and lost. "They make you turn off the lights at 10:00 p.m., but, with that woman crying all night and someone else screaming, nobody gets any sleep," El complained. "I'm tired in the morning, but they won't let me take a nap." On weekends at home, El often went to bed at nine and slept till ten or eleven, then took a three-hour nap in the afternoon. I couldn't understand how anyone could sleep that much.

I wondered what El was doing there in Spellman Two among these lunatics. What was really wrong with him? I thought of the term "nervous breakdown" as a nondescript euphemism applied to everything from a fainting spell to a serious psychotic illness like schizophrenia. It is a term so meaningless that it only conceals whatever lies behind the symptoms that lead to other labels like "neurotic," "disturbed," or "crazy"—also equally vague and meaningless. Scientific terms for mental disorders grew out of neurology, as psychiatry itself became an offshoot of that medical discipline. Freud himself had been a neurologist with an interest in the mysteries of mental problems that might or might not have an origin in the brain itself. But mind, not the brain, is often the source of mental "breakdowns" (excepting those with a genetic basis, or caused by identifiable brain disorders or injuries).

The first terms coined by Freud and other pioneers in the field of psychoanalysis and psychiatry were often inaccurate Latinisms that became general catchalls: *neurasthenia, dementia praecox, hysteria,* for example. At one time, El's condition might have been labeled neurasthenia. Whatever the label, however, the condition lies in the conceptual mind. Current studies in psychobiology show a relation between disturbances of the mind and the balance of chemicals in the brain, allowing treatment by means of drugs to correct the imbalance. Our therapist said El was "probably" schizophrenic and had prescribed Trilafon. It didn't do much, except exacerbate his impotence. Much of El's nightly rages followed directly on his failure to achieve an erection. Whatever might have helped—private talk therapy and new drugs—had not helped El so far.

An equally vague term, "stressed out," is in vogue. You can be stressed out if the car breaks down, if your kids need braces, if you hate your boss, if you can't lose weight, if you can't get a date for the weekend. The list of "stressors," as psychiatrists call them, is endless. High on the list of stressors leading to breakdown is the death of a loved one, a divorce, and a house burning down. El and I had not endured any stressful deaths at that point in our lives; El had seen his shack burn down as a child, and it was good riddance everyone thought. And we weren't yet divorced, though it was in the wind. "There is nothing either good or bad, but thinking makes it so," said Hamlet (Shakespeare 1961, II, ii, 255–56) pretending to be mad when, in fact, he was in a state of "nervous breakdown," neurasthenia, or just stressed out over the death of his father and quick remarriage of his mother.

When El was first admitted to St. Francis, I had been debriefed, so to speak, by a nurse who quizzed me on my version of what had brought El to Spellman Two. It was the most unpleasant, insulting, and cruel interview I have ever undergone. The nurse was clearly unsympathetic toward me, having prejudged me for reasons I cannot fathom. I have known nurses who have no sympathy for failed suicides who end up in their care, regarding them as crybabies who do not appreciate the gift of life. Their attitude is expressed as "better he/she should die than that nice cancer-ridden lady down the hall who is fighting to live." These nurses think suicidal patients deserve a scolding, not gentle hospital care. I learned this from a former student in a writing class, a respected nurse. I could not understand her callousness and lack of empathy for depressed and suicidal patients.

This St. Francis nurse had an equally unsympathetic attitude for the wife of a "nice" male psychiatric patient. Her attitude might have had something to do with the burgeoning women's movement, pitting "old-fashioned" housewives against "liberated" women like me, the new feminists. We no longer accepted the status quo as submissive wives. We were seeking equality in the home and on the job. Maybe something in me aroused her hostility. I'll never know.

The interview began in the conference room, the nurse opposite me with a notepad and form she filled out as I answered questions. I never was shown this form afterward, to sign or comment on. She asked very personal and intimate questions from a list I presumed she was reading from the form, writing my answers on a separate notepad, probably for transcription later. I answered these questions as honestly as possible. "How is your sex life?" was one. "How often do you have sex?" was another. "Are you having an affair with someone else?" (A redundancy, but I didn't say so.) "Is your husband impotent?" "Do you have orgasms with him?" She asked question after question, relentlessly. This was not a Kinsey Report, neither had I volunteered for this sex study.

I lost a lot more points when the nurse got to the question, "What kind of work do you do outside the home, if any?" I said I was a graduate teaching assistant at NYU. Even worse, I was completing my doctorate. Working in "the city" was the most damning point of all. Many upstate New Yorkers regard New York City as a den of iniquity, and urban people as the source of all crime, immorality, pollution, and undeserved wealth. In addition to my infamous identity as a city woman with a high-toned job, I had admitted to having an affair. That did it: I had caused El's problems. The nurse apparently saw El as a meek, mild, adorable, and abused husband. I did not tell her about El's affair with Linda; she hadn't asked if *he* had had any affairs. This psychiatric nurse had already branded me with a Scarlet A.

I felt the sting of guilt, even without the nurse's unspoken condemnation. I blamed myself for adding to El's unhappiness, if not for the breakdown. One night at home, I'd heard him calling out my name in a dream. "I'm here," I said, but he hadn't heard me. At the same time, I was struggling with depression. I hoped that completing the PhD and teaching college would help me. As a professor and writer, I would be able to make a better future for all of us. Or so I hoped. El could sabotage it all. The affair with Ian would have to be resolved, one way or the other, now that El had gotten so sick.

El knew he was losing his control over me, which worsened his rage and feelings of impotence. Rather than being able to discuss our problems, he drove me further away with anger. The sticking point for me was the children. I was the child of a ruthless divorce by my father, which left my mother a querulous alcoholic and me with fears of abandonment. I was living proof that divorce could deeply and perhaps permanently damage a child's spirit. As bad as things were with El, I couldn't do this to my kids. I could not live with the guilt of hurting them, or El. Personal happiness cannot be built on the destruction of others.

At this crucial moment, Ian wrote and asked me to come live with him. I'd been waiting for this, and dreading it at the same time—I didn't know how I would answer. The time had come: I would have to choose finally between El and my children, and a lover who treated me as an equal, and as a desirable woman. Not having had sex with El for years had taken its toll on me, tipping the scales toward having an affair.

Seeing El in the hospital day after day, so utterly miserable, I knew I couldn't leave him. I wrote Ian a long letter explaining my position. I told him of my husband's illness, that he was too sick for me to abandon right now. Maybe we could wait a while, I hoped.

I wasn't being noble. Romantic love is not worth ruining the lives of a whole family. I would have blamed myself for the rest of my life for whatever grief befell my children. In the back of my mind, as well, was the fear that El might kill himself if I left him. I couldn't live with blood on my hands.

Ian never forgave me for turning him down. When we spoke on the phone, he was terse, stung by my refusal. He hadn't expected it. He did not answer my conciliatory letters, returning them unopened. I had lost him for good. I followed his public life for a while, his latest books and his readings. His name popped up when I wasn't looking for it, in reviews and articles in magazines. Eventually, I read of his third marriage. His new wife's photo was on the jacket of one of his books. She was beautiful, much younger than he. A few years later, I read of their divorce. So Ian was alone again. He was the only man who ever told me I was beautiful.

Two weeks in Spellman Two was enough for El. "Get me out of here," he said when I arrived for a Saturday visit. "They don't leave you alone in here." It wasn't a country club, as the doctor had told him. Every morning, he had group therapy—a waste of time, El said. Every afternoon, he had private therapy with the doctor and me—another waste of time, in my opinion. And expensive, as we had to pay for the private sessions out of our own pocket. El smoked and smoked, the one private habit permitted to patients. A perpetual cloud of smoke filled the dayroom.

It wasn't up to me to sign him out. He signed himself out two days before Thanksgiving.

We spent the holiday with our children as usual. No one commented on where El had been for the past two weeks, or why. No one asked if he felt better. No one asked if he would get his teaching job back. We ate the feast I always cooked: roast turkey, mashed potatoes, candied yams, stuffing, black and green olives, creamed onions, celery, cranberry sauce, apple pie, and pumpkin pie. We drank fresh apple cider. Life went on as if nothing terrible or momentous had occurred ... as if nothing had changed. Yet, all had changed—utterly changed. El's spirit had been broken, and with it, his long tyranny over me.

Spellman Two still haunts me.

After El died, I was cleaning out a file I kept of the letters and notes and Valentine's cards he'd given me over the years. We often left notes and letters for each other on the kitchen table, or on a pillow, after a fight. Once, to my delight, he left a note on my pillow the morning after we'd made wonderful love. "Thanks for a delightful evening," it said, "Love, El," written on a business card that said ELWOOD ADAMS. It was a joke, taken from a movie we'd seen about Walter Kerr, the film and play critic, written by his wife, Jean Kerr, a novelist. Walter Kerr had left a similar note on Jean Kerr's pillow the morning after lovemaking. My pleasure in El's note was enhanced by our shared sense of humor. I came across a letter dated December 25, 1985. This was the kind of letter El usually wrote, summing up the complicated problems of our marriage and his own enigmatic personality. It is one of his many apologies to me for his uncontrolled temper.

Dear Barbara,

I am sorry for not taking my medicine and becoming psychotic. I honestly thought I could handle my problems, but I see that it is impossible—you get in the quicksand before you know it. It is dangerous to go without it. When I become psychotic everything seems as right as an interpretation of "Cinderella," but of course it isn't. I feel guilty as hell for going under again—for surrendering to my illness, for losing my way, especially when I thought that, finally, I had it together. Now it seems as though that day is a long way away … that I must be constantly on guard, up the medicine when necessary, warn myself of a psychotic thought, fight constant fatigue with coffee and books. Lastly, I am very sorry that I have let you down again. I am going to try to be more vigilant in fighting the demons of the scourge I have constantly lived with ever since I can remember. It wasn't so much my mother and father but my grandfather Sam who gave me this illness, I think. I don't know just how, but I believe he was such a power in the family that my own folks didn't even count.

Love, El

Chapter XII

RE-CREATION

When summer came, El got a job with a friend who had started a new contracting business. He was a bricklayer again, while collecting paid sick leave from teaching. The pallor of misery fading, his skin regained its outdoor ruddiness. He had a reason to get up in the morning.

I had the summer off from teaching, where I was on the bottom rung of a tenure-track position. The pleasure of having a secure job for the future helped me relax. While El was at work, I prepared for the fall semester, reading and ordering textbooks. Surreptitiously, I continued to write poems.

We continued seeing the psychoanalytic therapist, who was glad to be wiping the egg off his face from El's brief hospitalization. Dr. W encouraged me in the career I had begun, but most of therapeutic time was spent on El, trying to get him in shape to go back to his teaching job. Out of frustration, I could always get the doctor's attention by telling him a dream. Dr. W was strict: "You must tell me dreams *first;* they are the 'royal road to the unconscious,' said Freud." As I dreamt every night, in Technicolor, from horror movies to a stroll in paradise— often three or four at a time—I had no problem grabbing center stage when I chose. "Tell them all," he insisted. Annoyed to rebelling, I would pick a dream to tell, leaving the others behind on the "royal road." Then I'd have to free-associate to an image in the dream—on and on, in a pointless maze of images. In my heart, I knew this dream interpretation was as reliable as the assumptions of a phrenologist who has read bumps on a skull.

Another problem was El's lack of interest in anything outside of basic eating, sleeping, and smoking. "What about a hobby?" asked the doctor. El didn't have any.

"He loves tinkering in the garage fixing things; he can fix anything from clocks to bathroom tiles," I said.

"What about making toy houses?" asked the doctor.

El looked up, stopped wringing his hands momentarily. "Toy houses?"

The doctor held his hands in the shape of a little house, about five inches square. "You've built real houses, why not toy ones?" Neither El nor I was impressed.

In the next few weeks, however, El went to a hobby shop and came back with balsa wood, wood strips, glues, paints, a kit of X-ACTO knives, and tiny figurines. He'd already built a workbench in the garage, with a vise, where he kept his boxes of nails and screws and a professional toolbox. Clearing a space, he began on a "toy house."

I was amazed. El had taken the doctor's suggestion to heart, unlike the dozens of suggestions about giving up smoking. El also had given up drinking at the doctor's remark when we first began therapy, "You are an alcoholic. You cannot drink." And El stopped. At once.

El took photographs of houses (photography was another hobby he took up at the suggestion of a friend who taught high school history). Then he copied the photos in wood. He glued glass windows in some and painted them in lively primary colors. One looked like our doctor's house, an old gray Victorian, but El painted it blue. Another looked like our house, painted yellow with black shutters, as it actually was. Then he made a church, a typical Protestant church, but painted it bright pink with white trim. One of my favorites is a sort of commercial building with big glass front windows, a flat roof with a TV antenna, and a chimney on top. The pièce de résistance in the piece, however, is the tiny figure of a man in a business suit glued to the first floor, looking out the front plate glass—like a trapped figure in an Edward Hopper painting.

El made multiple versions of the Victorian house and our house, giving them to our children and to the doctor and my aunt Bea. None was in scale to the others—the church was much larger; the business building, much smaller. Today, they might be considered masterpieces of "outsider art."

Thanks to his friend, Harold, a principal in our district, El returned to teaching in the fall as a learning disability specialist. He did not have his own classroom, but traveled to several elementary schools to teach small groups of children who were unable to learn at the expected level for their ages. El loved these students. Every morning, he made a gallon of fruit drink, packed a box of crackers, napkins, and paper cups and took them on his rounds. He recorded multiplication tables on tape and made a "slide rule" out of cardboard to help children memorize them. He read stories on tape so that some children could listen to it on headphones while others did multiplication tables. While some wrote their lessons, El worked with one child at a time on reading and math. At the end of the school year, each teacher was given a book budget of one hundred dollars to buy materials for their classes. El took a child's delight in buying books and educational toys. One principal objected to a deck of cards El used to teach numbers, as well as social behavior. But El was so successful in raising the children's scores that his student load—set by New York State at a maximum of twelve—went up to twenty.

Finally, our children had finished college and gone on with their own lives. They visited and came home for holidays. We did not talk about the past. It would take many more years for us to deal with it, to talk about it with individual therapists before we could actually talk to each other about El and our marriage. Even as adults, the children usually bring up the good memories of El's sense of humor, and, only rarely mention his terrifying temper.

It took me seven years to achieve tenure and the rank of full professor. I commuted to New York City two or three days a week, by car or train. I had late classes, and did not get home until eleven in the evening. El would be in bed, asleep. On weekends, I was stuck grading papers and doing preparations. El tinkered with his toy houses and listened to Red Sox ball games on a little transistor radio that picked up the games from a Connecticut station. Life was quieter, but El and I were increasingly distant. I could feel El's anger, barely contained, for my spending so much time—without him—in the city.

The college where I worked held a lecture series, inviting famous people to talk about their work: Edward Albee, the playwright; A. Bartlett Giamatti, the Yale professor and baseball commissioner; and Stanley Tucci, the actor, among others. The lectures began at eight in the evening and were followed by a reception. It was very late when I could leave politely, and I didn't get home until around midnight. One day, the well-known poet Robert Bly was invited to read and talk about contemporary poetry. I was eager to hear him. After a quick bite at Beekman Tavern, I entered the university theatre and looked for a seat near the stage. And then I saw Ian, sitting near the back. I turned and took a seat next to him. "Hello," I said smiling, "How nice to see you." I hoped my colleagues would not notice anything but ordinary courtesy between me and a professor who was also a well-known poet. Ian looked at me without expression. "Yes," he said. "Bly is a good friend." But I knew Ian had come to see me.

Bly began talking, but I couldn't pay attention. I wanted Ian to touch me, to take my hand. I wanted to leave the lecture and be alone with him. But we sat like two professors interested in a colleague's talk.

When Bly's talk ended, the audience clapped, and students approached him to get a book autographed. Ian looked at me. His eyes said, *Time for a drink?*

I reached out my hand to him. "Well, it was nice seeing you again. Maybe we can get together sometime," I said, and left. I had just regained my balance, putting Ian out of my life, and had achieved a truce with El. I had to do what I had to do, to keep myself from falling off the edge of the world.

"Yes, good seeing you." Ian turned away and walked out.

Driving home, I cried to myself.

I wrote a few poems for Ian—he would never see. He had sent me two poems. Words on a page can last a long, long time.

Computers had now taken over from electric typewriters. I had burned out three of them typing my doctoral dissertation. Now I used a PC for writing my poems and for course preparations. I tried to teach El how to use the PC, but he couldn't grasp it and just gave up. For his birthday, I bought a new electric portable typewriter with a self-correction feature. He put it on an old desk he'd refinished and put it in his bedroom. He started typing up his old stories, many still handwritten on old yellow legal pads. It was a nice sound, the quiet clacking of the electric keys, and nice to know that El was doing something constructive. My computer, in my downstairs study, was as quiet as a mouse as my fingers tiptoed across the keyboard.

When the academic year ended in May, El and I went traveling. Our first trip abroad was to England. I had mapped out my dream trip years ago, from London to Hampton Court to Bath, Salisbury, Stratford, Wales, the Lake District, Hadrian's Wall, Durham, York, Cambridge, and Oxford. It took us three weeks, driving in a clockwise circle from London. I touched earth where my beloved best writers had lived. I wrote notes in my travel diary; I wrote a poem to Ian.

Every summer, we took another trip. Later journeys took us to France, twice. I felt so at home there, practicing my schoolbook French fairly successfully. El loved the food. The amazing thing about our travels was how well El and I got along. We were born traveling companions. I drove the rented cars, and El navigated. We shared a passion for French food, though he could not drink any wine. I slept peacefully in a twin hotel bed, dreamless and without anxiety. El smoked on a hotel balcony. Every view, every cathedral, and every concert and museum filled us with mutual joy.

We came home with souvenirs for our children and photos to fill an album. Back to work, back to our polite, silent détente.

Then, without warning, our long-suffering psychotherapist, Dr. W, died. He had retired only a few months earlier. A family friend unknown to us wrote a letter to his former patients announcing his death. I was shocked and grief stricken. Despite my criticism of his methodology, I had relied on him to keep El under control. Dr. W was a kind, decent man—the sort I wish my father had been. In private, I wailed for him. El seemed affected too, but said very little.

I was teaching the top of the ladder in my career when El decided to retire. He was clearly tired, sleeping most of the weekends. The school district and teachers gave him a farewell party. One of the gifts was a ceramic casting of a Jack Russell terrier wearing an ID collar engraved with the name "Whiskey." We had adopted the real "Whiskey" from my sister, who had found him as a stray in Dublin, Ireland. Hence, the name. He became notorious in our neighborhood, before the leash law was enacted, for battering down doors when a female dog was in heat. The local dogcatcher had picked him up so many times, she automatically called us to come and get him—and pay the fine. El and I couldn't stop laughing at the little ceramic copy. I put it in the front window as a sort of joke; it was where Whiskey used to sit, looking for action. A few years after he died, at age eighteen or so, I got a call from the dogcatcher. "I have Whiskey, here. Do you want to come get him?"

"He's dead."

"Oh, I'm so sorry. He was quite a dog." The dog she had caught was most likely one of Whiskey's offspring. The ceramic Whiskey is still in the window.

El's retirement brought new tensions to our taut situation. I needed to work on weekends, and asked him please not to interrupt me until I had finished. There was no door to my spacious room, and the door to the garage led off it. Because cars came into and left from the garage, foot traffic naturally led through my big room. On his way out, he'd stand in the opening with no door, not speaking. I'd have to turn from my desk and ask, "What?"

"Do you want anything from the store?"

When he got back from shopping, he'd make me brunch: perfect eggs, over easy; crispy bacon; and home fries. "Come and get it!" he'd call. I loved him for showing he still cared about me.

El had nowhere to go, nothing to do in particular. A men's reading club met once a month. Each one picked out a book in turn. El asked me, "What should we read?" He only read whatever someone else suggested, and then, a few pages at the beginning and at the end. He read in bed. "You must read sitting up, in a chair," Dr. W had commanded. El sat like an Egyptian frieze figure, stiff and one-dimensional, in a chair. For ten minutes. Then he got up, went out on the porch to smoke, and went to bed—to read. The other guys thought El was brilliant, even though he'd actually read so little of the book under discussion.

When our children were spread out, we decided to rent a house on Cape Cod, inviting any of our children who could to spend a week with us. We loved it so much, we rented a house each summer. El had been retired for a little over a year when we rented a nice house in Eastham. Our first grandchild, Aaron, was eighteen months old, so we were very happy when our son Sam and his wife Barbara decided to stay with us for a week. I took photos of us, the last time El would be in the picture with us. In one, El is sitting outside with little Aaron on his lap, El's muscular arm holding him safe. El is grinning, his eyes crinkling with happiness. Aaron, tow haired and blue eyed, takes his grandfather's love for granted. His father Sam is bending toward him, grinning with pride and joy.

We went to the beach—Nauset Beach—with its long, wooden stairs climbing down to the steep dunes. We spread blankets and chairs. Sam and I led Aaron to the edge of the surf, but he wasn't much taken with the pounding waves crashing at his feet. His fair skin burned. His mother, also fair-skinned, slathered herself and Aaron in sunscreen and dressed him in a shirt and floppy hat. Sam gave him a shovel and pail, and, together, they built a big sand castle to fend off the waves.

The exodus from the beach began around four in the afternoon, sun-soaked families struggling up the stairs with beach umbrellas and coolers, tired children carrying pails, dropping shovels in the sand. We packed up our things and began climbing the long, steep stairway, Sam and Aaron and Barbara leading the way, El and I last in line, El behind me. Ten steps up, El called, "Barbara." I turned. He was gray, gasping. "I can't breathe."

Chapter XIII

CANCER JOURNAL: EMOTIONAL TRIAGE, 1992–1993

July 25, 1992

The doctor at Medicenter Five in Brewster said El has pneumonia. He collapsed today, climbing the fifty steps up from Nauset Beach. He has a fever. The doctor, a woman, gave El a prescription for antibiotics and told me to make sure El rests. "Rest, rest, rest," she repeated. Then she stared at me very oddly and added, "Make sure you take these X-rays to your family doctor as soon as you get home."

"Should we go home right away?" I asked.

"No, no hurry—at this point," she answered.

August 1, 1992

We left our nice rented house in Eastham this morning, and stopped to pick up El's X-rays at the Medicenter in Brewster on the way home. I took out the films and the radiologist's report as I walked back to the car to see if I could understand them. My knees went weak. I couldn't make out the X-rays, but the radiologist had typed out his analysis of them in pretty clear English: *a large abnormality in the upper lobe of the left lung; pneumonia or a malignant tumor more likely.* El read the look on my face, but neither of us said anything. We were silent on the five-hour drive home. The doctors at either end were safely out of my line of

146

fire as I speculated on how long "the large abnormality" had been visible on X-rays. El had had X-rays the year before, and another set taken in March when he went to see our doctor for a persistent cough. Hadn't Dr. M seen "the large abnormality" then?

August 2, 1992
Dr. M (I call him Doctor Iceman now) confirmed the radiologist's report today. "It's a malignant tumor, about the size of a grapefruit. It can't be cured. A year." Thus he told us, his shorthand answers to our questions. Nothing could be done!

"Maybe a surgeon can get it out?" El asked Dr. M to recommend a surgeon. Dr. Iceman referred us to a local surgeon, Dr. Q.

August 5, 1992
Dr. Q says that, according to the CAT scans, blood tests, biopsies, and X-rays, the tumor hasn't spread. He says he can get it out—he thinks. "Do you want to go for it?" he asked, smiling like a car salesman. We had good insurance plus Medicare, so he had nothing to lose.

El rubbed his hands eagerly and said, "Yes."

"As soon as possible," Dr. Q said. We set the date for next week.

August 14, 1992
Dr. Q cut a slice from El's back as big as a watermelon and cracked three ribs to get at the tumor. But he couldn't get it out. He sewed him back up with the thing still there, still growing second by second. "I can't get it out," Dr. Q told me in the waiting room. His voice was shaking. I nearly fainted. Anne and I cried and hugged each other.

"What will we tell Dad?" she asked.

"I'll tell him, when he's out of recovery," said Dr. Q. I called Dr. Iceman.

"What now?" I asked.

"It's inoperable," he snarled. "You can go for radiation, but it's only palliative, not a cure."

"Pall*i*ative?" I asked, mispronouncing it.

"*Pall*iative," Dr. Iceman corrected. I asked him about the X-rays he'd taken in March. "That's a fair question," he said with more sympathy. "The tumor was definitely already there."

147

"And you didn't see it? You didn't notice? Did you even look at the X-rays?" I won't sue Dr. Iceman because his partner is Dr. MC, a good friend. But I'd like to kill him. With a knife. A gun. My bare hands. With poison in his Nicorette chewing gum.

August 20, 1992

Dr. S, the radiation oncologist, talked to me for an hour while El was being measured for radiation treatment. I told him how disgusted I was with Dr. Iceman and Dr. Q; I said that I'd wanted El to go to New York City for better doctors. Dr. S nodded, saying he could refer us to one in Sloan-Kettering, if we wanted. He'd been trained there and still had contacts. He showed me a garish medical diagram of the lungs and where the tumor had grown around El's *hilum* (a nucleus of connecting nerves, blood vessels, and an organ), and how nearly impossible it was to cut it out without severing the windpipe. "Then why did that asshole Dr. Q say he could and put El through that pointless torture?" Dr. S, tight-lipped, said he couldn't say anything against a colleague. But maybe there was a chance that a genius of a surgeon at Sloan-Kettering could get it out.

As we spoke, his assistant came running in with an X-ray. "Oh, God!" cried Dr. S. "His lung's collapsed. We can't wait for pinpoint measurement. We'll have to start radiation immediately!"

September 1, 1992

After ten radiation treatments, El's lung is still collapsed. He is now suffering radiation sickness as well and can't eat with the burns on his throat. He is losing weight and strength rapidly. Dr. S asked El today if he'd like to see a surgeon at Sloan-Kettering who might be able to operate again. El hesitated, thinking of his still-healing ribs and scars. When we got home, he called Dr. S and said, "Make the appointment."

September 3, 1992

I carried El's CAT scans, X-rays, and test results in large manila envelopes to give to Dr. B at Sloan-Kettering. Dr. B studied them, then said, "First, we have to open up the collapsed lung again. If that works, I think I can get the tumor out; I'll probably have to take out the whole lung." He wore a wine-dark turban, and was no taller than I, but I felt great trust in Dr. B. I didn't think he told lies.

Classes start in five days. I have to write course outlines and get ready somehow. If I don't go back to work, I'll go crazy.

September 10, 1992

Dr. B was able to open up El's lung with a laser. It's got air in it again. He told El that he has to build up his strength to get through another grueling operation. Dr. B sent him to a nurse who teaches breathing exercises. She gave El a regimen of deep breathing on a plastic tube with a ball inside. He has to blow the ball up the tube with all his breath—easy for me, with two good lungs. Very, very hard for El. He has to exercise every day on the stationary bike and walk around the block as well. She gave him a high-fat, high-calorie diet. Since the radiation stopped, his throat is getting better.

September 12, 1992

El has pneumonia again. Dr. MC put him in Cornwall Hospital and is giving him intravenous antibiotics. Dr. B can't operate until the pneumonia is cleared up. I feel better now that our friend Dr. MC is taking care of El, until Dr. B takes over. Dr. Iceman has done enough damage already. El is in good hands as I go back teaching.

September 24, 1992

Dr. B checked El out today and said he's strong enough for surgery now. He's gained a little weight and the pneumonia is gone—for now.

October 5, 1992

El had to have more pre-op tests today at Sloan-Kettering and is staying until it's over. I've been driving him back and forth on days I'm not teaching. His breathing is down to 40 percent of normal. They want to see if he will be able to manage with one lung following surgery. Tomorrow is the big day. Tonight, the kids and I gathered around El to give him our hope and love. As we stood by El's bed, a woman with gray hair came in and said, "I'm a nun. Would you like me to say a prayer before your surgery tomorrow, Mr. Adams?"

We looked at each other. "Why not?" we answered, all together.

Jim, our devout Catholic friend, is saying special prayers. So are the people who have called, or stopped me as I shop in the supermarket, "El is in our prayers," they tell me, touching my arm. She said a religious prayer, as I prayed to science and the skill of Dr. B.

October 6, 1992

We won! Dr. B removed El's whole left lung. It took four hours while Anne and I waited in the lobby of Sloan-Kettering. The nurse came in periodically to update all the families and friends waiting for patients undergoing surgery. Murmurs of hope filled the airy room. When our nurse came, we looked up hopefully and she smiled. It wasn't easy, Dr. B told us later. The post-op CAT scans show that his other lung is clean. The biopsies of the removed tissue show only three lymph nodes with cancer cells. Dr. B is optimistic for El's future. He is a kind, decent man, as well as a genius of a surgeon. He shook my hand, and I wanted to hug him. But he is a devout Sikh.

October 28, 1992

El rides the exercise bike and does his breathing exercises every day. He complains of chills, but Dr. B doesn't think they are significant. I'm getting through the semester with the help of friends and my housecleaner. They come in relays, bringing food and keeping El company while I'm at work. Luckily, I have a sabbatical for the spring term. We'll go to Florida for a few days. Maybe El can go to the literature conference with me in Kentucky in February when I read a paper. It's so good to be getting back to normal tasks!

November 6, 1992

I spent two days in New Orleans by myself, reading a paper for a communications conference. Aunt Bea stayed with El so I could get away. I had to have some time to myself. It was life restoring, though I feel guilty for leaving El and not taking care of him myself.

December 3, 1992

Dr. F, the cardiologist at Sloan-Kettering, put El on medication to control an irregular heartbeat caused by the surgery. El is also taking Cardizem for high blood pressure, plus two kinds of painkillers. The surgical wounds are still painful. The kitchen shelf is beginning to look like a pharmacy.

February 28, 1993

Marco Island, Florida, soothed El and me with its warm Gulf breezes. He slept and relaxed by the pool as I swam and walked along the beach watching the pelicans. He managed the trip to Kentucky very well and was good company on the long drive. He said he'd prefer driving to flying. My paper went well. El applauded me. He is still my greatest fan. I'm writing again. I think we've licked the cancer. His skin color is returning to its normal ruddiness.

March 13, 1993

El had two odd fainting spells, once in the garage as he was about to go out, and once in a store. His skin color worries me—it looks gray. And he's got a little fever and night sweats again. Pneumonia in the other lung, maybe. Maybe nerves. Dr. F, the cardiologist, can't find anything wrong to explain the fainting spells. El's heartbeat is still irregular, but not serious, the doctor says.

I've nearly finished writing a novella. I asked El if he'd read it when I'm finished.

March 28, 1993

El cried when he finished my novella. He said that, even though he'd known all the things I'd written about before, he had never understood how deeply they had affected me. His tears moved me to tears. How would I ever find another man like El who understands me?

April 15, 1993

Dr. B gave El a clean bill of health: no cancer anywhere! No more CAT scans, he said. Just X-rays, in three months. We did it!

May 27, 1993

We left for London today, as planned, despite El's persistent chills and fever. A virus, probably, Dr. Iceman said. I was very angry that El went back to him. He gave us antibiotics to take with us on our trip to

London, Scotland, and Amsterdam. I don't trust Dr. Iceman. I can't help but worry.

June 15, 1993

El is clearly very sick again. We both know it, but we don't say anything. He takes Tylenol every four hours to keep his fever under control. In between, he shakes with chills. Then he breaks out in a soaking sweat. He changes pajamas twice a night. Still, we managed to enjoy some blessed moments in Amsterdam and Scotland. El's favorite was the Van Gogh Museum. Mine was the Scottish Highlands, the misty lochs and mountains, and the sheep grazing everywhere, even on precipices. It makes me realize how one can cling to life, even to danger, even in places it seems impossible to gain a foothold.

June 17, 1993

We got back yesterday. I was supposed to leave for Maine today, to read a paper at the National Poetry Foundation Conference on 1930s writers. But El is too sick for me to leave him.

June 18, 1993

Dr. MC put El back in Cornwall Hospital. He has pneumonia again—in his only lung. Dr. MC ordered a set of CAT scans of El's chest and abdomen, a bone scan, sputum tests, blood tests, and a bone marrow biopsy.

June 21, 1993

Dr. MC told us that there are some "nodes" on El's right lung. Very small, he said. *What does it matter if they're small?* I thought. *It's cancer, and it will grow and grow until it smothers El's remaining right lung!* I feel myself beginning to crack—I can't eat, I can't sleep. My head spews out fantasies of El's slow suffocation, of his funeral and which poem I will read—Dylan Thomas' "Do Not Go Gentle into That Good Night," Alfred Lord Tennyson's "Ulysses," or one of my own. I've written five poems about El's cancer and my feelings of abandonment. I wonder if I should have his body sent back to New Hampshire for burial, where he was born, where his heart has always been. He told me once that he didn't want to be cremated. I think of throwing myself into his grave, like Hamlet into Ophelia's. I think of turning on the engine in my car parked in the closed garage, in my house where nobody but me will be home anymore.

June 27, 1993

El has been in the hospital for eight days, on intravenous antibiotics. They're sending him home now with Cipro, an oral antibiotic. They can kill the pneumonia, but not the cancer. Dr. MC told El he should go back to Sloan-Kettering as soon as he can.

July 1, 1993

I carried the new CAT scans, X-rays, radiology reports, and test results to Dr. B today. He studied them and examined El. "I'm sorry," he said, shaking his turbaned head. "It's the cancer again. There are four nodes we can see in the right lung, and probably many more so small we can't see them on the CAT scan. I can't remove them."

"What's to be done?" I asked.

He shrugged. "Chemotherapy, if you want." Dr. B looked directly into my eyes, telling me the horrible truth with his dark, human eyes.

El said he wants to try chemotherapy. Dr. B set up an appointment with the chemo department at Sloan-Kettering. I know Dr. B did all he could, and I am grateful to him. Judging by his eyes, I know he thinks chemo is useless. I do not want El to undergo chemotherapy. I've read all the literature about it from the American Cancer Society, the National Cancer Institute, and from technical articles sent to me by Maggi, my half-sister, who is an oncologist. Treating lung cancer with chemo is useless at this final Stage IV, and its side effects are ghastly. If it were my body, I wouldn't put myself through its poisonous torture. Just make me comfortable until the cancer wins.

But El is desperate, willing to believe there is still a cure to be had. He wants chemotherapy at Sloan-Kettering, though he could have the same treatment at a hospital near our home. Dr. B gave me back all the CAT scans, X-rays, and test results in the big manila envelopes. "You'll need these for the chemo department," he said.

July 6, 1993

I got a bill on my American Express card from the hotel in Maine where I was to have gone for the conference. I had forgotten to cancel it in the worry and pressure of El's sickness. They charged me for one night. A penalty for forgetting and staying home to take care of my mortally ill husband.

July 7, 1993

The chemotherapy department waiting room is darker than the surgical waiting room. It is crowded with hopeless-looking patients, many of them bald and yellowed, and their sad families. The nurses, aides, and orderlies all wear midnight blue lab coats with the Sloan-Kettering logo in red, darkening the mood even more. I wonder what ghoul thought up this ominous color code? After a long wait, we were ushered into Dr. Y's office. He and all the doctors wear white lab coats, but I can't get over the feeling that they are really studying white mice in cages.

The silver-haired Dr. Y looks like the television doctor played by Robert Young. He studied El's reports and films slowly, without looking at either of us as we sat in his chilly office. Dr Y finally spoke, without looking at us yet. "You'll need a fine-needle biopsy to determine if those 'nodes' are tumors or only infections." If it was just an infection, he added, with his back to me and to El, who was sitting on the examining table, then the "nodes" could be treated "less drastically." Our hopes rose slightly. But if chemotherapy were given and it was only an infection, he went on, still not looking at us, it could "kill him." "Therefore," he concluded, swiveling to face us at last, "You must have the needle biopsy before we can determine a course of treatment."

I let out my breath. Maybe it was only an infection. I clung to this straw of hope.

Dr. Y continued, "But if they are tumors, then, of course, we must try chemotherapy. There are two kinds: conventional and experimental." He warmed to his subject, explaining that "conventional" treatment could be administered in a hospital close to our home, with doctors trained at Sloan-Kettering. The drugs, two plus Cisplatin, would require two days, back to back, with a hospital stay for the Cisplatin on the second day. By contrast, the experimental protocol, using Edatrexate and Cisplatin, could be administered only at Sloan-Kettering. His eyes brightened, "The experimental treatment is at least as effective as conventional treatment, and has a 50 percent 'response rate.' This does not mean that it *cures* half the cases; it means that in half the patients treated with the experimental drugs, the tumors shrink—that is, 'respond'—for a while." He peered at us over the top of his half-glasses. "Do you understand?" he queried, as if we might be slightly retarded children. "Outside of Sloan-Kettering, the treatment has a 30 percent response rate at best," he said, nailing home his point. I knew from all the literature I'd read, and even from Dr. Iceman, that the usual response rate of lung cancer to chemo was only 10 percent. *Why bother?* I thought. It wasn't, in any a case, a cure. Just a dangerous, sickening delaying tactic of the inevitable.

But El clutched at this last hope. Dr. Y, seeing he'd caught a live one, strongly urged El to choose the experimental protocol. He said he was "the perfect candidate" (read, "hopeless terminal case") as his type of cancer did not respond well to conventional protocols. (Tell me about it, you bastard.) He stood up, told us to think about it, but not for too long. I could not say what I really thought since El was so eager to have any chance at all. If El agreed, Dr Y said he would call the radiologist to set the date for the biopsy. We were getting the rush treatment, I felt, before reality could set in and change El's mind.

El asked, "How long will I live if I don't get chemotherapy?"

After an endless pause, Dr. Y answered, "Five or six months."

"How long will I live with chemotherapy?" El ventured.

"That depends. There are no guarantees," said the slick snake-oil salesman.

"Okay," said El. "I'll do it—the experimental." Dr. Y all but rubbed his hands with glee. He called the radiologist immediately. The biopsy would be performed this week. El would initially be admitted as Dr. B's patient, until El formally signed the release for experimental chemotherapy. Signed up with Death and the Devil's apprentice, in my opinion.

July 13, 1993

Dr. B's secretary phoned at eight in the morning and said that the admitting office wanted El to be at Sloan-Kettering by one that afternoon. I was furious. "It takes us two hours to drive to the city, and we still have to get dressed and pack. It's impossible to make it by one."

"Okay," she said, nonchalantly, "Make it two, then," and hung up. I feel as if we've been demoted from the heroic surgical unit to the back wards of do-it-yourself chemistry. And being treated accordingly.

We made it to Sloan-Kettering by one thirty. I parked in the S-K garage and took El upstairs in a wheelchair. He was admitted to the posh fifteenth floor again, for surgical patients. The biopsy will be done tomorrow. I drove back home right away, as I expect El will come home either Wednesday or Thursday after what Dr. Y calls "a simple procedure." "We're admitting him only as a precaution, since he has only one lung and we have to stick a needle into it," said the careful doctor. "If the lung deflates, they can handle it in the hospital." *How,* I wondered? How do you blow up a punctured balloon? *Suppose they can't "handle" it? Suppose El loses the power to breathe with his only lung?* "It would be awful if the lung deflated as you were driving him home," said the astute Dr. Y, invading my thoughts. Now I understood why our friend, Dr. MC, had decided against the needle biopsy.

July, 14, 1993 (Shira, our second grandchild, is born) Bastille Day
When I arrived this morning, and leaned over to kiss El, he whispered, "We have a granddaughter. Sam called." We both burst into tears. I couldn't hug El, for fear of hurting him. I brushed back his hair with my hand, his hair still thick and more brown than gray. Shira, our granddaughter, had been born while I was on the road driving into the city. She was our second grandchild, Aaron's new baby sister, born on Bastille Day. El will get to see her. Will he make it to his sixty-seventh birthday on July 20?

"How did the biopsy go?" I asked.

"They didn't get enough tissue, they said," El croaked. "They'll have to try again tomorrow." His voice had almost gone completely. How could they put him through this torture again? I am boiling mad.

Soon after, the radiologist came in and said they'd have to do the test again, that they had missed the "teeny-tiny nodes" with the "teeny-tiny needle." He simpered and smiled as if he'd just filed El's nails instead of put him in jeopardy for his life. They were doing "the simple procedure" tomorrow, Thursday.

I quelled my anger in front of El. "I'll see you tomorrow," I said. "I'd better get home and do some errands." I drove home in a rage. I've been driving, every day, to Sloan-Kettering and back—four hours of driving every day, besides doing what I can to comfort El. I am trying to do errands, to eat, and to rest in the few hours I have each day before going back to the hospital in New York. I have no time for anything else—to write, to go to aerobics class, to even read the newspaper. My body is knotted and aching in every joint. Crying storms hit me without warning, day and night. I can't get to sleep, and, if I do, I wake in the middle of the night. I sit up, writing out my helpless rage in my journal. As I drive past West Point coming and going to New York City, rage makes me want to drive my car off the cliff on Storm King Mountain—down, down, down to the Hudson River.

July 15, 1993

I got back to Sloan-Kettering at noon today. El was already back in his room. "Good!" I said. "It's all over."

"No," El whispered. "I panicked. Blood was leaking out of this tube all over the bed. They wouldn't give me time to change my pajamas. I couldn't get my breath—they'd laid me on my stomach inside the CAT machine and I couldn't breathe. My oxygen level dropped to below 50 percent from 98 percent. Dr. BT told me to lie still, take deep breaths. I couldn't lie still. I was scared. I'm sorry. They couldn't do it." This speech had taken all El's strength. He looked weak and vulnerable, the victim of sadists.

I flew into a fury. "It wasn't done!" I screamed. "Why didn't somebody call me? Are the doctors coming to see you this afternoon?"

"Calm down. I just panicked. You're upset."

"You're damned right I'm upset!" I stormed down the hall to the nurses' station. "Are *any* of my husband's doctors coming to see him this afternoon?" I shouted at the impermeable, unbreakable glass.

The nurses, doctors, aides, and various people who always hang out at a nurses' station stopped what they were doing and saying and looked at me through the glass with the tiny porthole for talking with outsiders. "I don't know," a nurse at the switchboard answered.

"They damned well better!" I yelled even louder. "Nobody has had the decency to tell me a damned thing! How many times am I supposed to drive in and out of the city? I don't even know the name of the doctor who was supposed to do this procedure. Who is this radiological klutz, anyway?" I demanded.

I stomped back to El's room, my pulse racing, my face hot. I felt elated, ready to do battle with anyone who dared lie to me. I sat down in the Naugahyde chair for visitors, my sweaty hands gripping the armrests. El whispered, "What did you do?" He was too weak to lift his head. I suddenly realized I couldn't move. A woman in a white Sloan-Kettering lab coat came in and introduced herself—Dr. L, a social worker. In a soothing voice, she asked me what was wrong, was there anything she could help me with. Through clenched teeth, I described the aborted procedure, the torture to my husband, my outrage at being kept in the dark. "The 'simple' procedure," I growled, "turned out to be extremely dangerous, and they are planning to put my husband through all that danger again. What is the point? They *know* it's cancer. They *know* they can't do anything more to help him." My pulse slowed, and I had to stifle sobs as I told the social worker that I was sick of being treated as if I were invisible or stupid because I'm only a wife. "I don't even know the name of that fumbling radiologist who was supposed to do the biopsy. Every nurse pronounced it differently, so I had insisted that one nurse find out and write it down for me." I drew the crumpled slip of paper from my skirt pocket. Dr. L said she'd talk to El's doctors right away and find out what was going on. She'd be right back.

Time stopped as I sat in the chair, my back sticking to the slimy Naugahyde. All at once, Dr. N, Dr. B's fellow, came bouncing in on the balls of his feet. He barely nodded to me, and scolded El as if he were a child: "Now you see why it was necessary to put you into the hospital for this test." He all but tsk-tsked. "If you had two lungs, we could have done it out-patient, as usual. We'll just have to do it again tomorrow." He smiled and walked out.

Then came the unpronounceable radiologist, Dr. BT. He was short, pudgy, unctuous, and sweaty. "Doing a fine-needle biopsy in a man who has only one lung is extremely dangerous," he said. "The 'nodes' are so tiny that they are hard to get at for the tissue sample needed." He turned slyly to me and asked, "Do you have any questions?"

"Yes," I barked. "Why didn't you give him a sedative? It's a scary thing to have to go through. Don't you realize how nerve-wracking it is for him?"

"Oh, it's very dangerous," whispered the fat Dr. BT. "Sedatives lower the oxygen rate, and he has only one lung." Why do the doctors keep telling us what we already know—that El has only one lung? "Very dangerous indeed," he repeated, his eyes widening. He shook hands with El and with me. The greasy, soft hand felt like the proverbial dead fish.

Then came Dr. K, Dr. Y's partner in chemotherapy, trailed by his fellow, a bleached blonde with long red fingernails, which she kept studying with a bored look. Dr. K explained that El had to have the biopsy done again, just to make sure the "nodes" weren't an infection. He said it would be done tomorrow, grinning as if he were talking about a delayed delivery of a Sears washing machine. He never looked at me once, exiting the room trailed by his red-fingernailed fellow.

Last came gentle Dr. B. He gave me a quick, appraising look, then went to El's bedside. "Mr. A, what's the matter? This is just a simple test. You shouldn't worry. We'll give you a sedative before the biopsy tomorrow so you'll feel better, and a sleeping pill tonight so you'll get a good rest." El smiled for the first time today. Then Dr. B turned to me. "Are *you* all right, Mrs. Adams?" I couldn't speak, my chest so tight I felt as if it had been bound with wide bands of adhesive tape like a mummy. He sat down on a stool and took my hand, his kind, dark eyes peering intently into mine. "Do you want to ask me anything?" I shook my head.

I managed to say, "You've said everything that had to be said."

He nodded, holding my hand until I felt some of his strength reach my heart. "If you have any questions, just call me." Dr. B left, followed by his smiling fellow I hadn't noticed till then.

Dr. L, the social worker, returned. I had not moved from the Naugahyde chair, having lost all feeling as well as the ability to move and speak. "Did the doctors come? Do you feel better now?" she asked. I sat like a stone. "Would you like to talk to someone?" she prodded. I saw her lips moving, her white lab coat, but could not speak. "We have a support group for families of cancer patients—would you like to join it?" I glared at her. I *hate* groups where everyone beats on themselves, confessing terrible secrets and sins—a secular and ultimate *mea culpa*. "We also have an excellent doctor," she persisted. "Would you like to talk to him? He can see you today, if you like."

El, watching and listening to all this, croaked, "Yes! She needs to talk to someone!"

"Do you feel as if you're going to explode?" she asked kindly. I held my breath, choking back tears, and nodded. "Do you want to talk to the doctor?" I looked at my icy feet in sandals, the sand from Cape Cod ground permanently into them. "I'll call him right away. He'll be here within an hour," she said, hurrying off.

I hung my head, my body going limp, wondering if I could get to the window, open it, and jump. We were on the fifteenth floor, but the windows were sealed. Anyway, I didn't have the strength to get out of the chair, let alone smash through the window.

At precisely three o'clock, Dr. R strode in, wearing the ubiquitous white lab coat with the red Sloan-Kettering logo, a vertical arrow with three horizontal bars in graduated lengths across the shaft. "Mr. and Mrs. Adams? Hi, I'm Dr. R." He then turned immediately to me and said, "Come on, we'll go talk in my office." Youthful energy emanated from his six-foot-four body. I found I could move my arms and legs again, but still couldn't speak. I got out of the sticky chair and followed him, barely keeping up with his long, rapid strides down the corridor. I felt like a naughty child being taken to the principal's office for a dressing-down.

Dr. L stopped us and said we could use her office on this floor. She unlocked it for us. "It's better than waiting for the elevators to get to my office on the third floor," said Dr. R. He gestured for me to go in and closed the door behind us.

The windowless office was as cold as a refrigerator and not much bigger. The desk was piled with the social worker's papers, beside a filing cabinet also with papers on top. The only decoration on the walls was a case of butterflies pinned and labeled. It made me feel just like Prufrock—helpless and pinned to the wall, being studied dispassionately by a scientist. Dr. R sat in the social worker's chair, and I sat in the other, our knees almost touching. My hands and body were shaking with cold and terror, but my armpits were dripping sweat. Dr. R said something I can't remember. I said something I can't remember. Then he asked if I felt depressed. "I can't eat, I can't sleep. I can't even read," I admitted, staring at the dull linoleum floor.

"Why not?"

"I can't focus, or keep my mind on the book." I dared to look up and into his eyes for the first time. He had a kind face, an honest face. I took a deep breath and said, "I'm sick of doctors and their lies. They all lie. I don't trust them anymore. I *hate* them."

For nearly an hour, I poured myself out. When I'd finally run out of steam, Dr. R suggested that medication might help me feel better. "You've had these depressive episodes before, it seems. Have you ever taken antidepressants?"

"Once, for a few weeks. Then I threw them out. I hate medicine. I can ride it out. All I need is some sleep. If you could give me something to help me sleep, I think I'll feel better and I'll be able to handle things." We negotiated about medication for several minutes, Dr. R urging me to take an antidepressant, but I was adamant—no anti-depressants.

Finally, he said he could give me a very mild drug to help me sleep, Restoril. Looking at his nametag attached to his lab coat, he said, "I'm a PhD so I'll have to get the prescription from a psychiatrist on our staff. I'll bring it to you in a few minutes." He checked his watch. Time was up. "Would you like to talk with someone again?" he asked before we left the icy office. I was beginning to feel flash-frozen. "I could recommend someone outside the hospital, or you could ask to see someone else here, or me. I'd be glad to talk with you again."

I clung to this strong, kind young man like a drowning person clinging to a lifeguard. I nodded. "You," I said. We set an appointment for the following week.

Walking back to El's room, my body felt looser, released from the invisible mummy wrappings. "Feel better?" El asked. I nodded, not willing to reveal how angry I was at his doctors.

Dr. R came in a few minutes later and handed me the prescription for Restoril. He smiled and said, "I'll see you next week." I felt as if I'd won the lottery. I had wanted help so much, but had been too proud to ask anyone for it. Besides, I didn't know whom to turn to. Sloan-Kettering's psychiatric service came out of the blue, it seemed, a godsend. I smiled to myself: when Dr. R asked me why I wanted to speak with him, I'd answered cheekily, "Because the social worker wanted me to." He'd grinned. "So you're doing *her* a favor," he teased. Dr. R reminds me of my good friend Jeff, to whom I can tell almost anything. But I'm still afraid of Dr. R ... afraid he'll want to put me in the hospital. It isn't the first time I've thought of suicide.

"You see," whispered El, "I knew you needed to talk to someone. That's what I told the social worker before you came today. I had to fill out the patient profile form again; they lost the one you filled out. I wrote that I wanted them to help you, that you needed a psychiatrist. When she came to pick up the form, she asked me about it. I told her, 'Get that lady someone intelligent, or she won't sit still for five minutes.'" El was saving my life; I couldn't save his.

July 16, 1993

I drove home earlier than usual and beat the rush hour traffic. I ate something, took a Restoril capsule, and was in bed by eleven. I was amazed to wake in daylight, at six in the morning for the first time in months. It's Friday. Nothing gets done in hospitals over the weekend.

When I got back to Sloan-Kettering, El was back in his room, the biopsy done successfully this time. He was relaxed from the tranquilizer they'd given him—thanks to Dr. B. They got enough tissue, they told El. But because it's the weekend, we won't get the pathology report till Monday.

The nurse came in and I told her I'd been driving sixty-five miles each way every day for a week, expecting that El would be coming home in a day or two. She sympathized, having a relative who lives not far from me in the mid–Hudson Valley. She said she would check with the resident and Dr. B to see if El could go home tomorrow. In a half hour, she came back and said they would take an X-ray, and if it looked okay, El could go home in the morning.

I drove home that afternoon, again beating the rush hour plus weekend exodus, feeling better than I had in a month. I took another Restoril and slept soundly.

July 17, 1993

El called me at eight o'clock this morning and said the X-rays are okay and he can come home. "Get here by noon," the nurse said. I got to Sloan-Kettering exactly at twelve, and the nurse who discharged him, a pretty redhead from Galway, got us out quickly by sending me down to the pharmacy for El's prescriptions. "It's the weekend, and nothing happens unless you make it happen," she said. We talked about Dr. B, what a great surgeon and even greater human being he is. "I can't say as much for chemotherapists," I said.

Nurse Anne K put her hands on her hips and said in her Galway brogue, "I never met a chemotherapist I liked. Just get what you want out of them, and don't expect any bedside manner."

July 19, 1993

Dr. Y called Monday morning at nine. His Ivy League voice, well aged with high status and income, came over the impersonal wires: "We have the pathologist's report; we're dealing with the same 'material' as before."

El was on the upstairs phone, I on the downstairs. He'd lost his voice almost completely because of a "node" pressing on a nerve, the doctors said. "You mean lung cancer," El croaked as loudly as he could.

A long pause. "Yes," said the silver-haired chemotherapist.

"You remember we discussed two kinds of treatment, the conventional and the experimental? Have you thought about it since then?"

Dr. K, Dr. Y's assistant, had come to talk to El in the hospital Friday evening, before we had the results of the biopsy. "The chances of its being an infection seem very slim," I said angrily. "This whole horrible week was unnecessary in my opinion."

"Oh, no! We've been fooled sometimes," Dr. K said. Then he pressed on with his sales pitch: Edatrexate plus Cisplatin. El would get out-patient treatment at Sloan-Kettering two days, back to back. He wouldn't have so many side effects that way, he said. It would work even better than the conventional protocol. It's worked well on many patients so far. Blah, blah, blah. Then, showing he had a bedside manner after all, Dr. K added, "We haven't seen fur growing all over them, yet." Ha, ha, ha, he laughed. He sounded exactly like a Sears appliance salesman, down to the tasteless joke. His Barbie doll fellow, blonde and red-nailed as ever, lurked wordlessly behind Dr. K, examining her precious nails again. How did she get into medical school? Become a doctor? For that matter, how did anyone like Dr. K get to be a doctor? They must have studied with Frankenstein.

"Yes," said El. "You explained it before. I'm going for the experimental. I want it done here at Sloan-Kettering." Dr. K grinned happily, as if he was getting a big commission on the "sale."

El's chemo treatments begin on July 29 and 30, a year to the day almost since he got sick with "pneumonia" on Cape Cod.

I haven't written anything all year except cancer poems and this journal. I've never seen a dead person. Oh, yes—I saw El's father lying in his coffin, his leathery skin darkened with alcohol and death that no rosy cosmetics could conceal.

July 20, 1993 (El's sixty-seventh birthday)
I goofed it up badly with Dr. R yesterday, burbling on and on about my difficult marriage and my mother's death and how angry I was at having my work interrupted by El's illness. A pure, incoherent, selfish mess. "You're giving me mixed signals," he said. "You said you didn't want to talk about the past, and now you're talking about it." I hate it when I go on about the past, yet frequently find myself talking about it, thinking about it, and writing about it. "Why do you feel so guilty about El's having cancer? Why do you act as if it's your fault?" Dr. R asked, interrupting my obsessive thoughts, stopping my babbling and making me think about the present awful reality.

"When my mother died, my sister said it was my fault," I said.

"Just because someone says it's your fault doesn't mean it's necessarily true, or that you have to believe her," said Dr. R. An amazingly simple observation! Why did I never think of that? He's a great psychotherapist. Dr. R's final comment today was, "You have every right to be angry because your life has been put on hold."

I bought El a new glider rocking chair, with a soft padded seat. He sits in it to watch television.

July 21, 1993, 10:15 a.m.
Just knowing I have another appointment with Dr. R next week makes me feel better. Out of my incoherent babble, I've begun to organize my thought on paper, making a list of the reasons why I feel so guilty about El's cancer.

  1. I'm angry because my life had been put on hold, because I spend all my time nursing El and taking him to hospitals.

2. El has always resented my having any interests in life except him, so now he's got what he's always wanted: my undivided time and attention.

3. Would people expect a husband to quit his job and cease all activities to tend a sick wife? Why is a wife expected to be a nurse to her husband, when she has a full-time career that she loves? A husband would find a female relative or hire a nurse so he could keep on working at his career.

4. If I am to survive after El dies, I need to keep at my work and outside interests.

5. If El gets better for a while, then there's no problem. But nobody knows if he will or not, and how long he will live. So it's impossible for me to make plans or start a writing project.

6. I feel guilty for enjoying myself—my work, aerobics classes, writing, seeing people, eating good food, drinking red wine—when El can't enjoy any of them.

7. Dr. M, the kind radiologist who sent us to Sloan-Kettering, said a year ago, when El was given no more than a year to live, that I had to start to detach myself from his illness if I wanted to survive.

July 21, 1993, 2:00 p.m.

8. This is not life. El's life has been taken over by doctors, nurses, and a bushel basket of medications. He has to keep a list of what he's taken and when, or he'll lose track. He takes his temperature every hour and writes it down—a whole, long list of temperatures.

The nightmares have come back. They had all but ceased years ago, cured by a long-ago analysis. Now they're back full force, invoked by a real demon—cancer—evil in the flesh. One night, I dreamed El was in the hospital, walking down a corridor with an IV attached to his arm, and smoking a cigarette. I screamed at him, but he kept smoking, leaning away from me to take deep drags. This dream is factual, evoked by having seen many patients at Sloan-Kettering go outside wheeling IVs to have a smoke. This dream tells me how angry I am with El for continuing to smoke, even after high blood pressure, surgery for an aortic aneurysm, and all the doctors telling him to quit if he wanted to live. He laughed at the behavior-modification course he took at a local hospital. He snickered at hypnotism. He kept smoking as he wore the nicotine patch. Now, it doesn't matter, so I guess that's why those patients keep smoking outside Sloan-Kettering.

Another night, I dreamed that El asked me to take him for a ride in a horse-drawn hansom cab through Central Park. I hate those hansoms because of the way the horses are abused. But to please El, I agreed. It cost a fortune, and I was paying for it. This dream describes the outrageous cost for the treatment of El's cancer and the abuse of the patient that it entails. This expensive "ride," moreover, is even frivolous, given the incurable nature of El's lung cancer once it has metastasized. I've lost count of how many doctors we've seen—from Cape Cod to Cornwall to Newburgh to Sloan-Kettering—the internists, surgeons, radiation oncologists, medical oncologists, chemotherapists, specialist nurses, and lab technicians.

9. Another reason I feel guilty: this expensive treatment hasn't amounted to a hill of beans. El is still mortally sick. Money keeps pouring out, like water through a sieve.

July 29, 1993, 9:00 PM

El's first chemo treatment was today. We stayed at the Franklin Hotel last night, at Eighty-Seventh and Lexington. Small, but clean and convenient.

We arrived at the Adult Day Hospital (ADH) of Sloan-Kettering on the seventeenth floor at eight in the morning. Nurse Terry H put El in a two-bed room and said she'd start the treatment as soon as she took his history.

I stayed with El till ten, helping with the history and list of medications he takes. The receptionist gave me a lunch menu too, so I can have lunch with El. Nurse Terry hooked up the eternal IV. El's veins have started to "roll," she said, so she had to do it twice, using a warm compress to raise the vein. Then she attached the first of two liters of saline to flush out his kidneys. They had already analyzed the quart of urine El had collected since seven o'clock the night before. His kidneys, they said, were fine. The nurse noted his swollen ankles, the sores in his mouth, and his raspy voice. She said all that would improve, once the chemo started working. She explained the side effects: "Don't believe everything you hear. Your hair will thin, but may not fall out." She gave us a booklet on the side effects of the drugs being administered and showed us a ten-minute slide film on chemotherapy. Then she brought ointment for the ghastly sores inside his mouth and on his lips, and told him to wash his mouth with a solution of baking soda when we got home.

At ten o'clock there was nothing to do but sit and wait for the drugs to drip slowly into El's veins. He was comfortable as possible, so I left to get some air and exercise. You can get sick just sitting in a hospital as much as I have been in the last year. I took a cross-town bus on Sixty-Seventh Street to Madison Avenue, intending to go to the Metropolitan Museum. Instead, I decided to walk and window shop up Madison, stopping first at a coffee shop for a heavenly scrambled egg and coffee. El and I had not slept the night before, anticipating the first chemo treatment. I needed the food and caffeine to get me through the long day. It was warm and sunny, and as I browsed in shoe stores and Books & Co., my mood began to lift. I walked faster, feeling stronger. By twelve, I decided to walk back to our hotel on Eighty-Seventh and check out. I was sweating and my clothes were soaked—it felt wonderful. I got to the hotel and finished packing. I brushed my teeth and stripped off the sweaty clothes and took a quick shower. When I was cool again, I put on a clean skirt and cotton shirt and checked out.

I got back to the Sloan-Kettering garage ($13.50 a pop—a "bargain") at one thirty. El was finished with the Cisplatin dose and was being flushed again with saline. My lunch tray was waiting. I surprised myself by eating most of it—baked chicken, cabbage salad, fries, and club soda. El was only able to drink a milk shake and eat a spoonful of Jell-O. Nurse Terry told him to go easy on the food so he wouldn't get nauseous. The antinausea medication had been given before the IV, and it seemed to be working.

All at once, El began to complain that he was short of breath. The night before, he'd been snapping at me, wondering why *I* should be upset—after all, *he* was the one who was dying, not me. Even though he'd been instrumental in getting psychological help for me, I knew he was jealous of my talking to Dr R. At death's door, El was still jealous of any man who spoke to me out of his sight. I am not going to be snookered out of this one; I need Dr. R too much right now to give in to El's jealousy and temper. I suspected that the shortness of breath he was feeling now was mostly anxiety. Nurse Terry called the chemotherapist on call, Dr. P. She said if El's breathing didn't get better, he'd have to stay overnight. I said, "I think he's panicking. His breathing is the same as it's been for the last week." El, looking grim, but unwilling to stay overnight in the hospital again, agreed. He said that Xanax had helped him after Dr. B's surgery, when he'd had "the willies" every night. "Great idea!" said nurse Terry. She called Dr. P back, who agreed it was a great idea and he'd send up a prescription for Xanax right away. She didn't wait, though, hurrying to the floor pharmacy to get him a Xanax he could take immediately. "He can ride home with you in a mellow mood," she said. The nurses at Sloan-Kettering are the antithesis of most of the doctors: human beings.

At 3:15 p.m. Nurse Terry told me to go get the car and bring it around to the front entrance. "I'll bring your husband down at 3:30 so you can beat the rush hour." I got the car and pulled up to the entrance. Nurse Terry came, pushing El in a wheelchair. She'd been with him without a break since eight o'clock this morning. She wrote down the phone number where we could reach the duty nurse twenty-four hours a day, and the dosage for the antinausea medication El would have to take.

On the two-hour drive home, El was giddy and silly, mellowed out on Xanax. I stopped to pick up some take-out Chinese soup, then drove home and got El into bed. He went right to sleep, still drunk on Xanax. After I ate the soup, I took a Restoril and fell sound asleep, thinking gratefully of Dr. R.

July 31, 1993

This week, El doesn't get any treatment, just a blood check. Then next week, he gets the second treatment of chemo. At the end of the next month, they'll evaluate him and decide whether to continue with these drugs, or try another. When the semester starts a month from now, we'll stay at a hotel every midweek while El gets treatment and I teach my classes.

El is very tired today and his mouth is full of new sores. His feet are swollen double their normal size, but his fever is under control with

Naprosin. His coughing has eased. I think I'll go crazy listening to him choke and gasp for breath. What is more frightening and heart rending than to listen to someone slowly suffocating to death? It's like being hanged slowly, or being buried alive until all the oxygen is used up.

There is no happy end to this. No end to cancer. El will live with it as long as he lives, and will die of it sooner or later. Sooner, most likely. Meanwhile, I must keep living somehow. I can't bear this torment of waiting for him to die. What kind of life is it for him now? Neither of us has a life outside of the demands of cancer.

August 2, 1993

10. The best, or worst, reason for my feeling guilty is this: since El got sick a year ago, my emotions have roller-coasted. There have been odd moments of exhilaration when I fantasize the end—the end of El's suffering from fever and choking, the end of the brutal side effects of the poisonous chemicals running through his bloodstream, the end of my servitude to cancer's grip on our lives. When El finally dies, I will be free—released from serving the sad living ghost he's become.

Our former psychoanalyst, Dr. W, defined marriage as a continuous conversation. After forty-one years, El's and mine has been the longest continuous conversation either of us has had. The moment of exhilaration passes quickly when I realize that our conversation as husband and wife is drawing to an end. It has already ended, in a way. Our dialogue is now that of a nurse and a patient: "How do you feel? What is your temperature? Are you hungry? Let me change your sheets and put on clean pajamas." El's answers consist of a shake of the head, a nod, a guttural "97.2" or "101.4." His voice is gone, the one that used to thrill me whenever I heard it on the phone, reduced to a raspy whisper. He has to write notes, now, unable to speak enough to tell me anything he wants. Neither of us says anymore how we feel.

My life has already changed drastically and irrevocably. El will die before me (unless I get hit by a truck or lightning, or shot by a random bullet). I will travel alone, eat alone, and live alone for the rest of my days. If I want company, I'll have to invite someone—a someone whose conversation will be a superficial substitute for the deep, often unspoken, conversation El and I had for so long. For all our violent arguments and irreconcilable differences, we could talk to each other and know we'd be understood as no one else could understand.

I've had to control my emotional storms with a drug to help me sleep and an incipient conversation with Dr. R whose job it is to help cancer patients and their families accept the worst news anyone can get.

August 4, 1993

Dr. Y was shocked by the change in El's appearance today. El has not been able to eat and he's so weak he can hardly walk. His trousers are falling off and his shoulder blades sticking through his skin like a concentration camp victim's.

Dr. Y asked me, seriously, for the first time, what *I* thought. Did I think that El had lost strength since the chemo treatment began? "Yes, he's much worse," I answered, restraining the urge to tell him what I thought of his "experimental" protocol in front of El. Instead, I described the painful mouth ulcers and severe, watery diarrhea.

Dr. Y flashed a light into El's mouth and winced. "We'll give you something for those," he said, writing a prescription for pain-killing lozenges as if it were a papal dispensation for his guilt.

"What's causing the sores and diarrhea?" I asked.

Staring at the wall, Dr. Y said, "None of my other patients on this protocol is reacting this way," making it sound as if it were El's fault that he was doing so poorly.

"Could it be the synergy of too many drugs?" I asked. "He's taking Xanax, Restoril, Naprosin, Digoxin, Lanoxin, Cardizem, plus the chemo and antinausea and antidiarrhea drugs." Dr. Y looked at me over the top of his reading lenses, as if to say, What could a woman, a nonphysician woman, know about synergy? He shrugged, then turned his back on me. Smiling at El, he said, "We've given you *enough* of the medication, clearly. We didn't stint. When you get over these side effects, we'll cut *way* back on the dosage. Of course, we'll have to cancel next week's treatment until you're feeling stronger." The bastard as much as admitted he nearly killed El with an overdose.

August 7, 1993

Sam and Barbara brought Aaron and our new granddaughter, Shira, for us to see for the first time. She was born on Bastille Day, three weeks ago. We've had no time to enjoy this blessing. El held her in his arms, sitting in an easy chair wrapped in the new royal blue plush robe I bought him. His swollen ankles and feet, propped on a footstool, barely fit into his sheepskin slippers. Even wrapped in a quilt, El is still shivering with chills and fever. Smiling at Shira, he said, "You done good, Barbara," to my daughter-in-law. The bad grammar was a joke, one he could never have made about his own writing.

August 8, 1993

El called me every fifteen minutes last night. Groggy from Restoril, I got up again and again to help him to the bathroom and then change his soaked and soiled pajamas—and the sheets. He had continuous watery diarrhea all night. I mopped the floor from his bed to the toilet, again and again. He began vomiting at about 4:00 a.m., spewing watery fluid across the room in successive jets that hit the wall. I asked if he felt nauseous, and he shook his head. I was terrified. I should have called the ambulance, but I couldn't think straight from lack of sleep. I bundled him in a blanket and drove him to Cornwall Hospital ten miles from my house. The ER doctor examined El, listened to my explanation, and looked unconcerned. "He needs hydration," he said, "not unusual with chemo patients." But El's fever had spiked to 102 F, even with Naprosin. The doctor decided to admit him while we waited for Dr. MC, our friend, whom he had called. I saw El to his room, kissed him good-bye, and went downstairs to wait for Dr. MC. At 9:00 a.m. he hadn't arrived yet, so I went home to shower and get some coffee. I felt so tired and tense I couldn't eat. I dawdled over a second cup of coffee, waiting for Amy, our daughter who was coming back from vacation in Vermont. She was dropping off a rental car at our house, and picking up her own car. I didn't think there was any hurry to get back to the hospital; El needed rest and professional care more than he needed my company.

Amy arrived at noon. We ate a light lunch, then she and her husband left for Manhattan. I got back to the hospital at 2:00 p.m. A candy striper stopped me at the reception desk and said I had a message from Dr. BB, who was on call for Dr. MC who was still on vacation. She led me to the intensive care unit. Dr. BB, MC's partner, met me at the door of the ICU. "El's had a massive stroke," he said. "On the right side. It's very bad." He touched my arm and added, "I wouldn't resuscitate him, if I were you." He put his arm around me as I sagged.

A nurse led me to El's bed. His right eye rolled wildly; his left eye was closed. He writhed, trying to get out of bed, but his arms were tied to the bed rails with strips of soft cloth. When he calmed down, I held his left hand and cried, "My darling, my darling." He opened his still-sighted left eye and squeezed my hand hard, three times. He had heard me, recognized my voice.

The nurse returned and asked me to come to the nurse's station in the center of the ICU. The individual rooms are arranged in a glass-walled circle for visibility, but offer patients privacy with pretty cornflower blue curtains. What a pleasant color, I thought, as I signed the form that said to let El die: the DNR, do not resuscitate. Dr. BB said that El would live for twenty-four to thirty-six hours at most. The nurse let me stay for an hour, though visits in the ICU are supposed to be restricted to fifteen minutes. "Talk to him," she said. "He'll know your voice." I did not want to go when she said I had to leave. But I had to go home and call our children.

When I was sitting alone in my kitchen, Dr. Y called, full of phony concern. He wanted to have El moved to Sloan-Kettering. "Why? For God's sake! This is a *stroke*, not cancer. You've tortured him enough. Go get yourself another guinea pig." I slammed down the phone. Had Dr. Y been in the same room with me, I would have beaten him with my fists.

10 August 1993

Anne, our younger daughter, arrived at eight o'clock last night. Her roommate in Ithaca had to track her down, as Anne was en route by car to Burlington, Vermont, for fieldwork with the Department of Environmental Conservation. By the time Anne reached Burlington, Lyn had arranged for Anne's immediate return with her co-workers, one of whom drove Anne to my house. The co-worker had to turn around and drive back to Burlington immediately. I took Anne to the hospital to see El. She gripped his good hand and said, "I love you, Dad. I know you can hear me." El opened his good left eye and squeezed her hand.

The nurse made us leave after a few minutes. "He's exhausted," she said. Anne and I ate takeout Chinese soup and fell into bed, exhausted ourselves. Much to my surprise, I fell sound asleep, the cordless phone beside me on the bed. It rang at 4:00 a.m. Dr. MR, another of MC's partners, said, "I'm sorry, Mrs. Adams. Your husband died at 3:45 a.m. He was in no pain and died peacefully."

Anne, wakened by the phone, came into my room. We cried in each other's arms. Then she made coffee and we started making a list of the people we'd have to call when daylight came.

August 13, 1993

El was buried today in a lovely rural cemetery with a view of Mohonk Mountain, not far from where we met forty-two years ago. It's beautiful enough to comfort me, though not quite as beautiful as El's beloved New Hampshire mountains.

The funeral director handed me ten copies of El's death certificate. He said I'd need them for settling legal and financial matters. Cause of death, it reads, written out by our friend Dr. MC, who had finally returned from vacation the day El died:

Bronchogenic carcinoma of the lung, squamous cell.
Onset: 1 year.
Other significant conditions: Rt. sided stroke.

August 19, 1993

Dr. MC called and asked me to sign a release for El's medical records from Cornwall Hospital. Dr. Y had called MC and asked for them, not having the guts to call me himself. "All right, M, but only because *you* asked me." In a rage, I drove to Cornwall Hospital, signed the release, and on top of the first page of El's medical records, wrote a note to Dr. Y: "Dr. Y. I am releasing these records to you only because MC asked me to. God help you and your patients."

On August 10, the day El died, Dr. Y had called to ask me how he was. "Dead," I said. After a long pause, he said, "I'm so sorry, Mrs. Adams. Has anyone mentioned an autopsy to you?" I also let a very long silence pass, before I said, *"No!"* and hung up.

August 25, 1993

Dr. Y sent me a letter offering condolences. The bastard is afraid I'm going to sue him for committing medical murder.

August 26, 1993
My first and only husband has been dead for sixteen days. The cancer cells are dead too. I can go back to work next week. But I don't know how long it will be before I can resume living my life. First, I have to do penance for outliving him.

Chapter XIV

POST MORTEM, 1943, 1972, 1977

I made my first dutiful journey to my mother's hospital bed when I was eleven, in 1943. I made what I thought would be my last visit to her on her deathbed, in 1972, when I was forty. I believed she was going to die when my stepfather called me from Ireland. "If you want to see your mother alive, you'd better come now." Mom and Eric had retired to Ireland a few years earlier to live with my sister Judy who was, at the time, attending Trinity Medical School. They were planning to live with Judy and her husband Dan *forever*. My sister had other plans; ultimately, she and Dan moved back to the United States for their residencies in New York, leaving Mother and Eric in Ireland. Meanwhile, I decided I had to see my mother before she died.

I got an emergency passport and borrowed the money for the airfare from my brother-in-law Dan. El and I were in the midst of a marital crisis, so the sudden trip to Ireland came as a relief from our troubles. I packed and left El and our sad-looking children. Unfortunate witnesses to fights between their parents, they thought I was leaving forever. It was an accurate sense of how I felt.

I arrived in Dublin on a chill, gray, rainy November day. My sister Judy picked me up at the airport and took me directly to the hospital. On the way, she said, "Mom is delirious, but she seems to be hanging on. The doctors don't know what's wrong."

We parked on a cobbled street next to a wall of wet, black stones. Despite the circumstances, I felt like a tourist. This was my first trip abroad, after all.

Judy led me into the centuries-old, stone hospital. We walked down waxed green linoleum corridors. Barrel ceilings rose above us. We smiled at nurses who recognized Judy. "Hello, doctor." Doctors who didn't recognize her stared at my thirty-year-old beautiful sister, swinging her long, chestnut hair. When we reached the nurses' station, a pretty Irish nurse, a redhead, greeted her, "Hello, doctor. Nice to see you again." Judy asked to see Mom's chart. Putting on a pair of glasses, she studied the clipboard (I didn't know she needed them).

The first time I had taken Judy to see Mom in a hospital, she was three years old and I was twelve, my pigtails recently shorn and replaced with beauty-parlor permed curls. Acne assaulted my face. A sympathetic nurse saw me, the big sister, holding her little sister's hand in the waiting room and snuck us into Mom's room. No children under twelve were allowed in those days. Mom's eyes teared up, as always, hugging her baby girl. Judy looked forlorn … bewildered by her mother's apparent imprisonment in this strange place. But she didn't ask questions or cry. She knew better, watching me. Mom stroked Judy's hair. "You have your father's curly hair! Who combed it for you?"

"I did," I answered angrily. "When are you coming home?" I added.

"Oh, these doctors! Dr. BR said he'd see how the skin grafts hold up when I dangle my legs later today."

I was so used to seeing the dollar-sized round hole on my mother's right ankle, I wasn't disturbed by the oozing puss around the tiny patches of skin grafted onto it, bits of her own skin cut from her buttocks. Her "bad" leg was raised on a pillow, the ulcer seeming to be eating the tiny grafts. Judy played with the plastic ID bracelet on Mom's wrist. We had a collection of hospital IDs at home for playing "doctor."

When Mom was allowed to come home a week later, she had to keep her leg elevated. She lay on the living room couch, doing crossword puzzles or reading a new book.

A month later, she had to go back into the hospital again because the grafts hadn't taken and were decomposing. We were living upstate, and it would take us three hours to get to the hospital in New York

City, expecting to return later that day. Judy did not want to go. "My tummy aches," Judy said as we were leaving. Feeling her forehead with a gloved hand, Mom said, "That child can run a fever at will." Mom looked beautiful in a new suit and stockings, her ankle neatly bandaged underneath, wearing high heels and a lavender net over her upswept auburn hair. "Come on, we have to hurry."

In front of the tall, white buildings of New York Hospital, we met Aunt Bea, who was taking me shopping for the day. We waved good-bye to Mom and Judy. Uncle Billy, Aunt Bea's brother, was picking Judy up to go to the zoo. I would have preferred Uncle Billy and the zoo to a boring shopping trip with my spinster aunt, a voracious bargain hunter who loved scurrying from one section of Bloomingdale's to another.

At dusk, Bea and I returned to her apartment on East Eightieth Street. It had one window in the living room; a kitchen at the far end; a sofa bed; a table; two chairs; and a small, windowless bathroom. She had wanted me to stay overnight, but I dreaded sleeping on the pull-out sofa bed in the perpetual grayness of that apartment.

Bea told me to wash my hands and set the table while she made dinner. "Who do you love best?" she demanded. "Me or Billy?" I squirmed. "I love you both the same." I wanted to go home. She made me my favorite, steak tartare. There was nothing to talk about with Bea. We ate in silence. "Now I'll wash and you dry," she said.

The evening dragged on as we played go fish. The phone rang.

"Oh, my God! Is she all right?" Bea gasped.

I held my breath. Maybe Mom had died! Bea hung up the phone. "It's Judy! She has appendicitis and they had to operate!"

I had to stay overnight with Bea after all. The next morning, we took the bus to New York Hospital. Mom was waiting outside the recovery room. "Mommy!" I cried, so glad she was alive.

She hugged me and said, "Judy's okay. Dr. BR says they got the appendix, which had burst, spreading infection into her abdomen. But she's young, the doctor said, and she should recover. Penicillin should clear up the infection." My sister's fever of 102 degrees that morning hadn't been "faked" after all.

I spent another tedious day with Aunt Bea. We met Mom for dinner that night at my favorite Czechoslovakian restaurant. I had chicken paprika and *blinchiki* for dessert. Then we went back to the hospital.

Dr. BR met us outside her room, looking grim. He pulled Mom aside. Mom turned ashen as he spoke quietly. When he left, Mom said, "Judy has a high fever again, and has developed a rash. The doctors don't know what is causing the rash." That night, Mom slept in a chair beside Judy's bed. I slept at Bea's again. I thought I'd never get back to my own room, my school, my friends in upstate New York. I didn't want Judy to die. I didn't want Mom to be sick all the time. I just wanted to live my own life.

Mom called from the hospital the next morning. I answered while Bea was in the shower. "Can you believe it?" she said. "Dr. BR called in a pediatrician, finally! He took one look and smiled and said, 'It's German measles!' Those big shot surgeons can't even recognize measles!"

Despite her dependence on them, Mom held all doctors in contempt. No doctor knew more about her body than she did. "Not enough anesthesia," she said, waking in the middle of an operation. "I'm allergic to everything," she said, breaking out in rashes with every new medication. She was always right. The doctors, like the famous Dr. BR, were challenged to prove their expertise, but ended up catering to her choices of meds, to her demands.

Judy and I now entered another hospital, another deathbed scene, this time in Dublin. As machines hummed and water gurgled, it felt like diving into deep green, underwater oceanic depths. People in the room seemed to swim in slow motion. Eric, our stepfather, raised an arm slowly, his huge bulbous head tinted green like a moldy skull; a starched nurse leant forward over a white rectangle, a bed where the only rapid movement came from the flailing limbs of our mother, as if she had tentacles that were trying to wrap around an invisible enemy.

In the center of this white rectangle, Mom's face appeared like a pale full moon. Beneath the face, a blue-flowered hospital gown hung from her collarbones as one tentacle snatched the hem of the gown and pulled it up over her head. Her legs—two more tentacles—spread wide, black fur between them like a wig over the creature's livid lips. Another nurse appeared on the other side of the bed, and the two nurses then succeeded in pinning down my mother's wheeling arms and legs and pulling the hospital gown back down over their patient's private parts. Thick, mucus-laden noises came out of Mom's mouth, "Argh rike biichh leggoo."

Eric laughed. "Isn't she hilarious?" Judy smiled, turning to talk to a doctor who has just arrived in time to witness the scene.

I stood still, fascinated, as Mom continued to struggle free from the nurses again, and climb out of the bed. Her peculiar hazy state and cursing reminded me of a familiar nightmare scene. When Daddy was working in the city all week and we lived in the country, I would come home from school to a dark, silent house smelling of cologne mixed with gin, the blinds drawn in my mother's bedroom. She would be lying naked, the blue satin comforter on the floor next to empty bottles. Shaking her hard, I'd yell, thinking she was dead. "Get up, Mommy, please get up! Wake up! Judy's crying. She needs you!"

"Go 'way!" she'd mumble, flailing her arm. I'd shake her harder, crying.

"Fuckin' brat. Go 'way. Go to your father. You love *him*."

"Please, Mommy, I need you!"

One brown eye would open, then the other, watery and unfocused. A basilisk stare. "Get out, spoiled brat."

Dr. Reid came, time after time, setting his black bag down beside the empty gin bottles. Dr. Reid was a long-time AA member. He'd give Mom a shot, calming her down. When she was conscious, he encouraged her to go to AA. She finally went to a meeting, realizing my father was never coming back to her.

So here I was, in Dublin, to see her before she died—again. The fact that my baby sister Judy was now a doctor, planning on doing her residency in the United States, leaving Mom and Eric, who had moved to Dublin to be with Judy, in the lurch, so to speak, was more than enough reason for Mom's latest death-bed scene.

Mom's glassy brown eyes widened, then focused on me.

"I think she recognizes you!" Eric said cheerily.

I took a step closer to the bed, trying to look happy, my fists clenched tight in my coat pockets. Suddenly, Mom seemed fully aware of reality and glared at me with blood in her eyes.

"Get that kid pumpy out of here!" she screamed, pointing a swollen finger at me. "Get that kid pumpy out of here!"

"Ha, ha," Eric chuckled. "She doesn't know what she's saying, 'kid pumpy,' that's a new one."

I had no idea what my mother meant by calling me a "kid pumpy"; did she mean "puppy" or "pimpy" or "pimply"? As a teenager, I had suffered from severe acne, and it still afflicts me as an older adult. My father had the same bad skin.

The nurse quieted her, "Shhh. It's your daughter you're after talkin' to, come all the way from the US to see ye. Be quiet now, Mrs."

Another doctor appeared, handsome, black haired, in a tweed jacket. He shook Judy's hand. "Good to see you, again." They huddled in a corner, discussing Mom's chart.

Mom continued to writhe, babbling obscenities, the nurse holding her legs down so she couldn't expose herself again. Finally, they tied Mom's wrists to the bed rails with gauze. Leaning over, she tried to chew the wrappings off. I was shivering, though my sweater was soaked with sweat. Eric went to the bedside. "Now, Helen, you have to stay in bed until you get better." He patted her hand ... kissed her on the forehead as if she were a naughty child being punished and sent to bed.

Judy introduced the new doctor to me. "This is my older sister, Barbara. Barbara, Sean. We met at Trinity," she said.

Sean smiled. "Well, the good news: your mother's out of danger. But the downside: it will be several days before she regains lucidity. We have to rid her body of the toxin slowly."

"Toxin? Was she poisoned?"

"Heh, heh," Eric muttered, his face reddening. "You know your mother."

I looked at Judy for the truth. She explained. "You remember when she had the clot in her intestine, and the gangrene? And they removed several feet of her small intestine?"

I remembered, of course, another deathbed scene back in the States. I nodded.

"Well," Judy explained, "they prescribed a powerful opiate, a derivative of morphine, to slow down her digestion, so the few remaining feet of healthy intestine could absorb nutrients. Without the drug, she'd starve to death, no matter how much she eats."

Eric butted in. "And your mother apparently forgot she'd already taken a dose ... or two ... I, uh, found the empty bottle after I couldn't wake her. She really likes that medicine; it makes her feel very good. She's slept like a baby for the first time in her life."

Laudanum, it sounded like. Liquid opium so beloved of Coleridge. I took a deep breath. A sigh of relief ... of resignation. Mom's new drug of choice: opium, in lieu of alcohol. Mom had been given a prescription to use it. For as long as she lived.

Sean said, waving good-bye to Judy, "Your mother will be good as new in a week or two."

My mother was *never* good as new.

Eric, Judy, and I walked to the VW parked on the cobblestone street outside the hospital.

"Let's go to the Abbey Tavern. We can have Irish coffee," Judy suggested. Though no one said it, we all felt we could use a drink. "Might as well show Barbara around since she's come so far to be in Ireland."

As I opened the back door of the car, my eye caught sight of a plaque on the blackened stone: "St. Patrick's Hospital, Founded in 1746 by Jonathan Swift, Dean of the Dublin Anglican Church, as an Asylum for Fools and the Mad." In my graduate studies, I learned Swift had suffered from undiagnosed mental problems and incurable headaches. In a mock eulogy he wrote for himself, "Lines on the Death of Dr. Swift," 1741, (he died in 1745), Swift wrote:

> He gave the little wealth he had
> To build a house for fools and mad
> And showed by one satiric touch
> No nation needed it so much.
>
> (Swift, 1962,79-80)

Feste lentina was the motto of St. Patrick's Hospital. "Hurry up and die slowly."

Judy and I flew home together on an Aer Lingus flight. The plane was full, the seats taken by an Irish rugby team heading for a game in the States. Fifteen burly footballers who played a sport with no holds barred, and a flock of Irish nuns holding prayer beads as we took off from Shannon. As soon as we were airborne, the pretty young flight attendants dressed in green wheeled out the drinks cart. Little bottles of whiskey, bottles of stout and ale, champagne, brandy, and wine flew off the cart like angels of mercy. Judy and I gratefully accepted two bottles of champagne. Less than an hour over the Atlantic, everyone was in party mode. Songs broke out, and the nuns giggled. The drinks cart came again, and nobody refused refills.

And then everyone had to pee at the same time. A line to the nearest loo blocked the aisles. I was relaxed, laughing at nothing. "Hello, darlin', where are ya from?" A ruddy-faced rugby player pinched my butt. "Sit down on me lap and I'll sing ya a song."

I was drunk enough not to mind, to smile and shake my head. When I got back to my seat, I warned Judy. The rugby guys were in full action mode, chasing every woman under fifty not in a nun's habit. The journey back to New York passed gaily, and the rugby team, legs and arms sticking out in the aisle, snored, exhaling a pub aroma.

Judy and I parted at JFK Airport, she heading for her apartment in Manhattan, and I for my home in the Hudson Valley. We had survived another death scene.

A few months before my mother's actual death, she wrote and said she and Eric were coming to visit with us over the holidays—staying for six weeks. This was October, and she said they were coming from Thanksgiving through January. I knew her: six weeks would become six years ... the rest of her life. She wanted to move back to the States and stay with Judy or me. Neither of us wanted her as a permanent guest. I wrote back and said she and Eric were welcome, for *two* weeks. Mom wrote back a letter, which I have somewhere in a box of old letters. It said, in part, "You blame me for everything! I'm not sure what we'll do. I have to think it over." I never heard from my mother again.

In January, as I was resuming my teaching duties at NYU, I got a call from Eric. He was in New York, on his way back to Ireland.

"Your mother's dead," he said. My heart stopped.

"Oh, God. Where is she?" I wondered how I could make it to the funeral in Ireland.

"Judy and I scattered her ashes in the Hudson River," he said. I could almost hear the heh-heh in his voice. Since I lived right near the Hudson, I could easily have been there. I would have liked the privilege of really saying good-bye to my mother. Mom was dead! I could hardly believe it. It was 1977. Mom was *really* dead this time. El would die sixteen years later. My father would die eighteen years later.

I did not find out some of the actual details for some time. Judy finally called and told me that Mom and Eric had flown to the States around Thanksgiving. They stayed with Judy in Manhattan until Christmas, or thereabouts. They had not said a word to Judy about their prior plan to stay with me and my family for six weeks; and neither they nor Judy told me they were staying with her in the city.

After one week, however, Judy had had enough, and had driven them to Poughkeepsie where they stayed with a former co-worker of Eric's. A widower, the colleague lived in an unheated house in the midst of an energy shortage. On New Year's Eve, the three of them sat in front of the fireplace trying to keep warm, drinking in the New Year. On New Year's morning, Eric stumbled upstairs and found Mom lying in bed, uncovered, dressed only in her underwear. She was unconscious, burning up with fever. Eric called an ambulance. At St. Francis Hospital, the doctors said she had pneumonia. She died on January third.

All this I learned a week later.

There's no place on earth like the world
There's no place wherever you be...
Never throw stones at your mother,
Throw bricks at your father instead.

(Brendan Behan 1958, 170)

In 2010, I learned from my sister that Eric had taken Mom's ashes to Ireland to scatter on the moors, but instead, left them there in the unopened can. He lied to me, getting his revenge. I never trusted Eric.

Chapter XV

LAST RITES

Parting is all we know of Heaven,
And all we need of Hell.
Emily Dickinson

Death is a black comedy, at least when it comes to the body.

A few months after El died, Bella, my stepmother, called. "How's Ellie?" she asked.

"He's dead," I replied.

"Oh, I'm sorry," she said. "Just a minute; I'll put Dave on. Dave! Come say hello to Barbara!"

My father got on the phone, "How's Ellie? How are the kids?"

I repeated, "El's dead. The kids are sad."

"Oh, I'm sorry. Are you still working?"

What I knew of death and its rituals was zero. When my relatives died, they disappeared like dreams in a sunrise. I often didn't hear of their deaths until long afterwards. Some died naturally of old age, some prematurely from alcoholism, cancer, or suicide. So what else is new? My stepfather Eric called me two weeks after my mother's ashes had been scattered over the Hudson River to tell me, "Your mother's dead." When my stepfather died some years ago, he was living in the United States, but my sister wanted his cremated remains to be buried in Ireland. Don't ask. It's a long story. I only know the tail end of the story—that his ashes were lost in transit and ended up months later on somebody's doorstep in Dublin. They were enclosed in what looked like a paint can, so it was a shock to whoever opened it. Judy eventually found the ashes and scattered them in Ireland.

In El's family, the humor extended even to the fierce patriarch, Sammit. At a family reunion held in the Etna Baptist Community center to celebrate El's mother's ninetieth birthday, my son Sam and I, along with his wife and children, wandered across the road to the old cemetery. We were looking for Sammit's and May's graves. I found the site, remembering having visited it when I first moved to New Hampshire. We studied the dark stones with the still-legible letters spelling out "George" on one marker, "Mary" on the next, and "Georgina" on the third. Georgina, their foster daughter, had died in the 1918 flu epidemic.

When we returned to the party for El's mother, I told her about finding the Adams' patriarchal graves. She laughed. "That ain't the way they was laid out," she said. "A while ago, they had to clean and reset the headstones, and when they put them back, they got them backwards. George is where Georgina's marker is; Georgina is where George's is." Except for Mary, who else would know the difference?

An exception to my family's indifference to the death of a "loved one" occurred in 1995 when Maggi, my half-sister, called to tell me Daddy had died. She invited me to the funeral—a family first for me. She loved Daddy, as I still achingly did. We talked about his sense of humor and liveliness, which she said lasted right to the end. She wanted to have him buried in the Jewish cemetery in Omaha, but was refused because Maggi had married a Christian. So Maggi bought a family plot in a nonsectarian cemetery. The Jewish service would be at the funeral home.

My husband El's death was my "first," the central fact of the rest of my life. "After the first death, there is no other," as Dylan Thomas said. A feeling of permanent abandonment struck me full force, reopening the deep wound left by my father's abandonment and my mother's emotional instability and alcoholism. El's death left me feeling alone, drifting on an ice floe that felt as if it were slowly melting in the cold sea.

I had no prior experience in dealing with a burial and a funeral. There were no handed-down lessons, no family funerals as models, and no religious rituals I had been taught. It turned out that handling the mundane matters of buying a coffin, picking out a cemetery, and deciding on who would say what at the service was a diversion, of sorts, from the fact of bodily decay. In the face of El's death and my helplessness to prevent it, it gave me something useful to do.

The doctor at Cornwall Hospital had called me at four in the morning to tell me El had died. Anne, sleeping in the next room, heard the phone. We got up and made coffee, then wrote down a list of people who had to be called. At nine, I called the rabbi of the Reformed Temple, which El and I had joined several years before. Hirshel was understanding and helpful, giving me the name of a reputable funeral director, Bob Engel. I called Bob and arranged to meet him later that morning. After Anne and I finished calling all our relatives and friends, we showered, then headed for Engel's Funeral Parlor in a nice old Victorian house with flowers decorating the fence out front. "I teach special education," he told us, "besides running this business."

"My husband was a special ed teacher too," I said, warming to this man whose private business often provokes silly gallows humor. Bob told us everything we needed to know, taking care of the sundry bureaucratic details that were already overwhelming me. "Get at least ten copies of the death certificate," he advised. "Tell me what you want in the obituary, and I'll see that it gets in the papers."

Bob brought us a color catalogue of coffins. It was like any other catalogue for furniture, I thought. This was like shopping for a permanent couch. Anne and I leafed through it casually. I felt as if I had fallen into a rabbit hole. Jews believe in the simplest coffin, Bob told us, pointing them out. Anne and I picked out a plain wood coffin for a modest price. "We can put a nice Star of David on top if you'd like," Bob suggested. Anne and I burst out laughing. Bob looked startled. How to explain our complicated family's nonreligious history to him?

"No, I don't think that will be necessary," I answered, as soberly as possible. But every time I thought of El's devout Catholic mother gazing on her eldest son lying under a Star of David, I started giggling again.

"One more thing," Bob said, "but not right away—you'll want to look at monuments for the grave. I know a very good stonecutter, honest and reasonable. David Cohen, in Rhinecliff." David Cohen would turn out to be another of those ironies of the whole piecemeal ritual I was putting together to honor El, please ourselves, and offend none of El's family: David Cohen, born and raised in the Hudson Valley, looked, dressed, and talked like an upstate yokel. I have no idea what, if any, religion he practiced. But he was honest and reliable and reasonable in cost.

Bob asked, "Where is the family burial plot?" I must have looked stupid. Such a commonplace thing was unheard of in my family.

"We don't have one," I answered, feeling ashamed by my family's eccentricity. The one fact I was going by was El's wish: that he be buried, not cremated. Had I been able to afford it, I would have sent his body "home" to New Hampshire for burial in his beloved hills near Hanover. "I'll have to find one," I said.

Anne and I got in the car and went cemetery hunting. We started looking around New Paltz, where El and I had met. Bob Engel had mentioned one, so we headed there first. We found the caretaker and looked around, but shook our heads. It was too close to a main highway where the traffic noise disturbed the peace of the interred, and was dark and gloomy. Vaguely, I had a memory of seeing another cemetery on the other side of town. El and I had found it on a back road when we were dating and looking for a private place to make love.

Back home, I looked it up in the phone book, called the caretaker, and made an appointment to see available plots. Anne and I drove back to New Paltz up Route 208, turned off on Cedar Lane for a quarter of a mile, then turned right onto Plains Road that began where the apple orchards ended. We followed its leafy trail past pleasant houses and empty fields till we came to a field of hay. Next to it was the New Paltz Rural Cemetery. The caretaker was cutting grass with a tractor. He turned off the engine and climbed down, leading us to a plot right under an ancient maple and opposite an equally elderly tamarack. El was the one who had taught me that the tamarack, or larch, is the only coniferous tree to shed its needles in the fall. I loved this tree. Facing west from the plot was an unobstructed view of Mohonk Mountain where El and I had spent many a night in his car parked near the old golf course. "This is it," Anne and I said simultaneously. "Look at that tamarack," she said. I bought two plots. I could not imagine spending eternity anywhere else except beside El.

Back at Bob Engel's, we planned a simple memorial service at Temple Beth Jacob, with a private burial for us and El's family who were driving down from New Hampshire. Everything was ready now, except what we would say and who would deliver a eulogy. Anne and I went through El's boxes of writing and picked out some of his poems and stories for the service. She put them together in a pamphlet, with a cover made of a photograph of flowers El had taken for the Camera Club. She had dozens of copies made to hand out to the mourners. Each of my children planned to say something about their father, except for Steve in Alaska, who was tending his dying wife.

I booked rooms for El's brothers and sisters at a nearby motel. I had invited El's mother to stay at my house, but she preferred staying with her youngest daughter at the motel. She couldn't stand being in the house where her oldest son had spent most of his adult life.

The day of the funeral, we left early for the cemetery. I drove my own car; I wanted to have that much control, leading the procession, since nobody else knew the way. When we arrived, Bob Engel and his assistants were standing beside the open grave, wearing black suits and yarmulkes. We got out of the cars and lined up in two rows along the grave.

The sight of El's coffin suddenly made his death a horrible reality, and my knees went weak. Our children surrounded me: Sam stood on one side, Amy on the other, holding me. Anne, crying very hard behind me, was held by her friends. El's mother stood with us, despite her infirm legs, refusing to sit in the wheelchair. Her youngest son Bob held her. Finally, a brief silence, and then the rabbi was saying a prayer and throwing a handful of earth on the coffin. I found myself unable to bear looking at it. I could see El inside, wearing the navy blue blazer, white shirt, striped tie, and gray slacks I'd picked out and given to Bob. Even his white Jockey underwear and T-shirt. Bob had been very discreet when he'd come to pick up El's clothes. After joining us for a cup of coffee in the kitchen, I handed him the shopping bag of clothes. "Did you remember underwear?" he whispered. It was ludicrous, but somehow it mattered. And then the coffin was lowered and El was gone.

The Temple memorial service was a little easier to bear. Rabbi Jaffe led us in the Lord's Prayer in English and Hebrew and said the Kaddish. Then Jim, El's best friend and a professor of English, delivered the eulogy. Jim is very good at this kind of thing, delivering celebratory poems at his friends' birthdays and anniversaries as well. He said that there had been *two* El's—I held my breath, for fear that El's darker side was known to others, as the children and I knew it. But Jim described them as follows: "the one who was talkative and insightful and humorous when alone with one or two friends; and the one who was quiet, distant, and shy at parties and in large groups. But later, in private, El made it clear that he had not missed a thing at the gathering."

I let my breath out, relieved and grateful to this kind friend, a devout Catholic.

Then Anne read one of El's funny stories and had the mourners laughing quietly. She left copies of the little booklet for anyone who wanted a memory of El to save. Amy, usually shy, got up next, remaining composed, and read a sweet essay she'd written about the things she loved in her father. Finally, Sam, our youngest, got up looking disheveled and tired—his second child Shira had been born only three weeks earlier—and read a few notes he'd scribbled, then just spoke off the cuff about the father he loved and missed, who would not see his grandchildren grow up.

Soon, I found myself standing on the bema, reading a piece I'd written about how El and I had met in college on United Nations Day. We had been together for forty-one years, and I would miss him. Then, it was over. No one had broken down. There were no flowers, no music, as is customary at Jewish funerals. I liked the silence. And I liked not smelling the sickening sweetness of dying flowers. The faces in the pews were a blur, so I still am not sure who came to El's memorial, or who was absent.

When we got back to my house, my friends Jess, Lucy, and Bev had spread the funeral feast—finger sandwiches, cakes, coffee, tea. El's mother sat on the sofa and I on a comfortable chair in the living room as the women served the food and beverages. The men took off their jackets and ties, people went to the bathroom, doors opened and closed, and the noise level rose to a normal level of conversation. The smokers went outside to smoke. Someone brought me a plate of sandwiches and urged me to eat. I heard the voices of people talking, reminiscing about El, and laughing. I hadn't seen El's brothers and sisters in a while and listened eagerly to the New England inflections I would never hear from El's mouth again. The voices surged and receded around me as I sat in my black linen suit, which I'd bought for work, not a funeral. Nobody rushed to leave. Everyone ate hungrily. Lucy asked if I'd eaten anything. I couldn't swallow. "You need a stiff drink when everyone leaves; two stiff drinks," Lucy said. I nodded. "Have enough to knock yourself out." I couldn't wait.

Everyone admired Sam's two children—Aaron, my four-year-old grandson, and Shira, my three-week-old granddaughter. El had sat in this very same chair the week before, holding Shira. She'd never know her grandfather. Aaron was old enough to ask where Grandpa was. "He's with God," said his mother. I thought it was a good answer, and wished I could believe it myself. My daughter-in-law had stayed in the house with the children during the burial service, but she'd come to the Temple for the memorial, keeping the children outside the sanctuary. As the mourners filed out, Aaron peeked inside, reading out loud the Hebrew words on the wall. Lucy was astonished by my beautiful blond, blue-eyed grandson's intelligence. People hugged me or shook my hand. I was numb, smiling mechanically. As the funeral meats were consumed, Barbara nursed the baby and Aaron ate a peanut butter sandwich. Life was moving forward, leaving El behind farther and farther, receding into the past more quickly than I could comprehend or acknowledge.

By 9:00 p.m., everyone had gone home except Anne. She was staying with me for a week. Her friend Bill had come to the memorial service to shore her up, and another friend, Sue, came the day after the funeral from New York City. Sue was supposed to bring bagels and lox for supper, but when she finally got off from work, she had to run to catch the train. Luckily, we found a cooked chicken in the freezer left by a friend of El's who hadn't been able to come to the memorial. We defrosted the chicken and made a salad. I had no appetite, but the two young women ate heartily. I drank a stiff vodka before bed and slept for an hour. Then I woke in the dark, and stayed awake till morning.

Anne finally had to go back home to Ithaca, back to work. "Don't worry," I said, "I'll be too busy to feel lonely." Classes started three weeks after El's death, and I went back to New York and my hectic job, grateful for the distraction from my sorrow. My colleagues greeted me with sympathy, patting my hands, "You wouldn't know it to look at you," said one, rather left-handedly, but not unkindly.

A week after Anne left, I drove to Rhinecliff and met David Cohen. I looked at various headstones, things that seemed ordinary and alien at the same time. They were gaudy, ugly, flowery, and not suited to either El's taste or mine. Then David showed me a bench monument, and that seemed just right—a place to sit, meditate, and remember while gazing at Mohonk Mountain. David mailed me a tracing paper sheet a month later with the lettering that would go along the front edge of the pink granite bench ("You'd be surprised how often people find misspelled names and wrong dates," he said, "so I always have it checked before I start cutting"). In big capitals in the middle it would read ADAMS, with smaller letters reading Elwood W. on the right, with the dates, July 20, 1926–August 10, 1993, beneath it. On the left, it would read, Barbara B., and the date, March 23, 1932– …

Until winter snows daunted me, I went to the cemetery every week, crying by El's raw grave. I sometimes walked around the cemetery and found graves of several people I had known in childhood, including one of my childhood friends' husband who had died of a heart attack at forty. Like me, she had put her own name on the headstone, with the blank left for her date of death. I found it comforting to see so many names of people I had known growing up in this small Huguenot college town that had been the next best thing to a family for me.

On December 1, four months after El's death, Steve called: Regina, his young wife, had died. Regina had been diagnosed with lung cancer almost simultaneously with El's. Steve had had to take care of Regina by himself, without family and only a few friends nearby. The cancer had metastasized to her brain, so she had been flown to Seattle for radiation treatments unavailable in Alaska. The radiation, in fact, hastened the spread of cancer cells. By the time she died in the dead of an Arctic winter, Steve was unable to control her: she had lost her mind.

I could barely endure hearing the horrific details. Steve's imagination worked overtime, alone in Anchorage, enduring Regina's entombment above ground. She could not be buried until the spring, when the ground thawed. Steve was haunted by the image of Regina's frozen body.

On December 3, just three days after Regina's death, my sister Judy called. "Henry's dead," she said. "He hanged himself." Her second husband, Henry, had been a psychiatrist, but had quit or lost one hospital job after another, and was unable to sustain a private practice. Judy, also a psychiatrist, and I, were separated by nine years and our parents' divorce and remarriages. She had been raised by Eric, our stepfather whom I abhorred. We were not close as a result, sending cards on birthdays and Christmas to keep in touch. So I was stunned by her announcement. "What happened?" I asked.

"Henry was in the hospital, under suicide watch. They were supposed to check on him every fifteen minutes. He tied a sheet over the shower head and hanged himself."

I couldn't take it in. Three family deaths in a row: El, Regina, and now Henry. Are multiple deaths worse than one? "Pelion on Ossa," Ian used to say when I talked of my problems with parents and husband. I had to look it up: a Greek myth in which giants piled the mountains of Pelion on top of Mount Ossa in order to reach the heavens; hence, trouble atop trouble. My husband's death tore out half my heart; the others were just part of a chronic disease that afflicts the living. I had met Henry only a half-dozen times. Judy had told me only a little of his difficulties.

I went to Henry's funeral. Judy had arranged everything: flowers everywhere, Henry's photographs (failing as a psychiatrist, he had tried to switch to photography with no more success), and a large photo of Henry, a handsome man, beside the coffin. Aunt Bea, the only relative Judy and I had in common, had refused to come. She and Henry had hated each other in their competition for Judy's attention. Henry did not allow Bea to see Anna, my niece, and Judy's only child. Judy's friends and Henry's relatives filled the funeral chapel.

She had found a young Reformed Jewish rabbi to say a few prayers, and then Judy took over the lectern. Wearing glasses, Judy read from a prepared script, describing Henry's photographs with a pointer. Then she explained why Henry had killed himself: "Post-traumatic stress disorder." I have no idea what was really wrong with Henry. Judy's diagnosis did not explain his difficulty in communication with anyone.

Then Anna, Judy and Henry's daughter, a beautiful tall teenager, got up. She spoke movingly, without notes, about her father and the trips he'd taken her on, and the fun she'd had with him. Poised, tall like her father, and more beautiful than her beautiful mother, she was a brave sixteen-year-old. Her voice caught, and she let the tears run down her cheeks.

Two deaths in one December week. A week in hell, I told my therapist, Dr. R. He was leaving for vacation but said I could contact his colleague if I needed help. And, if things got really bad, he added, I should consider going into the hospital.

The snowfall that winter broke records. My neighbor helped me clear the driveway with El's big snow blower, which was too heavy for me to handle. Sitting by the fire that crackled in the fireplace El had made of stone, I felt El getting colder and colder. I wished I could keep him warm.

The spring thaw finally came. David Cohen called me in April to tell me the footing could be poured for the bench. A week later, I went to see it. It was solid, enduring. Beautiful. I sat on it, stared at the pink-tinged clouds sailing over Mohonk, and spoke to El, continuing the conversation we had had for forty-two years.

I left a stone on the bench and went home. Another ritual I'd learned.

Chapter XVI

BEGINNINGS

Making notes on "Sailing to Byzantium"
I take out insurance
To cover the lonely voyage.

I tried to expunge El from my life—get rid of every last trace of him. I threw out, tore up, gave away, or buried every scrap of his existence. Clothes were easy. Sam took his father's new tweed overcoat he'd hardly worn, and his suede leather jacket. For a memento, he took his shaving brush and mug. I gave El's sports jackets and one good suit to my housekeeper for her husband. The rest—pants, shirts, socks, and shoes—went to the Salvation Army bin. I saved one of El's sweaters—charcoal gray with an argyle pattern—to give to our older son Steve when he moved back to New York from Alaska. That's a half-truth, however; I really kept it to hold against my face and breathe in El's aroma whenever a crying jag hit me. I did eventually give it to Steve, who still wears it. Sam left the suede jacket on the commuter train.

Our daughter Amy took a folder of her father's poems and compiled some of them into a little book she made on her computer—eight years after El died.

Sam took the carton of El's pieces—essays and stories written over four decades, most of them unfinished, all but a few still in his loopy, big hand on yellow legal paper. Now and then, Sam mentions one he's read. When the family gets together, one of the children will bring up El's "Thunderjug" story—or another one—and we all laugh sadly.

I kept leftover copies of the funeral booklet Anne made, along with letters and notes El wrote to me. One day, sorting out a box of school supplies El bought for his classes, I came across an audio tape he made of a children's story by Hawthorne—"Feathertop." I put it in my car tape player. El's soft, resonant voice with its New England accent filled my car. I stored it in the file I reserved for El. It is the only way I can still hear his voice whenever I want.

The house we'd lived in together for nearly thirty years bore evidence of El everywhere: the fireplace he built from stone, the flagstone floors in the family room and front entry, the do-it-yourself repairs to the bathroom tiles, the garage filled with his tools. El prided himself on the one skill he'd acquired from his father. Most of our furniture was old, ugly, and battered—makeshift purchases made to suit an immediate need: beds to replace cribs, six dining room chairs bought on time so we could all sit around the table for meals, a sleep sofa that weighed a ton where El and I slept to give the children all the bedrooms.

Room by room, I dismantled my house—it was *my* house now. Piece by piece, I threw out the old furniture, old dishes, old flatware. I replaced the rickety dining room chairs with solid antiques reupholstered in blue brocade. The pine coffee table I replaced with one made of bird's-eye maple. I bought new stainless flatware for everyday, and saved the sterling silver I inherited from my grandmother Abbie for special occasions. A year after El's death, I bought a new bed: mattress, box spring, and sleigh frame. The deliverymen took away the one in which El and I had slept side-by-side, made love, and fought, for decades. I couldn't bear letting any other man sleep in that bed with me.

The house needed major renovations. I would not have to overcome El's objections to get them done. A new furnace so I could sleep in safety. The old one conked out periodically, always in the dead of winter. In summers, El used to put air conditioning units into the bedroom, the living room, and the downstairs room where I have my office. The older they got, the noisier they got. No way I could lift out those heavy units and put them in the windows, then take them out again to store for the winter. Global warming was just hitting the news, so I had central air conditioning installed and slept on cool, dry sheets—no longer slick with sweat and the sweet aromas of sex.

The most expensive renovation was the kitchen. The old particleboard cabinets were literally crumbling on the inside, the knobs were coming loose, and the doors were not closing or fitting in their jambs. I had new cabinets installed made of solid light oak, then added a tiled backsplash and Corian countertops. Sometimes I just stand in the kitchen and look at it. My children love it and approve: "You love to cook, Mom. So it's worth it."

But El had left his indelible mark everywhere in my house, on me, in me. What remains is both material and incorporeal. Material: the stonework in his fireplace, his patio; the brick chimney, the slate floor, and the ceramic tiled kitchen floor. He would shit a brick if he saw the two tiles cracked by the workmen who installed the new kitchen cabinets. I've had the chimney and patio pointed up, but otherwise, all of his stonework is as solid as the Rock of Gibraltar. Every day of my life, I am in touch with the man who built them. Whoever buys my house when I'm dead will not see what I see: the Stone Man.

Sometimes I can still smell El's hayfield body odor in a closet, in a bedroom. Before it was eaten by cancer, his body exuded the aroma of pines and fresh streams full of wild trout. As I sit alone at night reading in front of a fire glowing in his fireplace, El is still sitting opposite me staring into the flames. His thoughts are far away, and he's wringing his hands—the woe of the world in those nervous hands. I sit down to eat a meal I've cooked for myself. El sits in his place, smiling, sniffing in the aromas. "Boy, no one can cook like you, Bobbie," he says to me.

Periodically, I have to clean out my bookcases and shelves. Three rows of bookshelves fill three walls of my study in the downstairs family room. El built them of brick and wood for me. There are hanging bookshelves in two bedrooms, a bookcase in another, and two more bookcases downstairs. When I can't stuff in one more book, I read the titles on the spines and make ruthless judgments about which are expendable. A pile of discards goes to a nearby nursing home, another to the annual library book sale. I came across John Irving's *Cider House Rules* a few years after El died. It's a yellowing paperback with dog-eared pages. I should throw it out, but it's one of a handful of books El read straight through, and maybe the last one he read. I put it back on the shelf. I still have his copy of Shakespeare and Pepys' *Diaries*. Tell me what you read, and I'll tell you who you are, the saying goes.

When Steve, my oldest son, moved in with me a year after his wife died in Alaska, he tore into the garage and cleaned it out. I had to watch to make sure he didn't throw the baby out with the dirty bathwater. El had built a workbench and piled it with tools, a metal toolbox, coffee cans of nails sorted by size, sandpaper, cutters, bolts, steel tape measure, coils of wire, and mason's tools. He'd screwed on a vise that will never come off. Somebody took his mason's level—I can't remember who. Steve claimed his father's trowel, the brickie's true badge of honor, and used it to repair some of the concrete in the garage floor, breaking down in tears. Anne and Sam divided up the tools I couldn't use ... the electric drill and jigsaw. Steve used his father's gas-powered chain saw to cut up trees for firewood. I've kept screwdrivers, wrenches, hammers, tape measure, and nails.

El also put up two long storage shelves in the back of the garage. They were piled with useless things: empty boxes, old blankets used for dog beds, old Ping-Pong paddles, badminton rackets, drop cloths, El's ice skates (I could not bring myself to throw them out, remembering how he skated—a sixty-year-old man learning to ice skate, pushing an aluminum lawn chair ahead of him), my ice skates, a folding camp table and stools we used once on a picnic in the Berkshires, a box of El's material for building toy houses. The detritus of a life that serves no purpose any more.

I gave the gargantuan, gas-powered snow blower to my neighbor who had helped me shovel snow the winter after El died. I bought a jazzy, light-weight, electric-powered one I can use in snow up to six inches; for deeper snow, I hire a plow. The first summer alone, I cut the grass with El's self-propelled lawn mower. But it had a manual pull cord to start, and, being left-handed, I couldn't pull it easily. I gave the mower to Anne who needed it, and hired a man to cut the grass. I like my independence.

My fear of electricity prevented me from some repairs, like replacing a broken fixture in the closet. I broke down and cried, and then called a handyman to put in the new one for me. You could say that having enough money to hire help when you need it is part of being independent.

I have a recurring fantasy, now that the house is updated, transformed to my liking. It's this: if El came back and saw the house now, he'd be very angry. He'd look around, and be really pissed at the loss of his expensive electric tools and the abuse of his chain saw Steve used to cut down dead trees. El was always mad at Steve for not taking care of his tools, or losing them. El accused me, or Steve, of "stealing" them quite often. But El himself had usually mislaid them. He'd look where Steve had patched the garage floor with his trowel and explode: "You can't do anything without fucking it up!"

But once he got over being mad at me for "hiding" his things and changing the house, in my fantasy El would calm down and say, "I like it. Looks good." Then he'd mix up a batch of mortar and go outside to point up the cracks in the stone patio, and the mortar seams in the chimney. That's the way he was. Half mad, half gentle.

El had been a good helpmate. "I married a Communist; I married a Fascist. Neither one took out the garbage," said a message I read on the ladies' room wall in Chumley's. But El did take out the garbage, and cleaned up dog vomit and children's messes as well. He sat up all night with our daughter Amy when she had bronchitis, holding a blanket over the crib and the steamer to stop her coughing. He fixed broken lamps and broken toilets, kept our old cars running.

But I still felt El's criticism or approval in every thing I did. "I told you we should have bought one," he said in my dreams, when I bought myself a microwave soon after he died. Out of pride in my cooking and fear of radiation, I had refused to get one when he was alive. Eating alone, however, it made sense. I went alone to see *Schindler's List*, thinking El would have been moved to tears by the film, and by the common humanity I felt in the theatre that night. He would also have gotten angry, rubbing his hands, and muttering, "Those dirty bastards, the Nazis—I'd like to get my hands on them." Out of loyalty to me, El had joined the Reformed Jewish synagogue when I went through a spell of having to "belong" to the Jews, to affirm my Jewish half. He seemed to be truly devout while I only paid lip service. A week after seeing *Schindler,* I saw *In the Name of the Father,* arousing *my* wrath at the English treatment of the Irish. I did not realize I had such a strong sense of loyalty to my Irish half till then. El, a "half-breed" like me—Irish mother, Yankee-English father—would have sympathized with the Irish too. I missed having El beside me in the movies.

When I went to Cape Cod a few days after El's funeral, El "came" with me. I was searching for him in the last place where we had been happy together, just before discovering he had cancer. I sat alone on the sand at Nauset Beach, staring at the ocean. I felt like Sylvia Plath, "where the sea pours bean green over blue/ in the waters off beautiful Nauset"(Plath 1961, 49). El was just beyond the breakers, I felt, and if only I could swim out and reach him ... I dreamed of him frequently— alive, standing near me, silent. I called out his name. But he never spoke.

El was with me everywhere.

The only place where El did not appear was Manhattan. At my university job, I had an identity independent of him, one I had made for myself. Twice a week, I was alone from the time I left my house at eight in the morning until I returned home at eleven in the evening. On weekends, I couldn't sit still in the house. Being able to sit still alone in a room, said Pascal, is the hardest thing to do. I hiked on Minnewaska, and walked across the Newburgh-Beacon Bridge; I went to shopping malls just to look like I had something to do. I kept losing weight. The fun part was having to buy new clothes a size smaller.

The stages of grief so unctuously described in self-help books— denial, anger, bargaining, depression, and acceptance—do not come close to explaining my feelings for those first years after El's death. Depression, anger: Yes. Bargaining, denial: No. Guilt! Lots of that. I've felt guilty since I was twelve years old, blaming myself for my father's leaving and my mother's breakdowns. I am to blame for any defect in my marriage, in our children. Acceptance? I can never accept the death of a healthy, rugged man of sixty-seven.

I started seeing other men, a strange sensation after forty-one years of marriage to the same man. I felt like a weary teenager, dating men in their sixties and seventies. It was peculiar, disorienting, rarely fun, mostly boring. But at least I knew I was still alive and could have a man in my life, if I wanted. Of course, I could hear El commenting sarcastically on each of my elderly "boyfriends." "Are you stupid? Look at these jerks:

"*Number One*: An old lecher who had a penile implant; a Jewish Buddhist with a house in Woodstock decorated with Virgin Marys and little Buddhas;

"*Number Two*: He said he came to my funeral? He said he was my friend? Hah! He's a motorcycle freak, a cripple who has to use a pump and rubber ring to get it up—his penis must feel like an icicle (it did);

"*Number Three*: What kind of bachelor won't let you sleep in his apartment? Is he a bluebeard, or just a creepy slob? He sure likes to camp out in our house every weekend, free bed and board."

Number Three, "Jonah," came the closest to obliterating El's eternal presence in my life. He looked good, in Brooks Brothers shirts, was good in bed in terms of sheer mechanics, but lacked any real joy and spontaneity. He in fact *performed* the part of being an experienced bachelor, a ladies' man, a navy vet, a literati with a degree from Penn. His act wore thin after three years, and my sexual appetite was sated. Our last fight tore off his mask, leaving him without any prepared "lines." In my house, we sat watching TV, *Gone With the Wind.*

"Look at the smile!" Jonah said, "Look at those pecs!" he said. I hate this movie, and Gable never gave me the hots. An odor crept through the air: a common human exhalation—a fart.

"Was that you?" I asked, my nose turned up.

"Who, me? I don't do that!"

"Don't be silly. Every mammal does."

"Not I!" he insisted, looking offended.

"Well," I said, "it wasn't me, and I don't have a dog to blame it on."

Jonah grabbed his duffel bag and left, never to darken my doorstep again. El would have "coldcocked the sonofabitch." I would have applauded this time.

One thing I was able to do now would have been impossible were El alive: go to writers' workshops. He would not have tolerated my absence for a week or two. He would have called me every day and then tormented me when I got back. Any time I was not in his actual sight, El assumed that I was in bed with another man. His jealous rages made my life nearly impossible. When he was alive, I did my best always to be in the house when he got home from work, except when I was at work.

I had some reservations about their worth, anyway. After all, Emily Dickinson, Walt Whitman, George Eliot, Jane Austen, Hemingway, Shakespeare, Anne Bradstreet, and every other great writer up to the mid-twentieth century hadn't ever attended a writers' workshop. There weren't any. Maybe the first was Breadloaf, inspired by Robert Frost, in the 1940s. Now there are hundreds of them offered in the United States, in Europe, the British Isles, and Canada. Their ads in *Poets & Writers Magazine* mushroom every year. Still, I wanted to try one, to test their value and my own worth as a writer.

I first signed up for a poetry workshop that met Friday evenings at the National Arts Club in Manhattan. It seemed perfect—Fridays were the hardest to get through, facing the lonely weekend. I felt excited and nervous getting ready for the first class. Being in Manhattan one evening a week for fun would be a treat.

The Poetry Society of America, which sponsored the workshop, had a tiny room on the second floor of the Arts Club. Nicholas Christopher, the workshop leader, sat at the head of a large conference table surrounded by fifteen participants squashed in as best we could. The walls were crowded with books of poetry from Aiken to Zukovsky. Except for one other older woman, the other participants looked young enough to be my grandchildren. Nicholas looked about forty. I was terrified. I had published a lot of poems, but had not had professional feedback since graduate school when M. L. Rosenthal had given me his acerbic encouragement.

Each Friday, one of the workshop students was "at bat," his or her poem having been distributed the week before. After reading the poem aloud, the writer had to sit with mouth shut until everyone else had thrown every possible criticism at it. Nicholas, an astute critic and a fair umpire, supported or rejected their criticisms, and praised the poem when praise was due. The styles and techniques of the poems varied considerably, as did the quality. I discovered that I was the only participant who'd published anything.

In the third week, it was finally my turn. I read "Middle C," my latest poem about El's death, my obsessive topic. Its imagery was taken from my renewed interest in playing the piano. Neither Nicholas nor the young participants knew the technical words I'd used: arpeggio, flats, middle C. Vicky, the only other "old woman" in the group, did play piano, and explained what the terms meant. She went on to criticize my pronunciation of "Guido," "It's pronounced 'Gee-do,' not 'Gwee-do,'" she asserted. To her credit, Vicky apologized at the next class: "I looked up 'Guido' and your pronunciation was right—'Gwee-do.'" I stopped worrying about being compared with Vicky—a lonely old woman dabbling in poetry—and began trusting myself.

The next summer, I was accepted for a weeklong workshop in fiction writing and given a partial scholarship based on my samples. The Old Chatham Fiction Workshop was led by well-known editors and agents from New York City. The roster delighted me. These famous editors and agents would help me crack my problems in writing fiction, I hoped. It was in an ideal location in bucolic Columbia County in upstate New York, the workshops held in a handsome, but un-air conditioned Quaker conference center.

The thirty or so attendees were divided arbitrarily into groups of five or six. Each day, a group had a different workshop leader—an editor or an agent. Each participant had submitted two stories beforehand, and everyone in their group was given copies to read for the workshop. To my dismay, I was first "up" in my group, led that day by Robert Glusman, a senior editor at Farrar, Straus, & Giroux. He began line-editing sentence by sentence and attacking the story line. I went stone deaf, pretending to take notes as he spoke, but I simply couldn't absorb what he was saying. Later, I tried to make sense of the gibberish I had written down, but it was useless. I was ready to pack up and go home. The Quaker camp was "dry"—there wasn't a bar for thirty miles—so I consoled myself with the flask of cognac I'd brought to ease insomnia.

I steeled myself for the second round a week later, determined to learn if I could write a story at all. The workshop leader this time was Faith Sale, another well-known editor I very much admired. She offered an overview and gave me several useful suggestions that I absorbed with only a minor wince. She asked the others in the group for their input. This story was stronger than the first one, but I was afraid the subject matter was too revealing. Elizabeth said it was so powerful she had not been able to sleep after reading it. John said it had moved him to tears. One man hated it; another said it was too painful. Faith noted that they had all been moved by it. That is the power of writing. In the two weeks at Old Chatham, I found I was not at the head of the class, but not at the bottom either. There is a *lot* of worse fiction than mine.

Two years after El's death, I saw an ad for the Spoleto Writers' Fiction Workshop, led by Rosellen Brown and Reg Gibbons in Spoleto, Italy. I had just finished reading Rosellen's novel, *Before and After*, set in New Hampshire, and I sensed a kinship with the novelist, meeting an empathetic mind through her book. Reg was a literary critic whose work I knew slightly. I sent in an application along with two stories and was accepted.

As I was packing to leave for Italy in August, I made a last-minute change in one of the stories I was bringing for analysis, substituting a nonfiction piece, "Cancer Journal," for a weak story. What the hell, I thought. It was my work, my money, and I needed professional feedback.

It was very hot and dry when I arrived in Rome, along with twenty other workshop participants. We had flown in from all over the United States and Europe, gathering at Fiumicino airport awaiting a special bus that would take us to Spoleto. After waiting three hours for everyone to assemble (one of the women participants had had her purse snatched; three kinds of police pursed the thief who had to be questioned, and the victim had to bear witness before she was allowed to leave), we were finally ready to board the bus, but the driver said, "She no start." Rosellen, jet-lagged as the rest of us, looked stunned. We thought he was kidding. He wasn't. So we put our bags and knapsacks on the bus, climbed out and got behind the bus. "Push!" Rosellen yelled. The bus rolled a few feet, coughed, and started. I fell asleep and never woke up till we arrived in Spoleto five hours later.

The rattly bus drove up a stony path to the back entrance of Bambin' Jesu. A nun hurried us in. We followed her over cobblestones, dragging our suitcases. Emerging in a heavenly courtyard, Carole—the organizer—told us where our rooms were. I had asked for a private room with a "bath." Trudging up to the second floor, I entered a tiny cell with a small window cut into a foot-thick stone wall overlooking the burnt Umbrian countryside, two narrow beds along either side, a low but ample closet cut under the eaves, and a "bathroom." The tiny bathroom had a stone floor and no door. The toilet faced the sink, so close you could pee and wash your face at the same time. The shower was against the rear wall, with no curtain to divide it from toilet and sink. The five-foot-square room flooded every time I showered. In this climate, I wanted to shower five times a day, but we got only one fresh towel each day—a rough rag to mortify the flesh.

The convent was running out of nuns. Five elderly nuns had survived, and Sister Chiara—the youngest at sixty-five—was in charge of four fragile nuns in their eighties. Sister Chiara was the only one who could speak English, running the B&B business with a cell phone, in full nun's habit, streaking across the courtyard to and from her office. On the way to breakfast every morning, I passed a nun who was staggering under a heavy load of our dirty sheets and towels as she tottered toward the laundry. Another wizened nun watered the flowers in large tubs all around the courtyard, refilling a watering can slowly and patiently from a hose in a corner. I never could figure out why she didn't just unroll the hose to water them.

In the basement refectory, twenty writers and assorted musicians (the Institute Bambin' Jesu also included opera and flute workshops) sat at a long wooden table for a Spartan breakfast of fresh café latte and fresh hard rolls. We were given refills by an elegant, expensively-coiffed woman wearing diamond earrings and necklace, and high heels and stockings. She was a very wealthy widow, we were told, who donated her services and money to this dying order of nuns. The *Signora* was always cheerful and polite, as if we were not a scruffy bunch dressed in tank tops, shorts, and sandals, asking for more rolls, hot milk, and coffee. Jars of fig jam were set at intervals down the table, along with jugs of fig juice made by the nuns. Figs were the nunnery's only viable crop and kept our bowels in working order.

Our only time of solitude during the day was from 1:00 till 3:00 p.m—the *riposo*, the afternoon nap or rest time following a big midday meal. My room was airless, except for the small casement window. I had brought a small battery-operated fan with me that I directed onto my face and chest, allowing me to sleep. During the riposo, I sat up in my bed under the window and wrote the assignment for the next day's workshop, the fan blowing a warm, dry wind across my skin and the pages of my notebook. Despite the heat and the bizarre bathroom shower, I liked my room. I liked living in the convent. For the first time since El died, I felt truly like a new person and on my own in Europe.

We met at 10:00 a.m. in two large, airy rooms before it got too hot. Reg and Rosellen divided us into two groups of ten at random every morning, so no cliques would form. Marv Hoffman, a psychologist and Rosellen's husband, sat in as a student/facilitator. We wrote something new every day, free to choose genre, style, and interpretation of the assigned topic. I felt stimulated and wrote effortlessly.

We were to have a private conference with Reg or Rosellen about the writing we'd submitted. We had brought twenty copies of our pieces for everyone to read, leaving them in what began as neat piles on a long table in one of the conference rooms. I couldn't wait to hear what Rosellen had to say about "Cancer Journal."

At 12:30 p.m., we broke for the main midday meal, meeting in a restaurant in Spoleto, where we were treated like celebrities. Bottles of cool white wine and mineral water waited on each of several round tables. We sat anywhere, continuing to talk about writing as we feasted on excellent northern Italian food—Parma ham and melon, Caprese salads, veal, risotto, bread salads, fresh fruits. I suddenly realized that I was happy! I was having a good time with people I'd never met before. My former life married to El seemed like a distant dream. *This* now was my life.

Rosellen proved to be the catalyst I'd needed to leap forward. She and her husband Marv knew how to encourage while pointing out strengths and weaknesses in each person's work. One morning, Marv was crossing the courtyard and stopped me. "I just read your 'Cancer Journal,' Barbara. It's very moving. I think you'd like to read this book I just finished reading." He handed me *The Place He Made* by Edie Clark, a memoir of her husband who had died of cancer. They, too, were from New Hampshire. "It might have some bearing on what you're trying to do." I read it that night, quickly, and was amazed at the coincidences in my life, El's, and theirs. It helped show me the direction I wanted to follow.

One morning, Rosellen assigned us to write a piece with conversation. We had read a poignant story by Michael Cunningham as an example. During the riposo, half-dozing under the breeze from my trusty fan, I quickly wrote a piece. Since El's death, the phone would wake me in the middle of the night. I would listen, waiting to hear another ring, expecting bad news, but it stopped. I was never sure if the phone had actually rung, or if I had been dreaming. I imagined a conversation for my story, "Conversation in the Dark."

I volunteered to read first the next morning.

Conversation in the Dark

The phone is ringing. 2:30 a.m. The dial tone buzzes when I pick it up. No one there, again.

I scream at the dead phone. "Why do you keep calling me if you have nothing to say? It's been two years! You should have accepted reality by now. I *know* it's you. I called the phone company and had them check my line. The supervisor said there was no record of any incoming calls at 2:30 a.m. 'Maybe you were dreaming,' she said. What do they know? I'm a light sleeper, and my hearing is as good as a cat's.

"Damn you! Either say something or leave me alone! I've been looking for you for two years, in all your favorite haunts. You've always just left. Just once, I caught a glimpse of you last fall, as the sun was setting. You were standing on the hill in back of our house, you and your Uncle Allan, with fishing poles over your shoulders and a dozen fresh-caught brook trout hanging from a string. You looked so happy for a change. You always loved fishing. Remember the first time you cooked brook trout for me? I was hooked. 'They have no scales,' you said, gutting them, cutting off their heads, and washing them. Then you rolled them in flour and dropped the red-dotted silvery blue fillets into sizzling bacon fat, over hot coals. I never tasted anything so sweet. I knew then you would always take care of me. Why did you leave me? Traitor!"

The phone is ringing again. 2:30 a.m.

"Hello? Are you there?"

"Hello, Little Squaw. "

"It's *you*! Thank God! "

"You're not angry with me anymore, are you?"

"No, my darling. I'm not angry anymore. Please, talk to me—tell me how you are. I've missed you so much."

"I was so tired—you have no idea how tired I was. I've been catching up on sleep—two years already! Allan, who got here before I did, came by one day and said, 'Let's go fishing, El.' That was the day you saw me. We sure caught a lot of fish that day … over the limit. Allan always knew the best places to find wild brook trout. He kept them secret from everyone but me—not that it matters now. I never would have grown up if it hadn't been for Allan. You know how mean Dad was to me."

"I remember, dearest."

"I've been calling you, Bobbie, because I'm getting really sick of sleeping and fishing as much as I want. A permanent vacation isn't much fun after a while. Remember Prince Hal? 'If all the year were playing holidays, / To sport would be as tedious as work.' Hal was lucky, though. He quit fooling around doing nothing to win the war and become the king. I can't quit 'playing holidays.' I've been downsized for good."

"You always did love Shakespeare. I was so impressed by how much you had memorized."

"I'm sorry if I've been waking you up. I didn't want to let you go—I still don't. It hurts to see you having fun without me—I've been keeping my eye on you, you know. When I left, I was really pissed that you didn't come with me. I'm jealous—I've always been jealous—of your enjoyment of everything, your vitality. I knew you'd be all right without me, but I don't like it. Not one bit.

"God, was I tired! I couldn't go on any longer. Please forgive me for leaving you. I still—always will—love you. Anyway, it's about time you took care of yourself and not me. You took such good care of me. I was afraid you'd get sick by neglecting yourself for so long. You did break down, as I feared, when I had to leave for good.… I found you that nice Dr. R, didn't I? Give me credit for that, at least. I can see you're getting better now.

"Those guys you've been seeing—Good God, Little Squaw! Are you trying to prove that women can be just as stupid as men? At least you came to your senses and dropped the first two. And the third guy, Jack, you thought he was great. He seemed okay at first. But watch out—he's a phony. What's more, he's got the taste of a truck driver for diner food. He doesn't even appreciate your cooking, for God's sake! He makes me look pretty good, I think. I wasn't so bad after all, was I?

"Well, time to say goodnight. Goodnight, my dearest Little Squaw. Ma always hated it when I called you that, but you knew I meant it as a compliment—you could handle a gun and walk in the woods as good as an Indian. I'll be here waiting for you, when you're ready."

"Wait! Please don't leave me again! Stay a while. Talk to me, please! Where can I find you? Oh darling, I miss you so much. Don't leave me anymore!"

The phone is ringing. 2:30 a.m.

"Hello! Why won't you say anything? Why won't you talk to me anymore?"

"Because you're not listening to me anymore. You've figured out how to get along without me, finally."

6:00 a.m. The phone didn't ring last night. I must have slept too soundly.

The workshop participants sat in silence. "Who are the speakers?" Rosellen asked. They were baffled. "The caller is dead," she explained. Everyone looked mystified. "I can understand it clearly," said Rosellen. "She's talking to someone who died recently."

For me, it had been an experiment and became a catharsis. I told Rosellen later that it was based on the seemingly supernatural experiences I'd had after El's death, like actually "seeing" him once, in the sky at dusk. And I had heard his voice and felt his presence countless times.

As my personal conference with Rosellen drew near, I kept thinking about "Cancer Journal," trying to see what more I could do with it. Then, a truly bizarre thing happened. The night before our conference, I dreamed that Rosellen had to cancel it because a relative in the United States had died and she was flying home for the funeral. In my dream, we all flew home, but were supposed to return to Spoleto the following week. As I landed in New York, I couldn't decide if it was worth returning to Spoleto. I wanted to get to work on writing by myself.

After breakfast the next morning, I ran into Rosellen's husband Marv in the courtyard. I told him about my dream. He looked stunned. "No one told you last night?" he asked.

"Told me what?" I replied, puzzled by his sidelong look.

"Rosellen's mother died yesterday. We have to leave tomorrow for the funeral. We're doubling up conferences today to make the flight to

JFK tomorrow. We'll see you an hour earlier than we planned." I was stunned. I had not heard anything about Rosellen's mother's death before my dream. El's death had somehow heightened my sensitivity to feelings beyond the normal range.

I arrived for my one o'clock conference in the lobby of the only hotel in town, and the only air-conditioned room in it. Marv had told Rosellen about my dream. "You must have psychic power," she said. "I believe you have a special gift." Then she and Marv launched quickly into comments on my short story. "It reads like a European story," said Rosellen. "The characters are strong, well-defined, and the dialogue here"—she turned to a page—"is right on. But it needs more action, more analysis of the relationships, the *why now.*"

"An engine," agreed Marv.

Then Rosellen picked up "Cancer Journal." "This," she said, shaking it, "is powerful. I want to know what happened before—what led up to this. You need to expand it. It has the ring of truth."

I'd been afraid to show "Cancer Journal" to anyone at all before coming to this workshop. The night before, one of the participants knocked on my door and said how moved she and her husband had been by "Cancer Journal." Two others stopped me after breakfast to tell me the same. I was elated and stunned. I wasn't sure how I would expand it, but I was certain now that it was the right course for me.

That evening, before flying back to the States for her mother's funeral, Rosellen and Reg gave a reading on an open patio overlooking the terraced hillsides of Spoleto. Rosellen, looking elegant with her dark hair upswept in a roll and dressed in a graceful red print, read from a laptop—she hadn't been able to find a printer to print it out. It was a piece she'd been writing about her mother. Her voice cracked and tears welled in her eyes under the black Umbrian night. The sky filled with stars, and the air was sweet with flowers. When the readings were over, we took snapshots of the group with Rosellen and Reg and Marv, and of each other. We crowded around Rosellen, crying, as she hugged each one of us. When she got to me, she stood back a moment and said, "You're going to do fine. You're a serious writer," then she hugged me, tightly.

Appendix:
The Famous Thunderjug Story

Commentary on El's Story

El typed "The Famous Thunderjug Story" himself on the self-correcting typewriter I'd bought him. I have made only minor corrections in spelling, punctuation, and grammar. He wrote as he spoke, honing his stories to a polish, telling them over and over to our children, our friends, his students. As I typed El's manuscript into my computer, I could hear his voice—where he would pause, where he would laugh and shake his head, where he would wring his hands in alternating sweet remembrance and bitter anger.

Recalling how El told family stories, my children and I loved the one about Sammit's baptism and the epithet used by his grandfather, "Great Caesar's toenails, man! Are you tryin' to drown me?"

And we loved El's new epithets, especially when he was in a good mood. But I dreaded hearing his "whoreballs" and "cocksucker," ubiquitous as "and" and "the" in El's dictionary. Our favorite was "Standard futnuts!" It became a family code for anything interesting.

THE FAMOUS THUNDERJUG STORY
By
Elwood Adams

We were not homeless, but we were as close to being homeless as it is possible to be, and still have a home. My father had built it out of a torn-down chicken coop. It had no foundation, and you could look through the floorboards, if you had a flashlight, at the good earth, just a foot below. It had few windows, although there was an enormous piece of glass in front of the sink that had been salvaged from god knows where. My mother named it "the shack," and shack it was. I am sure that many slave quarters in the old south had more amenities.

There was no water, and no prospect of water. My grandfather Fields endlessly blasted with dynamite in a large excavation of solid ledge near the shack without producing a trickle of water. He enjoyed blasting immensely, and always had a big grin on his face when he carried a few sticks around with him in one hand with his cigarette in the other. This lack of water was strange because several dowsers had surveyed the same location and the apple crotch had twisted strongly down to that unrelenting ledge just below the ground that was as dry and devoid of moisture as a sand dune in the remotest desert.

So all the water had to be horsed in from my grandfather Sam's farm half a mile away. We used forty-quart milk cans. Water was always rationed, frozen in winter, and tepid in summer.

The toilet was a joy in itself. It was a kind of afterthought after the men helping my father build the house had almost run out of lumber. The architects had found some adjoining trees that served as uprights and nailed scraps of wood as children might to build a tree house a slight way into the young maple sugar orchard in back of the shack. Two young saplings about four inches through served as the doorless entrance to this woodsy retreat. Forest animals and insects soon moved in, or those already in residence simply stayed. It did have a roof of sorts covered with a couple of strips of tar paper left over from siding and roofing the little shack.

My grandmother Fields, who was rather stout, with large breasts, always had difficulty entering the facility. She could not, because of her breadth, assault the toilet head-on, but was forced to enter sideways, one big breast at a time, which, since she was a sweet and simple person, made her giggle. Sometimes, after this successful maneuver, she would exclaim, "God save us!" or "Jesus, Mary, and Joseph!" One always checked the readiness of the body for evacuation, the toilet being at a considerable distance into the grove from the main domicile. At night, it was not uncommon to see a deer, or meet a hedgehog in the doorway.

But back to the shack itself. There was one room that served all the many features of a common house. When we first moved in, there was no other access to the loft but a ladder where some of us had to sleep on cots. There was no floor in the loft, if I may call it that, just a few leftover boards that were warped out of shape and unsuitable for the sidewalls of the habitation. These boards were rationed out under the legs of beds, with a sensible runway to the ladder, and another to the pisspot.

Among many other things, my mother complained about the ladder, and justly so, for she was pregnant. My father, in due course, consulted with his brother Ben, a carpenter, and an agreement was reached. In a couple of months, Ben arrived with a truck and a staircase in pieces. It was soon assembled and erected against the east wall leading to the center of the shack so that it wouldn't be necessary to stoop when one reached the top. It was a great staircase of maple, by far the most splendid part of that extremely crude edifice. The stove nestled beneath the stairs, allowing no great loss of space, which was a most valuable commodity in a shack of one room and a loft for five people. This was not counting the occasional visitor.

Coming out the front door of our new home, there was quite a drop to the ground, but once again my father came to the rescue with a large boulder, which made the descent far less strenuous.

There was no direct route to the shack. To get there by car or horseback, one came by the field road that followed the fence from my grandfather Sam's farmhouse, about a third of a mile away. There was a stone wall around the front grounds, and over the stone wall, the Hayes' pasture, and the Paines' pasture divided by another stone wall. In order not to go backward on the way to school, my two brothers and I crossed the pastures, went over the three stone walls, and went through a fence to reach the town sheds. A short walk down a dirt road brought us to the main road and civilization.

I did not really feel deprived while living in the shack. I looked at it as a kind of adventure. There were all kinds of things to explore in the fields, pastures, and woodlands that surrounded the place. Maybe to feel deprived, one has to have something relative to compare it to, and I just wasn't aware of the relativity yet.

We moved into the shack in early spring when I was seven years old. It was 1933. Every little basin in the fields and woods was full of black water from melting snow. In every one of these depressions, there were frogs whose high peeps made of nighttime a stirring chorus under the bright moon. First, there were frogs' eggs in the little ponds: gelatinous globs of future pollywog, then thousands of tadpoles like giant sperm flipping their tails beside sunlit rocks. The frogs were hard to catch, but we soon got jars of pollywogs. Crows cawed in the almost silent countryside. There were no planes, no trucks, just an occasional car thundering over a distant planked bridge. This was the only interference with the songs of birds, the chatter of squirrels, and sometimes the distant bawling of a cow. You could hear the insects, the crickets, the flies—even the high hum of a mosquito. Millions of fireflies flew over the meadows and pasturelands on a summer evening. My brothers and I would have a contest to see who could catch the most. Everything was exciting and fun as we roamed our way through fields, pastures, and woodlands, making up games as we went along.

I have never bent birches, but I have swung maples, climbing up saplings, balancing on the trunk, then swinging out to the ground. They are much more fun than birches would be because they have more spring in them. It seemed as if there was always something to eat that summer too. In June, the strawberries grew red around the stones in the pastures. We would find patches of the succulent, wild berries, and spend an hour or two eating them. Sometimes, it was fun to gather a lot of them, and eat them all at once. Later, there were green apples. We used to pull young carrots out of the garden, take off the tops and clean them and eat them. Later, there were black raspberries in the woods and along the sides of the old dirt roads. We found patches of raspberries and blackberries too. You could eat peas out of the garden raw.

Often, we went fishing, catching trout in the brook that tumbled and sang its way through the valley. There were many pools and waterfalls along the way, water skates to look at, dragonflies that hovered in the sunlight, and choruses of birds. The water was so clear that you could see the polished stones on the bottom of the deepest pools. We always caught trout.

Trout are easy to clean. You don't have to skin them. We would take them out in the woods when we got home and dig a hole in which to put the heads and innards. Then my mother would cook them for supper.

And there were excitements that summer in 1933. Yes, quite a bit of excitement.

There were always plans in my family, or, I should say, schemes. A plan has something about it which would suggest order and direction; a scheme is concocted out on the battlefield of life and is more an act of desperation. Plans were beyond us. Everyone knew the limitations of the shack, and my father, pushed to the limits of desperation by my mother's complaints, was forced into action. Yes, improvements had to be made. He forthwith bought all the beer and spirits he could afford, and after consultation with his rather weird friends, decided what we needed was a well.

I can remember the selection of the diviner—the very nervous, hyperactive Uncle Bob. It was agreed that the best crotch for finding a vein of water was from an apple tree, although the reasoning escapes me—probably because someone once had been lucky to find the water table with an apple crotch. A diviner makes sure that the crotch will seem to bend down toward the earth by bending the limbs of the crotch in his hands, and then, unconsciously letting the tension-laden top go down where he believes water may be found. Uncle Bob was believed to be endowed with the magic touch, and it was believed that the tension applied to the stick had very little, if, in fact, anything to do with it. The crotch had a power of itself, and would only twist down where water was to be found. I can see him marching about the field and, finally, when he reached a low point by the fence, Bingo! He grimaced, seemed to fight with the power of the crotch as it twisted down to the ground.

"That's it," he said, grinning.

"You better make sure," said my father, and everyone nodded his head.

"All right, but that's it," said Bob, mentally marking the spot.

Sure enough, the stick would bend down only in that spot which was a little depression on our hilltop.

Digging began promptly but proved difficult. There were boulders and hard ground that required frequent use of the pick. The crowd thinned in inverse proportion to the difficulty of the task, and it wasn't more than a few hours before they ran into solid ledge: out of beer and out of spirits. My father came into the shack and said, "I guess we will have to get Benny."

Benny was my grandfather Fields, my mother's father. Most of my life he was out of work and so bored he was usually available. In the middle of the Depression, it was hard work to find work in the woolen mills in the surrounding towns, but I think even in good times he would not have worked a lot. He liked to scheme about getting on top of things. If he was digging, there was the possibility of finding gold and becoming rich, owning a large house with servants, and having a big car. His favorite fantasy, which I must have heard a hundred times, concerned the fish business. Say he had enough money to buy a truck (chances are, he'd have headed for the nearest place to buy booze). He would go to Portsmouth, New Hampshire, buy fish, take it home, and sell it at a nice profit. Soon, he would buy more trucks—Fields' Fresh Fish would make him rich.

Grandfather Fields, as I said, was usually available for my father's little schemes, especially if he could think of something that would need blasting, and the ledge where the well was supposed to be would require a lot of dynamite.

I think that farmers could easily get dynamite in those days for blasting out stumps, and for other uses around the farm. There seemed to be no trouble getting it and a device for setting it off. It was a black box with a handle that you pushed down with both hands—a sort of detonator. There was also a coil of wire hooked up to the dynamite which allowed the blaster to get a safe distance from the explosion.

When interested, my grandfather could really get going. He got himself a star drill and soon was drilling holes for the dynamite. I can remember him walking around with a stick of dynamite in each hand. My mother would say, "Don't get too close to the house with that!"

"Can't hurt you any. There's no caps in it yet." This with a big grin on his face. He was in his element.

When it came time to blast, we all had to clear out of the shack because the well was too close for comfort. We would all get a couple

215

of hundred feet back, and grandfather Ben would touch her off. A great crop of stones and rocks rose out of the well and pummeled the roof of the shack, the jagged ends making little holes in the tar paper, some rocks just missing the windows.

"God damn!" exclaimed Ben. "I guess I better put something over that hole next time!"

Not only was he blasting several times a day in the well, but seeing he was there, and it was really crowded in the shack, Ben got the idea that we ought to put on an addition. My father wasn't all that keen on it, but what the hell, if Benny wanted to dig a foundation for him, he'd go along.

So Ben dropped the well project, which had got a little tiresome anyway, and commenced to dig in back of the shack. He put up batter-boards, pulled some lines, and started to dig. But once again, just below the surface of the ground, he ran into ledge.

"Reat," he says, that was my father's nickname, "we've got to get a couple of cases of dynamite."

I know that there was something not quite aboveboard about the acquisition of the second consignment of dynamite. Little overheard scraps of conversation about a shack near a construction site that had cases of it. Maybe Henry could get some. Anyway, in a few days, Grandfather Ben had plenty of explosives which seemed to set him on fire with ambition. He pounded holes in the granite ledge as though possessed. Then he stuffed in the dynamite, put the electric wires in place, told my mother to fasten everything down, and sent us all up on the hill. I was pretty excited, and my brothers, younger than myself, were at least as keenly interested.

Grandfather Ben was between the shack and where we were. He turned, gave a big grin, spit on his hands, and touched her off. Immediately, there was a big explosion at the back of the shack. Dust boiled, stones flew, and when everything had settled, one could see that most of the tar paper was gone from the back of house. "My Land!" exclaimed my mother.

In spite of the constant blasting, there was very little progress. The poor shack was riddled with holes, and you could smell the explosive's odor and rock dust in the house. Ben just wasn't getting the same kick out of it anymore either—those holes in the ledge came pretty hard. I saw him sit one day, light a cigarette, and think about the situation. He came into the shack and announced that he had to find a job. He'd go over to Queechee and see if they needed a spinner tomorrow. The well and the foundation were to remain an unfinished dream.

The shack had its inconveniences to be sure. As I have mentioned, there was no water, no electricity, no plumbing, no wallboard, and now, in many places, no tar paper because it had either been blown off by the dynamite explosions or the flying rocks and stones had made holes in it.

Everything was all right, though, until one night when my father was entertaining a guest and we had the most terrific downpour. My father had returned from work with one of his bricklaying cronies, Frank McLaughlin. Frank came from one of the bigger New England cities, I think maybe it was Manchester, New Hampshire. He was a big Irish guy, good-natured and affable. We had an uneventful supper, and then the wind came up, thunder began to roll in the hills, lightning flashed through the big window over the sink, and the shack shuddered on its very foundation. Rain came in sheets. The wind roared. Water began to come through the wall in the back of the shack next to the uncompleted foundation, and we had to move the bed and the sewing machine. There were soon a few pitter-patters on the floor, and my mother got a can and put it under the leak. Soon, we had every available pot, pan, pail, jar, and even the frying pans under the leaks, which still could not be contained.

My father and Frank sat beside the stove partaking of old John Barleycorn. They were pretty mellow and philosophical about the whole thing as the wind roared, the lightning flashed, and thunder crashed outside, while the little drops made music in all the pans, pots, kettles, and cans, hissed on the wood stove, and steamed on the stovepipe.

"Reat," said Frank to my father, "we've got to do something about that roof!"

"I know it, Frank, we really should," answered my father, his speech a little slurred, "but I don't think we can do much about it tonight."

My mother was so disgusted and overwrought, she went up the maple stairs to the loft, walked the crooked boards, and went to bed. We all arranged our chairs so as to stay as dry as possible. "Can't we do something, Reat?" Frank asked.

"No, Frank, there's nothing we can do till tomorrow."

Frank told a story about being out of work the previous winter and running out of firewood. The house got cold, and the kids started to cry, so he took an axe and saw to the cellar stairs. When that was gone, he started to burn the furniture. He was evidently a man of action, but at the moment, his speech was blurred and he probably couldn't have got out of his chair without staggering.

"Reat!" he kept saying, as the rain hissed on the stove and plunked into the pans. "We've got to fix that roof! This is terrible!"

"Frank, I know it. We'll get to it first thing in the morning."

Just then, a large drop hit the globe of the kerosene lamp and it cracked and fell apart; the flame flickered and smoked. We all went to bed in the dark. The next morning, the sun was up and there was a beautiful, blue sky.

Sometimes, we would go down to my grandfather Sam's farmhouse and join him in whatever he was doing. One day, after it had rained, my brothers—Fred and Roger—went down with me to see what he was up to.

He had the horses hitched up to a homemade road scraper. "What yuh doing, Sammit?" I asked.

"Well, it's a good day to scrape the road and fill in some of those holes. The ground's softer after a rain."

"Can we go with you?"

"Sure, my chickens. A little more weight on that scraper will make it work better!"

So we all piled onto the scraper, he clucked the horses, and off we went scraping the road. The road was flat where the house was, on a little plateau, and then there was a fairly steep hill leading to the main road. We scraped all the way down the hill to Barnes Brook just before the main road, then took a rest.

"This used to be a main road. The town still owns it. They pay me to keep it up," Sam explained.

"Where did it go?" asked my brother Fred.

"It went up the lane which we use to drive the cattle up into the pasture now, past Chipmunk Knoll, over the land owned by the Water Company, past the 'Old Place,' and came out by the Jones's place.

Nobody uses it anymore, but the town is responsible for keeping this part of it up. They plow it in winter. Saves me a lot of work."

We headed back up the hill scraping the other side of the road, which had a high bank with a stone wall on top of it. Suddenly, when we were halfway up the hill, the scraper jarred a large rock loose on the steep bank. It came down, bang, on the scraper before anyone could move. We were all barefoot, including my grandfather, because no one wanted to get their shoes wet after the rain.

"Whoa! Whoa! Is everybody all right?"

"Yes," I said. "I'm all right." I hadn't felt anything. Then I looked at my second toe. It was flat, and blood was oozing out of it.

"No, I'm not," I said. "I think the rock hit my toe."

Grandfather Sam looked at my toe and said to my brothers, "You better get him up to the house and have May look at it."

I hobbled up to the farmhouse. By then, the toe was beginning to sting. My grandmother put some hot water and creolin into a bucket and had me put my foot in it. My toe began to throb. She put a bandage on it and I hobbled home. With every passing minute, my crushed toe began to throb harder.

My mother soaked it, too, but I was in agony. When my father got home, they decided that he should take me to the doctor who was in Lebanon, about five miles away. After we had supper, he helped me into the car and away we went.

Dr. Burnham had his office in his home. It was a nice brick house on a quiet street. There was a small waiting room with several people ahead of us when we arrived. We waited. He had no receptionist or nurse. It was the days when the general practitioner did everything from tonsils to anus, from deliveries to closing the eyes of a lost patient. He made house calls, and attended patients in the local hospital. Dr. Burnham was a step beyond creolin, and, when he was successful, somewhat better than prayer.

After a time, a patient came out followed in a minute or two by the good doctor. He was a tall man, around thirty-five or forty, dressed in a brown suit with a vest. He had a gold watch chain, wore spectacles, and there were long silences between his sentences.

"What seems to be the matter?" he asked my father.

"Stone fell on his toe. We thought you'd better take a look at it," responded my father.

Dr. Burnham turned to the other patients. "Can I take a look at this boy? It'll only take a minute." They agreed.

He put me on the table, unbandaged my foot, and took a long look at my squashed toe. Then he said to my father, "You'll have to take him down to the hospital. I'll be down as soon as I take care of these patients." He didn't say anything to me. It seemed to be between him and the toe.

It was the second time in my life I had been in a hospital. We waited there for quite a long time. Finally, the doctor came hurrying in. "Sorry, it's been a busy day."

They brought me into the operating room. I don't think they took my clothes off or anything. The doctor and my father huddled together and talked in low voices. I heard the doctor say, "So you want to stay here and watch? Sure you'll be all right?"

Then he went in back of me and fussed around. The next thing I knew he was putting something over my face. "Breathe deeply!" he said, giving the ether himself. I tried to sit up, but they held me down, and then I woke up sick as hell, my foot throbbing, in the shack.

"He's coming to," my mother said. "He's all right!"

"How did I get here? My foot hurts awful!"

"The doctor said to put some pillows under it. I'll get some," she said.

I don't think I was a very good patient. There were no painkillers in those days, and it hurt terribly, but in a few days I felt better. I asked my mother what the doctor had done.

"I didn't want to tell you this," she said nervously. "The doctor had to cut off your toe at the first joint."

"You let him do that!" For some reason, I was terribly, terribly angry. I was mutilated in some way, terribly mutilated.

"He couldn't do anything else. It was all squashed," she explained.

For days, I was so terribly angry I could hardly speak to my mother and father. But after a couple of weeks, I was able to walk and I felt better. Really, the lost toe never bothered me. In fact, it became something of an asset. I used to show the stub to my most intimate friends.

My mother told me years later that my father had fainted during the operation.

The toe was really nothing, but I nearly lost my life while we lived in the shack. One morning, I heard my father get up. I guess I probably heard him every morning because we were all right there, not so much as a partition in the whole structure. He made his way from their bed along the runway in the loft to the great staircase. Soon, the sound of the rings of the wood stove came; you could hear him assembling the kindling, then the splash of kerosene. There was a scratch of a match and a loud whoosh, the closing of the rings, and the adjustment of the dampers.

Pretty soon, between the pleasant smell of wood smoke, I could hear the frying of a rasher of home-smoked bacon, and the louder frying sound of eggs. I knew he was putting homemade bread on the back rings to toast. He was making a feast for himself. I could feel his satisfaction coming up with the smells and sounds.

Suddenly, I had to pee. The thunderjug, I noticed, was directly over the table. You could see the whole table through the open spaces in the island of crooked boards with the bacon and eggs, the toast, and my father, just getting ready to sit down. I was watching him, and hungry, when I should have been watching the crooked, loose board on which the night's solutions were so precariously standing. The second I did it, I knew that I had done something irrevocably wrong. I watched in horror as the pisspot was propelled into the air, made a perfect flip, and the turds and piss rained down on Dad, his rasher of bacon, his eggs, and his homemade toast!

A horrible growl came from my father as he ran up the stairs. I was too startled to move. My mother, who was sick, reacted instantly, and with almost the speed of light, somehow managed to get over the crooked footway to reach red-faced Dad at the top of the stairs. "Who did that?" he screamed, dripping with piss.

"Reat! Reat! It was an accident! You know those boards should have been nailed down! Don't, Reat, don't!"

Slowly, he turned and began to curse. It was a great curse with his whole construction vocabulary and anything else he'd picked up along life's road. He slammed the front door, as much as it would slam. The car roared to life, and he sped across the fields, sometimes, I suppose, actually leaving the ground. My father never loved me after that—to him, I was forever the Pisspot Kid! Sometimes, his mouth would quiver, even in old age when he looked at me, and I would feel an instant rage.

References

Adams, Barbara Block. *The Enemy Self: Poetry and Criticism of Laura Riding*. Ann Arbor, MI: UMI Research Press, 1990.

Adams, Barbara. *Hapax Legomena*. Lewiston, NY: Mellen Poetry Press, 1990.

———. *The Ordinary Living*. Lewiston, NY: Mellen Poetry Press, 2004.

Beers, Clifford. *A Mind That Found Itself*. New York: Doubleday, 1907. Reprinted with preface by Robert Coles. Pittsburgh: University of Pittsburgh Press, 1981.

Behan, Brendan. *The Hostage* in *Brendan Behan, The Complete Plays*. New York: The Grove Press, 1958.

Brontman, L. and L. Khvat. *The Heroic Flight of the Rodina*. Moscow: Foreign Languages Publishing House, 1938.

Chemotherapy and You: A Guide to Self-Help During Treatment. U.S. Department of Health and Human Services, Public Health Service, National Institute of Health. National Cancer Institute. NIH Publication No. 91-1136. Revised June 1990. Printed November 1990.

Clark, Edie. *The Place He Made.* New York: Villard Books, 1995.

Cox, Barbara G., M.A., Ed. S. David T. Carr, M.D. and Robert E. Lee, M.D. *Living With Lung Cancer: A Guide for Patients and Their Families.* Gainesville, FL: Triad Publishing Company, 1992.

Diagnostic and Statistical Manual of Mental Disorders: DSM IV, 4th edition. Washington, D.C.: American Psychiatric Association, 1994.

Dickinson, Emily. *Final Harvest: Emily Dickinson's Poems.* Edited by Thomas H. Johnson. Boston: Little, Brown, 1961.

French, Marilyn. *A Season in Hell.* New York: Knopf, 1998.

Frost, Robert. *The Poetry of Robert Frost.* New York: Holt, Rinehart and Winston, 1969.

Gilbert, Sandra M. *Wrongful Death: A Medical Tragedy.* New York: W. W. Norton, 1995.

Jamison, Kay Redfield. *Touched With Fire: Manic-Depressive Illness and the Artistic Temperament.* New York: Free Press, 1993.

————. *An Unquiet Mind.* New York: Vintage, 1995.

L'Engle, Madeleine. *Two-Part Invention. The Story of a Marriage (The Crosswicks Journal, Book 4).* New York: Farrar, Straus & Giroux, 1988.

Longfellow, Henry Wadsworth. In *A Treasury of American Poetry.* Edited by Allen Mandelbaum and Robert D. Richardson, Jr. New York: Gramercy Books, 1999.

Matthews, T. S. *Jacks or Better: A Narrative by T. S. Matthews.* New York: Harper & Row, 1977.

McGoldrick, Monica and Randy Gerson. *Genograms in Family Assessment*. New York: Norton, 1985.

A Patient's Guide: Memorial Sloan-Kettering Cancer Center. New York: 1991.

Patient Information Chemotherapy Fact Card: Edatrexate. Patient Division of Nursing, Division of Pharmacy, Department of Medicine. Memorial Sloan-Kettering Cancer Center. New York, 1990.

Patient Informed Consent for Clinical Research. Appendix A. #91-81A (3). Memorial Hospital, New York. Amended, 1990.

PDQ Information for Patients: Non-small cell lung cancer. National Cancer Institute. Building 31, Room 10A24, 9000 Rockville Pike, Bethesda, MD 20892. 1 August 1991.

Pearson, Drew and Jack Anderson. "Nixon Suppressing Visits to Psychiatrist." *The Times Herald Record,* (Middletown, NY). November 29, 1968, p. 69.

Plath, Sylvia. *Ariel*. New York: Harper & Row, 1961.

Plato. *The Republic, Book X; Ion*. In *Criticism: Twenty Major Statements*. Edited by Charles Kaplan. San Francisco: Chandler Publishing Company, 1955.

Riding, Laura. *Collected Poems of Laura Riding*. London: Cassell, 1938; reprinted as *The Poems of Laura (Riding) Jackson*. Manchester, England: 1980.

Riding, Laura and Robert Graves. *A Pamphlet Against Anthologies*. London: Jonathan Cape, 1928; reprinted NewYork: AMS Press, Inc., 1970.

———. *A Survey of Modernist Poetry*. London: William Heinemann, 1927; reprinted Folcroft Library Editions, 1971.

Sebald, W. G. "Interview." *The New York Times*. section E1, Dec. 11, 2001.

Shakespeare, William. *The Complete Works of William Shakespeare*. Edited by Hardin Craig. Chicago: Scott, Foresman, 1961.

Shelley, Percy Bysshe. "A Defense of Poetry." In *Criticism: Twenty Major Statements*. Edited by Charles Kaplan. San Francisco: Chandler Publishing Company, 1955.

Solomon, Andrew. *The Noonday Demon: An Atlas of Depression*. New York: Scribner, 2001.

Strong, Maggie. *Mainstay: For the Well Spouse of the Chronically Ill*. Boston: Little, Brown, 1988; New York: Penguin, 1989.

Swift, Jonathan. *The Poems of Jonathan Swift*. Edited by Padraic Colum. New York: Collier Books, 1962.

Trilling, Lionel. *The Liberal Imagination: Freud and Literature*. Quoted in *Bartlett's Familiar Quotations*. Boston: Little, Brown, 1980.

What You Need to Know About Lung Cancer. National Cancer Institute. NIH Publication No. 91-1553. Revised August 1987. Reprinted October 1990.